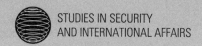

Published in

Association

with the

United States

Institute

of Peace

MARC SOMMERS

RWANDAN YOUTH AND

THE STRUGGLE FOR ADULTHOOD

Stuck

8/2015.

To all my
wonderful
EDC
Colleagues
—Marc

The University of Georgia Press   Athens and London

Published by the University of Georgia Press
Athens, Georgia 30602
www.ugapress.org
© 2012 by Marc Sommers
Photographs © 2012 by Marc Sommers
All rights reserved
Designed by Mindy Basinger Hill
Set in 10.5/14 Adobe Caslon Pro
Printed and bound by Sheridan Books
The paper in this book meets the guidelines for
permanence and durability of the Committee on
Production Guidelines for Book Longevity of the
Council on Library Resources.

12 13 14 15 16 P 5 4 3 2 1

Library of Congress Cataloging-in-Publication Data
Sommers, Marc.
Stuck : Rwandan youth and the struggle
for adulthood / Marc Sommers.
p.   cm. — (Studies in security and international affairs)
Includes bibliographical references and index.
ISBN-13: 978-0-8203-3890-3 (cloth : alk. paper)
ISBN-10: 0-8203-3890-7 (cloth : alk. paper)
ISBN-13: 978-0-8203-3891-0 (pbk. : alk. paper)
ISBN-10: 0-8203-3891-5 (pbk. : alk. paper)
1. Youth—Rwanda. 2. Youth—Rwanda—Social conditions.
3. Youth—Rwanda—Economic conditions.
4. Youth and violence—Rwanda. 5. Rwanda—Social conditions.
6. Rwanda—History—20th century. I. Title.
II. Series: Studies in security and international affairs.
HQ799.R95S66 2011
303.6'208350967571—dc23   2011029962

British Library Cataloging-in-Publication Data available

TO TOR

Who shared a passion

for exploring

other peoples' worlds.

Contents

Illustrations

Boxes and Tables

The only place that today's Rwanda resembles
is pregenocide Rwanda.

Central Africa scholar, private interview, 2008

The past is never dead. It's not even past.

William Faulkner, Requiem for a Nun, *1951*

Preface

Several years ago, I wrote that the central irony concerning Africa's urban
youth was that "they are a demographic majority that sees itself as an outcast
minority" (Sommers 2003: 1). Since that time, field research with rural and
urban youth in war and postwar contexts within and beyond Africa has led
me to revise this assertion. The irony appears to apply to most developing
country youth regardless of their location.

Research for this book underscores the relevance of this unfortunate irony.
Youth who felt overlooked and misunderstood ran like a deep, wide river
through the field data for this book. The irony surfaced in many ways, including in a theme linking the plight of urban and rural youth in an immediate
and concrete fashion: 200 francs ($0.37).[1] *Amafaranga magana abiri* was a
common way of highlighting the plight of a youth's immediate situation. In
rural Rwanda, 200 francs is the most common daily payment for cultivating
another person's farmland. That wage rests at the core of the plans of many if
not most rural youth. For male youth, those earnings are how they buy roof
tiles for a house they hope to complete. For female youth, the earnings go
toward personal care products and perhaps savings that might attract a male
youth. In Kigali, Rwanda's mushrooming capital, 200 francs is what it costs to
buy one plate of food in a simple restaurant. This was the daily focus of many
urban youth: to somehow get enough money to eat one hot meal a day (most
lacked cooking facilities in their residences). These activities circumscribe the
central findings in this book: the exacting adulthood requirements in Rwanda's
countryside and the desperation of city life for its urban youth. *Stuck* is offered
as a contribution toward a more accurate picture of contemporary Rwanda

and toward a deeper understanding of the powerful influence of two dynamic forces in youth lives across the world: masculinity and urbanization.

The two forces are linked. The first step to socially recognized manhood in Rwanda is to build a house. This sets the stage for a formal, legal marriage (as opposed to an embarrassing and illegal informal arrangement) and then children. Once a man can do this, and protect and support his children and wife, manhood is achieved. Yet research for this book revealed that attaining manhood is exceedingly difficult. Many male youth are caught on a treadmill toward the first step—building a house—which they know they may never complete. Rwanda, already among the world's highest ranked in population growth, population density, urban growth, and poverty, also has a traditional culture that is both demanding and unrelenting toward its own young people. Male youth drop out of school to start working in order to save to build their house. Then they get stuck. The fallout from this housing crisis is breathtakingly severe, and a common result is for male (and female) youth to escape adulthood requirements by migrating to an urban area, usually Kigali, where their main pressure is not obtaining adulthood but sheer survival.

The impact of this situation on female youth is profound. Because male youth get stuck, female youth get stuck too, since they cannot attain womanhood without having a formal, legal marriage and then giving birth to children. Rwanda's infamous genocide of 1994 (and its far lesser known civil war of 1990–94) has compounded this female youth challenge, since it is estimated that there may be eighty-eight men for every one hundred women in the land (Ministry of Youth, Culture, and Sports n.d.: 9). With polygamy outlawed, and if the above estimate is accurate, then perhaps 12 percent of female youth cannot marry because there aren't enough men to wed. A much more immediate fact is that so few male youth are able to marry because they are unable to complete their houses. In addition, the clock is ticking: while male youth strain to construct a house and consider the prospect of a life of public failure, female youth must marry before society considers them failures as well. Once unmarried women reach the age of twenty-eight, but perhaps just twenty-four or twenty-five (male youth and men debate the cutoff age), they are labeled "old ladies" or "prostitutes" and permanently forced onto the margins of society. Since no one can legally marry before the age of twenty-one in Rwanda, the window of marriage opportunity for female youth may be as narrow as four years. A male youth, by contrast, has more time to marry than female youth, but it's far from forever: by his early thirties, a single male youth faces public embarrassment if his house is not completed and he still isn't married.

The widespread inability of most male and female youth to become adults in Rwanda results in an array of negative social and economic concerns. These include illegitimate children, prostitution, the spread of HIV/AIDS, crime, a high urban growth rate, and an increase in school drop-out rates. Rwanda's government, together with some of its largest international donors, engages with youth concerns mainly through efforts to expand access to secondary and vocational education. Its disconnect from youth priorities is stark. Even after the government and donors doubled access to secondary education, few Rwandan youth are able to attend, and many youth drop out of primary school to start wage work aimed at becoming adults. Vocational education is available to even fewer youth. Meanwhile, as we see in chapters 5 and 7, government restrictions on house construction and on income generation make the task of attaining adulthood, and a stable economic existence, significantly more difficult. National and international institutions in Rwanda are focused on what they think youth *should* be doing, not on what youth priorities are.

The importance of masculinity in the minds of Rwandans shone through the research for this book and brought forth a challenging proposition: if one wants to help young women in countries such as Rwanda, one probably has to help young men first. The traditional dependence of womanhood on manhood appears to make this necessary. Clearly, this is a troubling suggestion, since exacting a measure of independence for and direct assistance to women often seems appropriate if not absolutely urgent. But not helping male youth may prove dangerous and destructive for female and male youth alike by undermining their prospects for becoming adults. Many youth, and nonelite youth in particular, may lack the ability, and sufficient agency, to escape adulthood mandates without risking harsh and perhaps devastating repercussions.

Urban growth is a central component of Rwanda's current transformation. Before the genocide, movement within Rwanda was severely restricted. Today, although the government hardly welcomes the surge of youth toward the capital (reports of harassment of urban migrant youth by the authorities were common), there exists at last some degree of an outlet from the extraordinary pressures in Rwanda's thickly populated countryside.

Whether Rwandan youth attempt to achieve adulthood in villages or migrate to town, the government's presence is commanding. The recent decentralization reforms illustrate this. One of the most sweeping changes has been the increase in regulations that has followed the enhanced empowerment of lower-level government officials. Many local officials have seized the opportunity to mandate change in their areas by administering fines if, for example, someone enters a market area in bare feet, does not send all his or her children to primary school, or fails to compost garbage properly. Still other mandates arrive from farther above. A list of "suggested" reforms that the Ministry of Local Government gave to *umudugudu* leaders (the lowest government level, at the village level) featured thirty objectives (see the appendix). Among them were the objectives of "bringing people to love their country" and "eradicating infiltration." All citizens are expected to know who is entering and leaving their community and to be a part of the "Eye of the Nation." Given the source of these suggestions, an *umudugudu* leader intimated that it would be difficult to disagree with or even modify them.

The list is but one indication of a nation that, despite regular government declarations to the contrary, remains infused with a sense of insecurity. It also illustrates the degree to which Rwanda remains on a war footing, maintaining its vigilance against the remaining *interahamwe* (those who work together) militia who helped carry out the genocide and persist as a fighting force just across Rwanda's border in the eastern regions of the Democratic Republic of the Congo (DRC).[2] They are also the notorious "infiltrators" who have, on occasion, slipped into Rwandan territory and attacked.

Internationally, Rwanda is seen generally either as a spectacular success story with dynamic leadership and a promising future or as an unequal society facing serious strains and bleak prospects. Although findings from this research detail a mixture of the two, the situation facing most Rwandan youth is significantly more serious than the glowing assessments allow. The Rwandan government tends to be sensitive about depictions of life in Rwanda that do not describe a nation and its citizenry as rapidly advancing forward. This governmental sensitivity impacted the way in which the research was proposed, undertaken, and discussed. *Stuck* began as a regional research endeavor funded by the World Bank, a research study on youth and gender in Central Africa (here defined as Rwanda and Burundi) aimed at finding out how youth were faring and whether they posed a risk to a return to violent conflict. Once in Rwanda, I was told by Rwandans working with international donor agencies to present the endeavor to government officials as a one-country study. Many in the government evidently believed that Burundi ranked far below Rwanda in terms of development, thus making such a comparison unsuitable. Rwandans and non-Rwandans with deep knowledge of the government's sensitivities also advised me not to mention the issue of violent conflict. It could only arouse suspicion about the underlying motivation of the study.

Once a satisfactory, nonconfrontational way of describing the research to officials had been established, government doors began to open. Officials of all ranks were available for interviews, and they were, in general, thoughtful and compelling. The experience shone light on qualities from both sides of Rwandan governance: engagement and, quite often, startling frankness set within established boundaries for discussion and action. At times, some officials seemed to push beyond those boundaries. When our conversations touched on the difficulties of reporting disquieting news to superiors, such as the virtual impossibility of meeting government housing objectives, I began to sense that they had decided to share the information with me instead, hoping that I might use it in my writing. The sources of all interviews for this book, including those with government officials, remain confidential.

Writing this book was emotionally draining because the tale it told was relentlessly sad. There were most certainly delights: research team members, and those supporting the research, were consistently professional and upbeat. Nearly all government officials were accommodating and generous with their time during private encounters. The youth that the research team interviewed were open, energetic, articulate, and frequently expressed a sense of humor about their circumstances. Many related that no one had interviewed them before. The experience surprised them, and they seemed to truly enjoy contributing to the research. And yet, the collective story they described was persistently discouraging. One colleague with years of developing country experience in both stable and war-affected contexts said that an early short version of this book was the most depressing youth report she'd ever read. Did I agree that Rwanda's youth situation was unusually gloomy, she asked, and if so, why was it so?

It is hard to say. I have interviewed youth in challenging circumstances in many countries and have found it difficult if not inappropriate to evaluate who is better or worse off. Certainly the research for this book details a youth situation that is, in many respects, frightening—many youth in Kigali face circumstances, for example, that have made them fatalistic in the extreme. It is also safe to say that, having made eight research trips to Rwanda prior to fieldwork for this book (the first trip began six weeks after the 1994 genocide had ended), most of which examined youth concerns, I found the difficult circumstances that Rwandan youth described during the 2006–7 field interviews much worse than I had anticipated.

Research is captivating because it yields surprises. This endeavor is no exception. Not only was the picture of Rwandan youth surprisingly dire, but it also contrasted sharply from findings with a similar sample of youth in neighboring Burundi. Peter Uvin, a longtime friend and former colleague at Tufts University's Fletcher School, and I have each carried out extensive fieldwork with Rwandans and Burundians over the years. The World Bank invited us to carry out related studies of youth in Rwanda and Burundi and we developed our methodology together.[3] The two landlocked, poor and resource-poor nations are famed for sharing a tragic fact: recurring and extreme ethnic violence involving the same two groups—Hutu and Tutsi. Yet here were youth from apparently analogous countries who had strikingly different views of their future. In some respects, the results were virtually the reverse of what we had anticipated. It was expected that Rwanda, with an expanding economy and international renown, would contain youth who were considerably more upbeat than Burundian youth. The opposite was the case. It was also presumed that most Rwandan youth, amid rapid development of their country's education sector, would feature education in their future plans, whereas most Burundian youth, living in a country just emerging from civil war, would not. Again, the opposite was the case. These two Central African governments, societies, and cultures are not nearly as similar as is often supposed, and the warm glow that increasingly surrounds Rwanda contrasts sharply with the cold realities confronting most of its youth.

Acknowledgments

I remember hearing, long ago, that Herman Melville's method for completing *Moby-Dick* was to write each day for twelve hours and chop wood for two. It is an admirable recipe for escaping a book's hold on its maker, and laying the work, finally, to rest.

Armed with central heating, modern life did not afford me many opportunities to approach Melville's feverish focus and fortitude. So I wrote in spurts, and found and made time to organize and analyze data, and then write this book. The best bursts happened in my home. It somewhat resembles Melville's western Massachusetts house: a small cottage in the New Hampshire woods, where e-mail access did not exist until recently, winters are frigid, and quiet is abundant.

The aim of the research for this book was, at its core, to find out what Rwandan youth are thinking and doing about their lives, and then use their stories to consider how male and female youth come of age (or not). While responsibility for the contents of this book falls entirely on me, every effort has been made to communicate youth views in this book without bias. Emphasizing an unbiased approach may seem peculiar and perhaps unnecessary to some. After all, the author is a social scientist and the reader will hopefully find that the book's findings and analysis are frankly described. Yet those familiar with the Rwandan context, and others where the government's presence and sensitivities are similarly strong, will recognize the utility in stating that the author has no ax to grind. Indeed, given how contentiously some Rwandan government officials responded to my preliminary findings, I will state again, and with additional emphasis, that *no one but me has responsibility for this book—neither its findings and analysis nor its conclusions and recommendations.*

The breadth and depth of this book could not have been achieved without the extraordinary efforts of the entire research team. The field contributions of the Rwandan researchers in 2006–7 were superb in every way: they were dedicated, detail oriented, conscientious, and incredibly productive. They carried out all aspects of their demanding work with good cheer, generosity, and unstinting professionalism. Although I have carried out research work in twenty war-affected countries for two decades, I've never worked with a better field research team. It was an honor and pleasure to work with each of them.

Thirteen graduate students from the Fletcher School, the Tufts University Graduate School for International Affairs, contributed significantly to the data analysis process. Special mention must be made to Xanthe Scharff, who helped to input, organize, and analyze the data, as well as supervise the contributions of other Fletcher students. A quick study, she generated a wealth of helpful insights; her work was steady and outstanding. Marcus Holknekt joined the research team before the other students, developing a system for inputting and analyzing respondent profile information. His work was stellar. The contributions of Angie Nguyen and Raul Chavez, who inputted much of the field data and helped with initial data analysis, and Amelia Cook and Natalie Parke, who also contributed to the analysis process, were also essential and well done. Thanks also to Noël Twagiramungu and Nils Baetens (a graduate student from Belgium), who each made substantial contributions to the document research. Subsequent bibliographic work by Claire Putzeys, Sujatha Sebastian, Regina Wilson, and Jessie Evans was equally superb. Near the end of the data analysis, the contributions and upbeat energy of Julie Guyot-Diangone of Howard University, and my research assistant at the United States Institute of Peace, were absolutely terrific. Excellent contributions to the final draft work were thankfully made by Michele Wehle and Amelia Hight, who helped me reach the finish line. The collective student work proved extremely helpful, even essential, and their uniformly high spirits made it fun to work with all of them.

Steady, patient, and always upbeat and helpful assistance were provided by my immediate supervisors (now good friends) at the World Bank, Maria Correia and Pia Peeters, with whom the contours and direction of this research originated. Maria's leadership of the project, and her verve and drive to assess the role of masculinity in youth lives, enhanced my focus on this elemental concern. I am grateful for her passionate and always insightful comments on this and related issues. As time went on, Pia became my point person for every research-related detail that surfaced, of which, unfortunately, there were many. Maria and Pia's patience and support to me and this project are sincerely appreciated.

Heartfelt thanks are also offered to a friend of many years, Peter Uvin, who led the counterpart research with Burundian youth, and Kimberly Howe, who contributed to the Burundian youth research. Together, we developed a shared

ACKNOWLEDGMENTS

methodology that guided the youth research in both countries. Peter also provided periodic feedback on the Rwandan research and writing. I continue to appreciate his contributions and generosity. I am grateful to the entire research team, in Washington, D.C., Medford, Massachusetts, and Rwanda, for their hard work and good cheer. Thanks also to Charles Matthews, Siobhán McEvoy-Levy, Matt Venhaus, Andreas Wimmer, Robin Wright, Rosalind Shaw, and so many others who have supplied invaluable insights and comments to the enterprise that ended up as this book.

An expression of gratitude is due to Rwandan government officials from the *umudugudu* up to the ministry levels. Nearly every official was accommodating with their time, interested in sharing information and discussing preliminary findings, and ready to lend a hand with logistical arrangements for the field research. The conversations about research findings with sector officials were particularly frank and fascinating. The late Abedy Kizito Ruzigana was memorably perceptive and inquisitive about Rwandan youth as well. I am also grateful for the generous hospitality of and input from the entire World Bank staff in the Kigali office, to Pedro Alba, the World Bank's former country director for Burundi, Rwanda, DRC, and Congo, for giving the green light to this endeavor, and to Ian Bannon (sector manager, Fragile States, Conflict and Social Development, Africa Region) of the World Bank, for his encouragement of this work. A word of sincere thanks is reserved for Nancy Grayson, executive editor of the University of Georgia Press, for enthusiastically supporting the publication of this book.

All of my writing and research projects over the past decade and a half, books and otherwise, have benefited from my position as a visiting researcher with Boston University's African Studies Center. I continue to value the collegiality, insights, and friendship that so many BU colleagues have offered over the years, including Timothy Longman, James McCann, Parker Shipton, James Pritchett, Edouard Bustin, and Joanne Hart at the African Studies Center, and Timothy Riordan, Seka Milutinovic, Tom Johnson, Edmond Deraedt, David Westling, Loumona Petroff, and the late Gretchen Walsh at the Mugar Memorial Library. I reserve a special word of appreciation for Thomas Barfield of the Anthropology Department. Across a great many years, Tom has regularly provided me with sage advice on a variety of academic, research, and publishing concerns. He has been an unstintingly generous colleague, mentor, and friend, and I remain full of gratitude for his support.

Special mention is reserved for my former colleagues at the United States Institute of Peace. I remain grateful for the opportunity to complete my book draft as a Jennings Randolph Senior Fellow in 2009–10, even though it cut a bit into my time for the book project they had originally supported (on youth, popular culture, and civil war in Sierra Leone). Thanks to my fearless leaders at the Jennings Randolph Fellowship Program, Chantal De Jonge Oudraat (formerly associate vice president) and Elizabeth A. "Lili" Cole (senior program officer); to Shira Lowinger (formerly program coordinator), Janene Sawers (formerly program assistant), Kathleen Kuehnast (gender advisor), Daniel Serwer (formerly vice president of the Centers of Innovation), and so many other wonderful colleagues who made writing at USIP so rewarding and productive, including Tara Sonenshine (executive vice president) and Valerie Norville (director of publications), both of whom enthusiastically supported Chantal's strong and sincerely appreciated backing for completing and publishing *Stuck*. My thanks to all of you.

Finally, thanks to my son, Isaiah, for his many insightful inquiries and comments about Rwanda and his youthful counterparts in that country. After a field research trip or a day of writing, our conversations always helped put what I was learning about Rwandan youth lives into fresh perspective.

STUCK

PART ONE

Introduction

YOUTH VIEWS

Youth in Waithood

Endless Liminality

Just before a wedding ceremony, the man and woman (or man and man, or woman and woman) who are to marry have identities as separate individuals. They are single. At the close of the ceremony, they form a union. During the wedding ceremony itself, the two people are no longer single but not yet joined. Marked by ambiguity, the period of the ritual transition has been called the liminal stage, in which people pass through "a cultural realm that has few or none of the attributes of the past or the coming state" (Turner 1969: 94). This period puts a person in "a limbo of statuslessness" (97) in which the attributes of the previous and the future identities do not apply. The liminal stage, in short, is the stage of becoming.

While governments and agencies tussle over the appropriate age range that defines what a youth is, being a youth is not, fundamentally, about a person's age at all.[1] Instead, it marks the transitional stage of life between childhood and adulthood, when a person sheds her or his identity as a dependent child and strives for social and cultural fulfillment as a recognized adult. "Youth" is a moving target not because it's so difficult to settle on an age range but because the phase of life it embodies is transition itself. Being a youth lasts much longer than a ceremony: it means experiencing the liminal stage of becoming for years. It may even become a state of permanent ambiguity, as cultural prerequisites for adulthood in many countries are hard if not impossible to attain.

Two situations—one in the Middle East, the other in West Africa—have inspired catchphrases to describe young people who are unable to shed their youth identities. In Egypt and across the Middle East, Diane Singerman has found that many young people are said to "experience 'wait adulthood' or

An increasing rarity in Rwanda: the large, socially recognized
wedding. The solemnity of these composed faces is no accident:
getting married and entering adulthood is a serious affair.
The groom and bride are in the center.

'waithood' as they negotiate their prolonged adolescence and remain single for long periods of time while trying to save money to marry."[2] Until youth marry, they remain in a "liminal world where they are neither children nor adults" (Singerman 2007: 6). A similarly punishing situation faces male youth in West Africa. Mats Utas draws the term "youthmen" from Abubakar Momoh's research in Nigeria to describe the "structural marginalization" of Liberia's war-affected youth:

> Due to economic crisis and increasing dependence on the central state in the 1980s an ever-growing number of young people in urban and semi-urban environments were excluded even from the possibilities of becoming adults. Possibilities to participate in the wage economy diminished and education ceased having any importance. With this crisis looming, many young men lost even the possibility to establish themselves as adults, by building a house, or getting married—even though they continued to become fathers, of children for whom they could not provide. (Utas 2005a: 150)

A "youthman" in West Africa is a young man who is too old to be a youth but culturally still cannot be considered an adult man. This situation affects young women, as well. In Liberia and many other countries in Africa and the Middle East, if young men cannot become adults, then neither can young women, since an adult woman's identity is often tied to, at the very least, becoming married in a ceremony that the couple's society considers acceptable (which tends toward a large, expensive wedding).

What Singerman and Utas essentially describe are situations in which the cultural prerequisites for adulthood are so hard to reach that "youthhood" becomes a kind of arrested liminality. They tie this to the inability of youth to find a job and, most of all, marry in the fashion that society will accept and recognize. The broader context reflects how youth demographics and the growth of cities are helping to sculpt current realities in much of today's world.

We are now in the age of youth. Today's human population is the youngest in recorded history. About half of all people are under the age of twenty-five (Barker 2005: 11). Nearly a quarter of today's population of 6.5 billion people (Leahy et al. 2007: 15) are youth between the ages of twelve and twenty-four. The overwhelming majority of people in this age group live in the developing world (1.3 billion of a total of 1.5 billion, or 86 percent of twelve- to twenty-four-year-olds) (World Bank 2006: 4). This cohort of young people in developing countries "is the largest the world has ever seen" (33). Since fertility rates are expected to begin to decline in developing countries in the coming decades, "there will likely never be in human history a youth cohort this large again" (Barker 2005: 11). The unprecedented expansion of youth in developing country populations has many outcomes, including, in many countries, an increasing difficulty in the ability of young people to become adults. Access to land is a case in point. Reasons for the difficulty for male youth to gain access to land can differ. In Sierra Leone, for example, elders control the access of youth to land (Peeters et al. 2009: 17) while in Côte d'Ivoire land shortages exist partly because some farmland has been snapped up by outside investors (Chaveau and Richards 2008: 532). As a consequence, African youth are more likely than older people to migrate to cities, and the shift seems to make particular sense "in land-scarce countries" because rural-urban migration is both unavoidable and "desirable as a way to improve allocation of human resources" (World Bank 2009: 1). Regardless of the reason, more and more of today's youthful world is urbanizing. The year 2008, in fact, marked a turning point in human history: for the first time ever, more than half of humanity are urban and not rural residents (United Nations Human Settlements Programme 2009).

Sub-Saharan Africa sits at the intersection of the dual trends of youthful demographics and urbanization. The growth rates of sub-Saharan Africa's youth cohort (World Bank 2006: 33) and its urban population (United Nations Department of Economic and Social Affairs/Population Division 2004: 7) are the highest of any region around the world. The sub-Saharan region also has the youngest population of any world region, and the growth of its youth population continues to be spectacular: having expanded by over 400 percent since 1950, rates are expected to continue to rise (World Bank 2006: 33). Rwanda, recently renowned for rising up from genocide, is also a densely populated, exceptionally youthful, and increasingly urbanizing nation at Africa's center. The circumstances arising there have created a youth crisis centering on the inability of most youth to become adults, where the circumstances of "waithood" are pervasive and the threat of male youth becoming entrapped as "youthmen" is real. In Rwanda and beyond, the implications of what might be called failed adulthood—or, perhaps, unrecognized or even unaccepted adulthood—are profound, and they emanate from the prominence of masculinity in gendered relations between youth. Since a female youth (in Rwanda and similar contexts) cannot be accepted as a woman until she marries and has children, she is dependent on whether and when male youth are able to become men. That prerequisite begins with building a house in rural areas. The next step is demonstrating an ability to care for a wife and children, which may require acquiring sufficient land on which to start married life and securing a means to providing for a family. Nearly all male youth who were interviewed for this book were stymied by their inability to reach the traditional first step to acquiring manhood: house construction. Even while admitting that they "had no choice" but to leave school so they could work to save money to build a house, many said that they might never complete it—and thus, never have an opportunity to be accepted and recognized as a man in Rwandan society.

The consequences of this state of failed masculinity extend from gender and urbanization to development, governance, and the character of a society's culture. The Rwandan case suggests that there, the paramount necessity for helping rural youth may not be education but housing. In other countries, it may be land reform or job training. In Rwanda's heavily regulated and controlled environment, another dominant challenge, particularly for Rwanda's urban youth, is finding viable economic activities that the government will condone. A push factor driving youth to Kigali, where youth constitute the overwhelming majority of residents, is that Rwanda's capital has become home to male and female youth who are largely unable to become adults in traditionally accepted ways and, given their fear of humiliation if they return to their rural homes without signs of urban success, may never leave Kigali—even to visit their childhood home. The urban context for achieving adulthood differed somewhat but was just as difficult. Male youth attempting to build a house in town risked having it destroyed by government authorities. Some said they could become a man in town by getting the sort of job that provided a steady income and the means to rent a house or apartment. Most single male youth viewed such a scenario as highly unlikely.

The dependence of female youth on male youth achieving manhood for them to reach womanhood suggests a pervasive sexism in the construction of female identity in Rwanda and beyond. This sort of adulthood mandate effectively calls for assisting male youth in order to assist female youth. In Rwanda's case, the rigidity of its culture concerning adulthood has helped create a situation in which fears of failure and humiliation are increasingly common for its enormous population of youth. Strict government regulations and policies, as detailed in this book, only make matters much more difficult for Rwandan youth striving to become adults.

None of these conditions, constraints, and perspectives is particular to Rwanda. The story of Rwandan youth that fills most pages of *Stuck* magnifies the significance of these issues through their telling.

Poverty, Urbanization, and Masculinity

Field research for this book aimed to illuminate the current situation of youth in Rwanda by featuring the perspectives, concerns, and priorities of Rwandan youth themselves. Through this research, the book also endeavors to shed new light on the plight of, prospects for, orientation of, and thinking about youth more generally. Three comments are necessary for these broad purposes to be achieved. First, the research sample was developed to reasonably represent the broad outline of Rwandan youth demographics: since the overwhelming majority of Rwandan youth are poor and have no formal education beyond primary school, nearly all youth whom the research team interviewed share this profile.[3] In addition, while the definition of youth for this research aligned with the Rwandan government's classification (everyone from age fourteen through thirty-five), 97 percent of the youth research sample was between the ages of eighteen and thirty-five. It is not entirely clear why so few youth under age eighteen ended up in the research sample. The research approach certainly did not target older youth. Although it is possible that some younger youth were in school during interview periods, many interview sessions took place during nonschool hours.

Second, researching urban youth in Rwanda remains new—so new, in fact, that my research team uncovered no substantial prior research on Rwanda's urban youth. While Rwanda's urban population remains fairly small (approximately one in five Rwandans live in urban areas), it will not remain that way for long: by 2030, it is estimated that 42.1 percent of all Rwandans will reside in urban areas (United Nations Department of Economic and Social Affairs/ Population Division 2006: 37). Making urban youth a central component of this research is thus aimed to provide a picture of an expanding Rwandan reality.

Third, particular attention was paid to the views and concerns of male youth. Approximately half of all of those interviewed come from this group, even though males may constitute as little as 44.5 percent of the population.[4] There are important reasons to highlight the needs and concerns of Rwanda's male youth. Rwandan male youth have an established history of being directly involved in violence. It has been argued by many writers about Rwanda's genocide that the sense of entrapment, frustration, and hopelessness felt by a great many male youth during the civil war years (1990–94) provided its organizers with opportunities to exploit, entice, and coerce tens of thousands of male youth into becoming the so-called "foot soldiers of the genocide" (Mamdani 2001: 233).[5] One of the interests of the World Bank (which funded the field research) was to explore the relationship, if any, between violence and youth. Such an interest is not unfounded, for in addition to precedence in recent Rwandan history, there is evidence that male vulnerability, powerlessness, and sense of impotence can lead, in its most extreme form, to violence, conflict, and war (Correia and Bannon 2006: 250). In addition, significant cultural and social pressures on male youth do not apply to any other population group in Rwanda. As is described in chapter 4, becoming a man in Rwanda requires male youth to build a house before getting married. It is difficult for most to achieve, and difficult in the extreme for many. While the frustration and fear of failure that the social situation produces for many Rwandan male youth is significant in itself, it is also the case that such circumstances are hardly Rwanda-specific, as similar expectations and pressures have been found to apply to male youth in many societies and nations in the world (e.g., Correia and Bannon 2006).

The situation facing male youth in Rwanda cascades and affects other Rwandans as well, chiefly female youth. In addition to a shortage of men in the overall population due to postgenocide realities, the path to marriage for female youth is further hampered by the inability of many male youth to meet the traditional marriage prerequisite: building a house. Highlighting male youth concerns thus also becomes one means for better understanding female youth trajectories and challenges.

Finally, the rise of male youth migration to cities, Kigali in particular, is partly an outgrowth of cultural and social pressures on male youth to become men. Male youth may go to Kigali, or to large farms, in search of employment that would provide a means to construct a house. But there are other reasons that have fueled the movement of male youth from rural villages to urban areas, including the fact that young men are "more likely [than women and old men] to migrate to cities as a reaction to conflict" (Barker and Ricardo 2006: 175–76). Yet even if male youth remained in the countryside, Rwandan government regulations were found to negatively impact their ability to achieve adulthood and economic stability.

Stuck is organized in the following way. The remainder of this chapter provides background about Rwanda's youth and the circumstances they face. Chapter 2 describes the research context and the methodology that was employed in the research for this book. Part 2 of the book describes rural youth lives, while part 3 describes life for their urban counterparts. The initial chapters of both parts 2 and 3 highlight government perspectives of and approaches to youth, perhaps an unusual approach for a book about youth until one considers the dominance of the government over everyday Rwandan life. The degree and nature of the connection between the poor youth majority and their government, in fact, proved to be a prominent theme in the research. The middle chapters of parts 2 and 3 depict everyday youth life in, respectively, the countryside and poor urban neighborhoods. The final chapters in parts 2 and 3 each address the gender dimensions of Rwandan youth life. Part 4 features concluding thoughts and recommendations. It also contains an examination of why the situation of rural youth in one location that the study team visited was, on balance, significantly better than any other visited area.

Youth in Rwanda

Rwanda has one of the poorest and youngest populations in the world. In a survey of 213 nations, Rwanda's gross annual national income per capita rank was 193 (World Bank 2011: 3). Three in four Rwandans are under the age of thirty.[6] Paradoxically, while Rwanda is the most densely populated country on the African continent and has one of the most rural-based populations anywhere, it simultaneously has one of the world's highest urban growth rates.[7]

The paradox illustrates how change in Rwanda is coming, and it is coming extremely fast: soon before independence from Belgium (in 1953–54), the capital, Kigali, had no more than three thousand residents (Voyame et al. 1996, cited in Uvin 1998: 116). In 2006, it had approximately 1.1 million. Rwandans are streaming into the capital at rates that are, for Rwanda, completely unprecedented: another million Rwandans are expected to migrate to Kigali in the next twenty-five years (oz Architecture et al. 2006: 51, 52).

Despite this extraordinary development, Rwanda largely remains a rural-centered nation. Most Rwandans subsist on precious little land that, as the population advances alongside entrenched land inheritance traditions, grows ever smaller. For farming families, it remains a place where "every centimeter" counts (Uvin 1998: 198). Rwanda's population growth rate is 2.9 percent annually, and projections estimate that its population will rise from 8.1 million in 2005 to 14.3 million by the year 2020, when there will be an average of 543 people per square kilometer (Ministry of Public Service and Labour 2005: 18). Such severe and advancing population pressure has been a longstanding focus of scholarly analysis and government concern.[8] A former Rwandan prefect, for example, publicly characterized land scarcity as "our time bomb" (Sommers 2006a: 90).

Notwithstanding Rwanda's noteworthy demographics, the tiny, landlocked Central African nation is best known for the shattering genocide that took place there in 1994. It was arguably the most efficient genocide in modern history, with an average of perhaps eight thousand people killed daily for a hundred days and at a rate that averaged, on peak killing days, one murder every two seconds (Peterson 2000: 252–53).[9] In the end, approximately one in eight Rwandans, and nearly three in four ethnic Tutsi, perished during the genocide. The 1994 genocide has overshadowed everything else arising in Rwanda (including the concurrent civil war), and has, naturally enough, affected Rwandan society in profound and pervasive ways since then.

The thread weaving its way through all of these events and trends, and a great many more, is youth. Two in five Rwandans are youth.[10] According to a city council official, two in three Kigali residents are youth. Nine in ten primary school graduates will not attend secondary school (Save the Children UK 2007: 2). While most youth remain pinioned to Rwanda's hillsides and engaged in farm-related activities, increasing numbers are launching into Kigali, searching, mostly without success, for regular work. Rwanda's president, Paul Kagame, has noted that there are over a million unemployed youth and more than a million underemployed youth in Rwanda (Ministry of Public Service and Labour 2005: 11). Perhaps one in four or five Rwandans, in other words, appear to be members of this collective group of unemployed and underemployed youth. A recent survey of Rwandan youth, moreover, found that 61 percent were single and living with their parents, and an astonishing 98 percent had no personal property (18). A quarter of Rwandans under the age of thirty-five are illiterate. The illiteracy rate rockets to over half (55.8 percent) in rural areas (27–28). The situation facing nearly all Rwandan youth is unquestionably dire.

Background

Rwanda's situation is exceptional, in part, because of ongoing impacts from the extraordinarily efficient genocide in its still-recent past. Among the results is that it maintains a multifaceted engagement inside eastern Democratic Republic of the Congo (DRC; formerly known as Zaire), including periodic clashes with well-armed, former Rwandan *génocidaires*. While the current regime's tendency toward social engineering and control is hardly a recent phenomenon in Rwandan history (Prunier 1995: 3), it has also broken important new ground, such as, evidently, being the first to allow rural youth an urban migration outlet within the country and the creation of important initiatives in support of youth.[11]

Rwanda is, moreover, unquestionably a country on the move. The government's brand of forward-looking change—the grand scale and rapid pace—grabs one's attention. The urgency is impossible to miss. Sweeping reforms are underway to change the housing of almost the entire population. Government authorities are planning to relocate many of Kigali's residents and require the renovation of much of its urban housing stock. It is also in the process of shifting almost the entire rural population into *imidugudu* (community housing areas) located near main roads.[12] Starting in 2001, the nation's adults have been required to attend *gacaca* (community-based courts) proceedings once a week that were designed to try more than one hundred thousand Rwandans imprisoned for allegations of crimes committed during the 1994 genocide (Kirkby 2006: 94). Concern over environmental protection has led the government to become one of the few nations to outlaw plastic bags; indeed, visitors are required to hand over their plastic bags at the airport

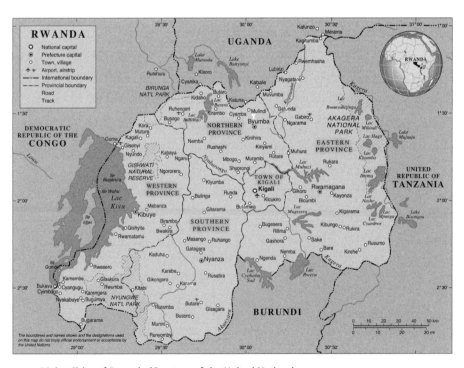

Major Cities of Rwanda (Courtesy of the United Nations)

before entering the country. Extensive education reform is underway. And as if this were not enough simultaneous change, the government has instituted expansive decentralization reforms, which extend from the president's office down to the smallest government officials, the *umudugudu* (community leaders).

This section provides context for the research findings and analysis detailed in parts 2 and 3. First, let's consider the divergent views of Rwandan realities before we turn to a review of specific issues that figured prominently during field interviews for this book.

GUSH AND ALARM:
ASSESSING RWANDAN REALITIES

Rwanda has made impressive development strides, recovering remarkably well following the 1994 genocide. The economy grew at an average rate of almost 10 percent a year between 1995 and 2005. The Government has introduced market reforms and privatized many state-owned enterprises. Economic and political governance has improved dramatically. The Government has introduced measures to promote reconciliation and peace. Poverty and mortality rates are down significantly, and immunization and literacy rates have risen substantially. These results are impressive.

Alfred Watkins and Anubha Verma, Building Science, *2008*

Rwanda is in a horrible situation; the main time bomb in Central Africa. It's a total dictatorship that oversees the smallest level of social life. It's become a nonsustainable state that is becoming more and more repressive and will explode one day. Planned work in Rwanda [by our agency] had to be canceled for political reasons, as there was no partner left who dared to say anything that the government might view as criticism. Except for some humanitarian implementers, nobody has a credible Rwandan partner anymore. Every nongovernment organization has become a semipublic institute. European social scientists don't dare speak out anymore, as they may lose the possibility of getting a visa to enter Rwanda.

International agency official, private interview, 2008

Rwanda is, by far, the quietest country I've visited in sub-Saharan Africa.[13] Banter and laughter are present but, during my dozen research visits to the country, are almost always muted. Unsurprisingly, Rwanda was exceptionally quiet during my first visit, just weeks after the 1994 genocide had ended. Yet even today, there are few spots in Rwanda that could be described as even a little noisy. While this is an unscientific observation, the subdued quality of most of its streets, restaurants, bars, and other public locales, particularly in contrast to the experience of visits to similar places in its neighboring nations, is striking.

Part of Rwanda's quiet is a direct result of the regulated nature of its society. While the airport can have an eerily hushed quality, it is only when one enters the city of Kigali that Rwanda's singularity arises. There are, for example, no street vendors because such irregular economic activity is outlawed (the exceptions are those hawking mobile phone cards and newspapers, but they are found only in certain locations). Selling food on the street and playing music outdoors in the evening, moreover, are both banned (Kron 2010b: 3). There is also little trash in most public zones because cleanliness is not only a matter of national pride but determined action: it is not uncommon to see people in matching T-shirts meticulously cleaning up streets and pathways. There are also few street children (many of whom were orphans from the civil war and genocide) in Rwanda's towns and capital because most were taken to a site that, for a brief period, attracted considerable attention. A report from Human Rights Watch in 2006, titled *Swept Away*, highlighted the government effort to collect thousands of street children and place them in a compound known as Gikondo.[14] Whether Gikondo is a center for rehabilitation or for detention is a matter of debate that was vigorously taken up by Minister of Internal Security Sheikh Musa Fazil Harerimana when he publicly condemned the report in forceful language and argued that Gikondo was a rehabilitation center for homeless children and "idlers" (Economist Intelligence Unit 2006: 14). For at least the handful of Rwandans whom I asked about *Swept Away* and the government response, the minister's condemnation was the first they had heard of the report. None had ever examined the report, much less visited the Human Rights Watch Web site. Over time and across many conversations, I gathered that visiting Internet sites containing mostly critical reports on Rwanda was uncommon, an apparent example of the risk aversion that figures prominently in the Rwandan youth research elaborated in this book.

Rwanda works. Efficiency, security, cleanliness, orderliness, patriotism, and hard, hard effort—these are featured hallmarks of the current Rwandan regime. They are also regularly praised by visitors, journalists, and many international agency officials. The country is pressed forward by the soft-spoken but dominant presence of President Kagame, a brilliant, serious, disciplined, imperious, resolute, intolerant, and, apparently, humorless former general who expects—demands—that all Rwandans be just as driven as he is and move in the direction that he and his aides have delineated. If the president and members of his regime can be stridently contemptuous of criticism in public, they can be inquisitive, courteous, and reflective in private. The only people who seem able to relax a bit in Rwanda are its few international tourists, who take in Rwanda's breathtaking vistas and visit the mountain home of gorillas. They also routinely visit the nation's genocide memorials. Rwanda is a serious place run by serious people.

It is difficult to draw a bead on this tiny, landlocked country.[15] Is it an engine of transformative growth and visionary reform? The answer would have to be "yes," and to a significant degree. At the same time, does its regime crack down on dissent and maintain a very high degree of social order? Again, to a significant degree, most certainly, and in most respects the current government has been unrepentant about its record on human rights, democracy, and social control. Contemporary literature on Rwanda is mostly unhelpful in gathering a balanced picture of contemporary life there because much of it is so sharply drawn between the upbeat and the downbeat.

Glowing accounts of Rwanda's current state are increasingly common. The movement from a nation shorn of many of its people (either from extermination or after having fled the country as refugees or fugitives of justice) right after the 1994 genocide to its current state has indeed been dramatic. Some of the writing about postgenocide Rwanda could not be more complimentary, such as the following description by Stephen Kinzer, in which contemporary Rwanda is characterized as having "recovered from civil war and genocide more fully than anyone imagined possible and is united, stable, and at peace. Its leaders are boundlessly ambitious. Rwandans are bubbling over with a sense of unlimited possibility. Outsiders, drawn by the chance to help transform a resurgent nation, are streaming in" (2008: 2). Philip Gourevitch highlights an array of specific achievements of President Paul Kagame and his government since the end of the genocide and civil war: "On the fifteenth anniversary of the genocide, Rwanda is one of the safest and most orderly countries in Africa. Since 1994, per-capita gross domestic product has nearly tripled, even as the population has increased by nearly twenty-five per cent, to more than ten million [as of 2009]. There is national health insurance, and a steadily improving education system. Tourism is a boom industry and a strong draw for foreign capital investment" (2009: 37). Gourevitch names other achievements as well: Internet availability is growing, cell phones "work nearly everywhere," "soldiers are almost nowhere to be seen" (37), and "there is incessant construction" of buildings of all kinds (38). He also mentions that Rwanda is both "the only government on earth in which the majority of parliamentarians are women" and "the only nation where hundreds of thousands of people who took part in mass murder live intermingled at every level of society with the families of their victims" (37, 38).

The countervailing viewpoint on postwar, postgenocide Rwanda is equally compelling. A key feature of this second perspective is the severely constricted environment for public expression and dissent. Transparency International's scores for Rwanda, already uniformly low, marginally declined between 2005 and 2007 in the categories of both "Accountability and Public Voice" and "Civil Liberties." They slightly improved in the categories of "Rule of Law" and "Anticorruption and Transparency" (Burnet 2008: 1).[16] Transparency International also notes that even if Rwandan parliamentarians are mainly women, they are also overwhelmingly of the same party: the ruling Rwandan Patriotic Front (RPF) (4). Civil society organizations in Rwanda only "speak publicly and influence policy decisions when their views are in line with those of the government and the RPF" and "are very careful to avoid criticizing the government, the RPF, the president or their policies" (4,5). Although Rwanda has legal guarantees of freedom of expression and the media on the books, "in practice the media are still tightly controlled by the government" (5). In addition, "The government and security forces continue to arrest, detain, or 'disappear' critics of the government, the RPF or the president" (8). Johan Pottier adds that non-Rwandans attempting to analyze Rwanda are, in his view, "hampered by the Rwandan government's insistence that outsiders should have no opinions of their own" (2002: 207).

Filip Reyntjens, in a scathing review of events in Rwanda in the first postgenocide decade (1994–2004), provides additional criticisms of the state of Rwandan governance. While he notes that the Rwandan government has publicly outlawed ethnic discrimination of any kind, including "even the notion of ethnicity," Reyntjens also asserts that the governing RPF effectively employs ethnic favoritism by reserving "access to power, wealth and knowledge to [ethnic] Tutsi" (2004: 187). He describes a "dismal" human rights record for the RPF "from day one," when it was a rebel movement that invaded Rwanda from neighboring Uganda in 1990. Reyntjens estimates that the RPF massacred as many as a hundred thousand civilians between when the civil war resumed in April and again in September 1994 (the genocide concurrently took place from April to June of that year) and tens of thousands more in 1997, during a counteroffensive against the extremist Hutu *génocidaires* in northwest Rwanda (194–95). He further cites numerous sources to suggest that, "before, during and after the genocide, the RPF killed tens of thousands of innocent civilians" (197).[17] The issue of how many people RPF soldiers may have killed during times of civil war or the genocide, or thereafter, is not one that I pursue any further here, except to say that attempts to negate or underestimate the immensity of the 1994 genocide, during which, by two assessments, more than three quarters of all ethnic Tutsi were murdered (Kuperman 2001 and Des Forges 1999, cited in Sommers 2006b: 143) (not including the perhaps fifty thousand moderate and other Hutu who were also killed), are preposterous and disingenuous.

A key component of the second, critical perspective is Rwanda's ongoing military engagement in the neighboring DRC. It is not an issue to which most proponents of the first, praiseworthy perspective, which highlights Rwanda's dramatic economic rise since the genocide, pay particular attention. But since the issue is troubling, significant, and (at the time of this writing) ongoing, it requires mention here. Gérard Prunier's book on what he refers to as "Africa's world war" in the DRC effectively draws out Rwanda's formative role in the conflict. Rwanda has staged military incursions into "the Zairian vortex" since September 1996 (2009: 75), which was first aimed at the refugee camps containing well-armed Rwandan *génocidaires* and perhaps two million Rwandan civilians. What followed was complex, brutal, and unusually deadly for civilians: estimates of civilian deaths since the beginning of the war in the DRC have reached 5.4 million people (Coghlan et al. 2008: ii).[18] Reyntjens cites reports estimating that two hundred thousand Rwandan refugees were "unaccounted for" (but most likely killed or scattered by Rwanda's army, he infers) and that, later in the conflict in the DRC, the actions of the Rwandan army and its aligned militia in eastern DRC "conveys an image of large-scale and deliberate atrocities" (2004: 205). Powerful contingents of the remaining Rwandan *génocidaires* continue to prey on civilians mainly in eastern DRC, as well as, from time to time, inside Rwanda itself. They constitute one of a broad array of domestic and international military forces that have cut a broad swathe of destruction, chaos, and plunder across much of the DRC and remain a prominent security concern for the Rwandan government.[19]

Two aspects of this war, both brought forth by Prunier, are relevant to this study. First, there is the nature of Rwanda's rule that Prunier argues emerged from the crucible of war and genocide in 1990–94 and continued during its experience in Zaire/DRC. Prunier asserts that "the mainly Tutsi RPF had decided to 'liberate' Rwanda and create a 'new democratic Rwanda' free from ethnic domination.... But what actually happened later bore no resemblance to these theories." Prunier describes the government approach that emerged as "a policy of political control through terror. The RPF seemed to trust nobody in Rwanda, not even the Tutsi [genocide] survivors who were felt to be 'contaminated'" (2009: 19–20).

Second, there is the international aid that "went on as usual" throughout Rwanda's military engagement in Zaire/DRC. For the year 2001, Prunier shares three estimates of Rwanda's military budget. The Rwandan government figure of $55.6 million is by far the lowest. The highest is $161.8 million, provided by the International Crisis Group. The international aid community, Prunier asserts, accepted the lower figure, using it to "justify its high level of aid [to Rwanda] in proportion to the budget by arguing that it did not contribute to the war either directly (through misuse of aid) or indirectly (by allowing military spending to be financed extralegally while civilian spending would be taken care of by aid)" (2009: 243). Prunier then calculates the value of raw materials that the Rwandan government imported from the DRC in 1999 and 2000. The amounts are remarkable: 8.4 percent of the nation's gross domestic product in 1999 ($163.6 million) and 7.1 percent in 2000 ($163.4 million). Neither the Rwandan government's active involvement in the DRC war nor its apparently substantial enrichment from it appeared to alter significantly the levels of international aid that it received. In Prunier's view, "international aid has—rightly—come under heavy criticism both for prolonging the war and for favoring" those opposing the Congolese government in the war, which included Rwanda (2009: 244–45). He then quotes officials from several major donor institutions that provided assistance to the Rwandan government while hailing its performance in reforming government services, reducing poverty, and boosting the economy.

Concerns over Rwanda's engagement in the DRC continue to the present day. Despite the fact that "Rwanda still relies on foreign aid for roughly half of its budget" (Gourevitch 2009: 46), the Swedish and Netherlands governments suspended aid to Rwanda late in 2008 after a United Nations report stated that the Rwandan government was continuing to support ethnic Tutsi rebels in the DRC (Voice of America News 2008). Paul Kagame dismissed the news by stating that "the people of Rwanda will just have to learn to live without foreign funding" (quoted in Voice of America News 2008). The Rwandan government continues to be publicly unperturbed by the prospect of losing its international aid contributions, which Prunier suggests is largely due to the fact that Kagame's "capacity to fine-tune white guilt as a conductor directs an orchestra" may be unsurpassed among African leaders (2009: 332).

What is to be made of these two broad characterizations of Rwanda as either a nation that "has made remarkable progress in rebuilding its politics, economy and society" (World Bank 2008: 1) or one that is marked by "authoritarian rule and renewed structural violence" (Reyntjens 2004: 179)? Are they mutually exclusive? Before attempting to answer these questions, it is useful to highlight two general differences between the two literatures. The upbeat assessments of Rwanda tend to be ahistorical, highlighting what has taken place since the end of the genocide, while many of the publications that criticize Rwanda's performance contain backward looks to pregenocide Rwanda. Second, the dissenters to the grand view of Rwandan progress tend to focus largely on the ways in which Rwanda's rapid security and economic success have been achieved.

This second difference suggests how two apparently conflicting optics for examining contemporary Rwanda coexist. Much has been made of the "Singapore model" being tested in Rwanda. In one article, the upside of this model, and Rwanda's interest in it, is characterized in the following way: "Rwanda's dream of becoming the Singapore of Africa—an information technology hub for the resource-rich nations of Eastern and Central Africa—is a point of pride for the government, a matter of concern for some Rwandans, and a curiosity for just about everyone else" (Baldauf 2007: 2). It is an unusual vision for a country as poor as Rwanda. The high-tech plans of Rwanda's government require an educated workforce, and while significant strides are being made, Rwanda is a long way from achieving that. As a result, if Rwanda were to attain its ambitious goals, it runs the risk of expanding inequality at the same time. Scott Baldauf notes that "several aid groups have criticized [Rwanda's high-tech ambitions] as an investment in the rich at the expense of the poor" (4).

Kinzer's generous assessment of Kagame's Rwanda is revealing in part because he was allowed an unusually high degree of access to the president himself. He comes away vividly impressed with Rwanda and its openly authoritarian leader. Kinzer's summation suggests that Kagame's style of leadership is what Rwanda needs—and seeks:

> Rwandan leaders have sought to shape a governing system that meets their country's unique needs in an unimaginably delicate period. Under the umbrella of authoritarian rule, they have stabilized their country and set it on a path toward a better future. That is what ordinary Rwandans care about. They have little interest in politics or ideology. Most sense that their lives are slowly improving. They are happy that President Kagame has centralized so much power in his own hands and are not fearful that he is becoming a dictator. (2008: 331)

It is not entirely clear just how Kinzer concluded that "ordinary Rwandans" are happy about Kagame's rise to dictatorship, or more particularly how, under an emerging dictator as sensitive to criticism as President Kagame, one might openly dissent from such a view.[20] Kinzer's assessment seems representative of the generous assessments of Rwanda's situation in that it is consciously carried out, effectively, with blinders. To see Rwanda in positive terms, it appears that one must be comfortable with, and deem necessary for now, the government's authoritarianism.[21] There is also a strong tendency for those such as Kinzer, who see Rwanda's current state in almost entirely upbeat terms, to set aside or relegate to the background troubling aspects of Rwanda's current situation. In Kinzer's case, for example, Rwanda's active engagement in the DRC is not worthy of mention in his closing assessment of Kagame and his regime.

Kinzer's mention, in addition, that "nearly every foreigner" who resides in Rwanda "reject[s]" criticism of Rwanda's human rights record (2008: 328) was not supported by my interviews with foreign officials there. While some were unhesitatingly positive about the Rwandan regime and its style of governance, many were not. A foreigner serving as an international donor agency official, for example, hastily closed their Kigali office door and window before our interview began. When I asked why they had done this, the official expressed their concern about any comments reaching the ears of Rwandan colleagues, since such concerns could then be reported to Rwandan government authorities. After securing my assurance that no comment from our interview would be connected to the official, the official launched into a heated description of how troubling information about particular economic and service sectors had to be sanitized or framed in positive ways before it could be shared with government officials or the official's Rwandan colleagues.[22] Other foreign officials also mentioned performing this kind of self-censorship, which essentially sounded like providing a positive spin on troubling information. Officials said that they soldiered on in support of this approach in spite of the discomfort it caused them. Quite unlike Kinzer's findings, then, research for this book clearly pointed to a government with a widely held reputation for having a thin skin when it came to criticism, insisting on a collective denial of disquieting realities and sanction against mention of issues that may not be mentioned, such as ethnicity, dissent, official policies that weren't working well, the RPF's conduct during the civil war and the 1994 genocide period, and the wars in the former Zaire/DRC.

The following comment from President Kagame helps describe what Rwanda has become—in terms of its accomplishments and the shortcomings of the style of governance in Kagame's Rwanda: "We have to work on the minds of our people. We have to take them to a level where people re-spect work and work hard, which has not been the case in the past. You have to push and push. I hear whispers of criticism, complaints that people are being pushed too hard. I have no sympathy with that. People have to be pushed hard, until it hurts. I push myself, many days until I almost drop dead" (quoted in Kinzer 2008: 6). This quote captures the essential upside and downside of Rwanda's current situation. The tall, wiry titan in firm control over Rwandans is unquestionably confident, determined, rigid, unsympathetic, and driven. He also has a strong sense of where he wants Rwanda to go and how he wants Rwanda to get there. At the same time, President Kagame assumes that Rwandans need to be moved ahead and work harder—or, in the parlance of Rwandan officialdom, become "developed." Excuses are com-pletely, thoroughly unacceptable. It is as if President Kagame is still General Kagame: giving orders and expecting them to be carried out on time and to the letter. These tenets are also found in the statements of the many Rwan-dan government officials who were interviewed for this book. Strikingly, the perspective also applied to the operation of some donor agencies as well. As a donor official explained regarding a troubling report on Rwanda that the official's agency never released, "You toe the [Rwandan government] party line here. If you don't, you're out. No one wants to look bad before their bosses. So you pretend that everything's OK" (see the Sample Selection section in chapter 2 about anonymity for respondents). The collective impression of these views and approaches is of a Rwandan government that is hell-bent on progress according to a blueprint that cannot be revised, and that it will toler-ate little or no public dissent—even, apparently, from donor agencies—in the process.

In this process, over and over again there was strong evidence that policy decisions had already been made and must be followed. All that was required from Rwanda's citizenry was stolid perseverance and complete loyalty to its hard-working government. A patriotic Rwandan is, among other things, a diligent one. Resisters run the risk of being castigated with a truly dangerous label: being supporters of "divisionism." Donor governments rarely criticize the Rwandan government publicly, which is an indication either that they see little to criticize or that they share their concerns in private—or some com-bination of the two.[23] Those raising issues of rights and freedoms are mainly foreigners who haven't lived through Rwanda's genocide and, according to Rwandan government supporters, cannot appreciate the government's drive to improve the nation and provide security.[24] At the same time, many of those raising concerns regarding justice and rights warn that ignoring such elemental issues just might lead to the return of extreme violence in Rwanda—a result, after all, that has repeatedly befallen past authoritarian regimes in Burundi and Rwanda alike. The recipe that the Rwandan government is following, in short, is both yielding impressive results and raising serious questions. These two slices of Rwanda, as illustrated in the divergent assessments of Rwanda's situation, turn out to be halves of the same pie. In so many ways in Rwanda, the ends justify the means.

THE BLUEPRINT

The electric sign above the supermarket across the street from my Kigali hotel spelled out, in English, a variety of goods sold in the store. "Blackcurrant chewing gum," the sign flashed. Then, "Gotta Have . . . The Wrigley Company." And then, the sign announced something that the store did not sell: "Vision 2020."

Rwanda's Ministry of Finance and Economic Planning released its now-famous *Rwanda Vision 2020* document in July 2000. The vision is based on what the document characterized as "a national consultative process." The contributors to this process shared a "broad consensus on the necessity for Rwandans to clearly define the future of the country." The core goal of Vision 2020 was "to transform Rwanda's economy into a middle income country." To do this, Rwanda will require an annual growth rate of at least 7 percent until the year 2020. The Rwandan government gave itself twenty years to attain this and other goals (Ministry of Finance and Economic Planning 2000: 3). The document frankly states some of Rwanda's daunting challenges: it is landlocked, it has a narrow economic base, weak institutional capacity, diminishing agricultural productivity, a "severe shortage of professional personnel," unseemly public debt, and the impact of a genocide that, in the words of the document's authors, halved gross domestic product in a year and "plunged" 80 percent of all Rwandans into poverty (8). The plan is daring if not audacious: to promote macroeconomic stability, create wealth, foster entrepreneurship, reduce aid dependency, eventually create a thriving middle class, and—crucially—transform Rwanda from an agrarian into a knowledge-based economy. The compelling conclusion of this short document captures the relentless drive, urgency, and exceptional focus of the Rwandan government, as well as its frame of reference—surprisingly, nations in East Asia:

VISION 2020 represents an ambitious plan to raise the people of Rwanda out of poverty and transform the country into a middle-income country. Some will say it is too ambitious and that we are not being realistic when we set this goal. Others say that it is a dream. But, what choice does Rwanda have? To remain in the current situation is simply unacceptable for the Rwandan people. Therefore, there is a need to devise and implement policies as well as mobilize resources to bring about the necessary transformation to achieve this Vision. This is realistic based on the fact that countries with similar unfavourable initial conditions have succeeded. The development experience of the East Asian "Tigers" proves that this dream could be a reality. (2000: 25)

The United Nations Development Programme (UNDP), together with the Rwandan government, produced a mostly bubbly assessment of the first seven years of Vision 2020. "Rwanda's experience shows that even war-ravaged least-developed countries can make progress towards achieving sustainable long-term development." The document argues that Rwanda is "sufficiently small to consider the option of scaling up aid," which is already one of Africa's highest, at $55 per capita annually (UNDP 2007: 1). Dramatically increasing aid to Rwanda is indeed proposed. "In order to overcome the trap of decreasing agricultural productivity, poverty and population growth," Rwanda will require what the document calls a "Big Push of investments across a range of key sectors" (86).

Three pertinent comments are relevant. First, Rwanda's increasing renown as a location for economic growth, stability, and private investment (to say nothing of its determined efforts to attain the Millennium Development Goals [Ministry of Local Government, Good Governance, Community Development, and Social Affairs 2007: 3]), and Kagame's "doctrine of security, guided reconciliation, honest governance and, above all, self-reliance" (Kinzer 2008: 3), is confronted by its need for unusually high levels of foreign investment.[25] Rwanda receives large amounts of international aid despite its assertive stance toward donor government support. Expanding the education sector, for example, is partly informed by a policy requiring that all foreign investments directly support the Rwandan government's existing national policies and plans. Rwanda is at the forefront of a fairly groundbreaking approach to assistance from powerful donor governments and agencies. Donors often have explicit interests in funding, for example, basic or girls' education, or education in a particular geographic region. But if they attempt this in Rwanda, a Rwandan official with the Ministry of Education explained during a research interview, then the Rwandan government "may decline their aid" (Sommers 2004: 92). Donor assistance, in other words, must support existing national government objectives or it may be rejected. It is not an attitude to which donors are accustomed. But such a government approach to donor assistance may be "the only way to ensure that an education system is truly coordinated" (93). And it certainly does not seem to have damaged donor eagerness to support Rwanda's education sector.

A second comment foreshadows research findings about youth in the Rwandan capital. Both the original Vision 2020 document and the 2007 follow-up report assert that Rwanda's urban growth rates are low but rising.[26] Substantial evidence indicates that the nation's urban growth rates are already sky-high. As noted earlier in this chapter, Rwanda remains a mainly rural-based population (for now) with an unusually significant urban growth rate. While its annual urban growth rate is no longer the world's highest, it is second, at 6.5 percent a year (Burundi's is 6.8 percent; UNFPA 2007: 90).[27] Kigali is also visibly mushrooming in size, something I describe in part 3. In development terms, the stance on urbanization in the two documents suggests that Rwanda's development plans are not adequately addressing the needs of its burgeoning urban population. Whether this represents a denial of Rwanda's increasing shift toward cities remains to be seen.

Finally, there is the question of whether Rwandan youth have gained the attention they warrant. The answer appears to be no. Even though Rwanda has one of the youngest human populations in the world, it has nonetheless been possible to observe that the literature on Rwanda "is conspicuously thin on information about youth in the postwar and postgenocide period" (Sommers 2006b: 143). The fact that male youth were foot soldiers of the 1994 genocide has indeed been noted by scholars. Many in the genocide militias "were unemployed young men," African Rights states (1995: 56). Alison Des Forges notes that both the RPF and those organizing the *interahamwe* (those who work together) militias were recruiting youth into their respective forces just prior to the genocide (1999: 129). What took place during the genocide itself was "a near-complete engagement of youth at the forefront of involvement and victimization," when "young people became killers and the killed, rapists and the raped, and looters and the looted" (Sommers 2006b: 146).[28] And yet, after the genocide, attention to male (and female) youth concerns is decidedly underwhelming, despite some determined government efforts. Rwanda's National Youth Council (NYC), its Ministry of Youth (formerly the Ministry of Youth, Sports and Culture), and its National Youth Policy are examples of the government's engagement with youth issues (the NYC is examined in chapters 3 and 6). That said, youth are mentioned only once and in passing in the government's Vision 2020 document (Ministry of Finance and Economic Planning 2000: 13), and just twice in the 2007 follow-up report (UNDP 2007: 73, 75). This suggests an inadequate recognition of Rwandan youth concerns.

HOUSING

Field research for this book (2006–7) took place when Rwanda was undergoing a radical (and still ongoing) housing reform. There is a government regulation that directly and negatively affected youth efforts to construct houses: the national policy mandating that all new houses in rural areas should be built in community housing areas known as *imidugudu*. According to two government officials in 2007, rural youth were attracted to newly expanding areas in the capital where irregular, unplanned, and illegal housing was expanding. There, house rentals were cheap and generally available. Rumblings of change had created a sense that the Rwandan government's master plan for transforming Kigali aimed to take down the illegally built houses and put up new houses. Details of how this would be carried out were unknown. As one Kigali government official commented during the interviews, "What's obvious about the master plan is that they don't talk about places where they'll relocate people."

Rwanda's rural areas continue to be informed by a state-led vision of social reorganization: the *imidugudu*, an updated Rwandan concept of community where, quite unlike traditional Rwandan life, farmers would no longer live on their land in family compounds known as *rugo* but beside each other in new *imidugudu* villages.[29] It is controversial—the literature on what many observers consider forced "villagization" is almost entirely, if not profoundly, negative—and in all of the areas where the rural research was taking place, it was barely observable. The plan is for *imidugudu* villages to have the benefits of "development": running water, electricity, and easy access to information (including the Internet), health services, and education. From time to time, and generally near the government sector and cell offices, *imidugudu* could be found.[30] They were easily distinguishable: lines of mostly mud houses with roofs made of shiny new *mabati* (imported, expensive corrugated roofing sheets). None of the *imidugudu* that we visited during the research period had the promised amenities with the exception of shared water taps in some *imidugudu*. Most Rwandans still lived as they always have: in traditional *ingo* on hillsides and in valleys, even though nearly all were under mounting pressure to soon move to *imidugudu*. In Kigali, most residents live in houses that are made of illegal materials (mud, mostly) (Des Forges 2006: 369) and therefore are increasingly prone to destruction by state order: an estimated 80 percent of all Kigali households are vulnerable to "expropriations or market-driven evictions" (Durand-Lasserve 2007: 7). The state, moreover, owns virtually all land in the capital (5). If one accepts estimates that 80 percent of Kigali residents and 94 percent of rural residents will be changing their residence because of government mandates (Human Rights Watch 2001: 1), the collective result is breathtaking: the Rwandan state is in the process of forcibly changing the residences of nearly all of its citizens. Unsurprisingly, one of the central findings of the research for this book is that there is a housing crisis in Rwanda and, secondarily, Rwandan government regulations and restrictions on housing are—intentionally or not—making a dire situation significantly worse for its youth. Rwanda's housing situation is hardly a small concern, particularly since it is tied to the nation's severe overpopulation and land degradation. To deal with housing in Rwanda, in short, is to deal with the burning land question. And that means playing with fire.

Social engineering runs at the core of the immense housing reform policy. An RPF official explained that the *imidugudu* idea originated during the civil war years with civilian committee members who had been tasked to develop postwar policies for the nation. A former RPF member who was involved in this committee work recalled that committee members asked themselves, "How do you change the way people are scattered to get them together, so they don't continue subsistence farming, and [in order] to make more farmland available?" From the outset, a specific method for modernizing agriculture and rural life was the RPF's goal. Subsistence farming was to be reduced, opening the way for a new way of living that was based on, presumably, cash crops and off-farm work. The answer was, in the official's words, "by creating centers. We built the idea around the youth. The idea was to put new houses around the school, market, and other infrastructure that communities need. Youth still wouldn't have land, but we drew up the principle of this plan, not the specific design of it. We have to change, slowly by slowly, the life of people." Even here, one can see that rural Rwanda's underlying problem—the land shortage—was not fully addressed by the mandates to create *imidugudu* and reform agriculture: youth still would not have land.

The RPF's vision for rural change got underway as an integral part of the Rwandan government's emergency response to a severe housing shortage that developed when over a million "old case" refugees from the surrounding countries (that is, mostly ethnic Tutsi who had fled Rwanda mainly in 1959–64) returned to Rwanda in the years 1994–98 (Van Leeuwen 2001: 630), in addition to an estimated 2.5 million "new case" refugees (that is, mostly ethnic Hutu who had fled the civil war and genocide violence circa 1994) returning from Tanzania and the former Zaire in the same postgenocide period; see the Differences section later in this chapter. In that period, "international organizations helped to build 250 communities with 85,000 houses" (Hilhorst and Van Leeuwen 2000: 264). As a result, "What started as an emergency project turned into a far reaching development programme" (264). The emergency situation engaged international organizations in the construction of huge numbers of new houses for Rwandans and, in the process, catalyzed the government's plans for wholesale villagization. Despite concerns among some international officials that the Rwandan state use of emergency housing to establish *imidugudu* was "a device to improve control over the population," international agencies largely supported the combined housing construction and villagization work because "the immense and obvious need for shelter" for the millions of returnees "turned the programme simply into a necessity" (Van Leeuwen 2001: 632).

The government's plans to reform land and housing in rural and urban Rwanda face five significant challenges. First, the connection between land and villagization is problematic. The *imidugudu* program's driving assumption is that villagization "would rationalize agriculture" (Pottier 2002: 195) because, "in the eyes of the new RPF government, the dispersed settlement pattern common in many of the rural areas of Rwanda represented a waste of space" (Van Leeuwen 2001: 631). Fewer people living directly on small plots of land, the government's analysis suggested, would pave the way for making rural land use more productive and market based. However, Rwanda's land reform process (officially underway with the new national land law in 2005) is complex, not least because, as Pottier warns, "policy makers have never produced evidence to show that land consolidation boosts productivity." In addition, Pottier notes that "there exists the vexed question of what compensation will be paid to Rwandans who become landless" from forced relocations (2006: 523, 524).

A second challenge stems from a fundamental component of the government's strategy to move all rural Rwandans onto *imidugudu*: restricting all new house building to *imidugudu* plots instead of the established tradition of building them on inherited family farmland. Since cultural norms demand that all male youth in Rwanda build their own houses before they can marry and be considered men, the restriction impacts them explicitly and directly. Furthermore, research for this book details how the shift to *imidugudu* is slow, arduous, and scarcely even feasible for most rural youth today. Interviews with cell- and sector-level officials of the government strongly supported this assessment. Interviews with these midlevel government officials, however, also illuminated the national government's steadfast commitment to changing Rwanda's landscape significantly and literally, regardless of any difficulty. "Emphasis will be put on the planning and development of improved rural and urban human settlements consistent with the contemplated sustainable land use and environment protection schemes," the Republic of Rwanda's Economic Development and Poverty Reduction Strategy for 2008–12 announces (Ministry of Finance and Economic Planning 2007: 40). Social engineering is a necessity, not a concern. In the same document, the government explains that "seven districts with the worst living conditions will be restructured, and their inhabitants will be relocated to better houses endowed with basic services" (40).

Third, and related to the difficulties rural youth face in constructing houses, is the availability and price of locally made clay roof tiles. Roofing is the most expensive housing material in Rwanda. A great many male youth work to save money to buy roof tiles because they can accumulate them over time. As is explained in chapter 5, a government regulation to protect woodland curtailed roof tile production and radically increased roof tile prices. Building a house, already difficult for nearly all male youth, became much more expensive.

Fourth, there is no precedent of success in the region. Van Leeuwen notes that Rwanda's villagization (and resettlement) program has "appeared to have similar shortcomings to earlier programmes" in Tanzania, Ethiopia, and Mozambique (2001: 625). The governments of all three countries eventually abandoned such programs because they were "expensive failures with varying adverse effects for the population and the development of the country" (626). Most prominently, the programs failed to provide adequate services, caused decreases in agricultural production and reductions in access to land, created a negative credit balance, and spurred negative environmental effects and communal disharmony (626–27). Rwandan government officials have argued that Rwanda is a case apart. Yet while it has been argued that the *imidugudu* policy is voluntary and therefore is not comparable to other attempts in the region (in the early period, some cases appeared to be voluntary) (633), interviews for this book with government officials about housing policy made it clear that this is not at all the case.[31] It has also been mentioned that local residents who lost land either during the creation of *imidugudu* or who were obliged to share land with refugee returnees without compensation created enduring local conflicts (Des Forges 2006: 363).

Finally, there are significant housing problems in the urban areas. The rationalization of land use in cities, as set forth in highly technical terms in the master plans for Rwanda's primary urban areas, faces the challenge of having 83 percent of Kigali's population living in illegal, informal settlements (oz Architecture et al. 2006: 52). Mud houses have been popping up in Kigali just about everywhere, climbing up hillsides and across valleys that were not previously part of the city. The extensive, expansive Kigali Master Plan has answers for all of this. The approach is almost entirely technical; social concerns are not its focus. The plan contains impressive discussions of water supply, storm water, wetlands, wastewater, waste management, transport nodes, and telecommunications. In terms of housing, however, reality has taken a different turn. Most Kigali residents live as renters in housing that is vulnerable.[32] In a situation common in many developing-country cities with rapidly expanding populations, the threat of eviction is common because securing legal housing is so difficult: "Individual housing constructions are authorized on land leased by public authorities, provided they conform to the same set of norms and standards. Few households can manage this, and most have no choice but to rely on informal land markets, and are thus exposed to eviction" (Durand-Lasserve 2007: 6). Informal housing is also endangered by private investors seeking land to construct new buildings. If the investors get approval from the city government on a site where informal housing exists, they can "negotiate the 'voluntary departure' of the occupants or their eviction" (6). The promise of compensation for the removal of one's house (reportedly, it does not always happen) is possible only for those who own houses, not for those who rent. Despite touted new housing for the urban poor, resettlement options are limited. Alarmingly, Durand-Lasserve notes that "the practice of eviction without fair compensation or without offering resettlement options is creating a population of homeless families" (6).

Regardless of the challenges to and the naysayers of Rwanda's approach to its colossal land and housing challenges, the government of Rwanda has been consistent, dispassionate, technocratic, and emphatically clear about what, in its view, must take place: radical land and housing change. The ambitious land and housing policies it has set forth are absolutely sacrosanct. In the process, the Rwandan government's determined forward movement consistently overlooks mainly Western criticisms of its human rights record by redefining what those rights mean within Rwanda. To Kagame, rights in Rwanda mainly concern eradicating poverty, not accessing various individual freedoms. As President Kagame noted,

> I don't give too much time to some of these criticisms. They are misplaced, out of context, made by people who are used to dealing with ordinary situations. Ours is not an ordinary situation. . . . For me, human rights is about everything. Even languishing in poverty as a result of colonization and other situations of the past violated human rights. If you solve that, you resolve the human rights issue. People in the West shy away from that and don't even want to talk about it. They run away from the significant blame that would be put on their shoulders. This is not just one person here or there. This is the killing of societies or nations we're talking about. (Quoted in Kinzer 2008: 323)

Led by its president and with virtually unfettered support from Western donor nations and agencies, Rwanda's society and landscape are being reinvented. For the Rwandan government and its many supporters, the urgency is clear. In the countryside, there are far too many people living on far too little land. In the urban areas, the explosion of unplanned housing is unacceptable. In both, environmental threats caused by land use and overpopulation must be addressed. Accordingly, sweeping, government-driven reforms aim to make land use efficient and effective while reorganizing and modernizing every city and village. The push to permanently change Rwanda's landscape and way of life is under way.

OTHER ISSUES

While housing and land together constitute the predominant context within which the lives of Rwanda's rural and urban youth play out, there are several other issues that require brief description, as they surface and impact directly on the lives of Rwandan youth in the countryside and its capital.

Difference. Public mention of ethnicity was outlawed in Rwanda in 2002 (P. Clark and Kaufman 2009: 9). The rationale was entirely understandable: a person's ethnicity determined whether a Rwandan might live or die during the 1994 genocide. Yet prohibiting open discussion of ethnic identities does not cause ethnic and other differences to vanish, particularly in a society as consumed by difference as in Rwanda. Underneath the prohibition on ethnicity is evidence that it remains influential. Prunier highlights an important yet largely overlooked fact about Rwandan demographics: the population only marginally declined after the 1994 genocide because ethnic Tutsi who had fled Rwanda at the dawn of independence (starting in 1959), known as "old caseload refugees," returned in droves. These returnees, however, were significantly different, as a group, from the Tutsi who had remained in Rwanda and perished during the genocide:

> the "old caseload refugees"—the Tutsi returnees coming from abroad—were sociologically quite different from the victims of the genocide. Roughly the same numbers came back (around 700,000) as had been killed (800,000). But the [genocide] victims had been ordinary Rwandese, with a majority of rural dwellers. The [returnee] newcomers were not peasants; they had lived in exile in situations where access to land was restricted, and many of them had no experience in agriculture. . . . [The returnees] tended to congregate in the towns and to look for and monopolize the moneyed jobs. (Prunier 2009: 5)

While it is not unusual for a former rebel army to position members of its military command and their supporters in influential government positions after assuming power, this certainly seems to have occurred in Rwanda. Villa Jefremovas, for example, observes that "the most powerful members of the current government are 'Ugandan' Rwandans who supported the RPF in the struggle for power" (2002: 125). Moreover, President Kagame's 2008 declaration that Rwanda had become an Anglophone country (Gbadamassi and Ghartey-Mould 2008)—making English the main foreign language, not the French language that the Belgians and French, close supporters of former Rwandan regimes, naturally preferred—further positions those with fluency in English (namely, former Tutsi refugees from Uganda) to take particular advantage of the new linguistic environment. Ethnicity of a sort appears to have remained significant in Rwanda and, reportedly, not just for ethnic Tutsi. Citing other sources, Jefremovas warns that "far from moving beyond ethnic labels, the RPF has conflated the term Hutu with *genocidaire* and rationalized the exclusion of Hutu who are not part of the RPF from negotiations on the basis that they are all *genocidaires*" (2002: 122).[33] The debate on the utility of banning public use of ethnicity in Rwanda remains white hot. For example, while René Lemarchand warns that the ban makes Hutu and Tutsi identities "all the more pregnant with mutual enmities" (2009: 75), President Kagame pushes back firmly: "Lemarchand's attempt to see everything Rwandan through the ethnic prism will not help bring Rwandans together" (Kagame 2009: xxiii).

Never mentioning ethnicity—in any way, ever—with respondents during field research for this book did not negatively impact this endeavor. Ethnicity neither came up in any interview nor was ever raised by an interviewer. One may presume that most poor youth were Hutu, since the overwhelming majority of Rwandans have long been known to be ethnic Hutu, and that some ethnic Tutsi, particularly those who had returned from Uganda as refugees, dominated government power. But making such distinctions were beside the point of this research, which concerns the lives of the poor and undereducated majority of Rwandan youth regardless of their ethnicity. In fact, the research findings drove home the point that class differences are exceptionally important in Rwandan society. While Rwandans regularly volunteered many kinds of difference during interviews, the primary reference point was class. Indeed, it is entirely conceivable that similar descriptions of dramatic class distinctions also would have surfaced had the research been conducted prior to Rwanda's civil war and genocide.

In addition, and due to the government ban, mentioning ethnic issues during interviews with Rwandans runs the risk of endangering the safety of interviewees as well as researchers, who would undoubtedly risk detention if they were found to be discussing ethnicity with Rwandan citizens. The research effort surely would have come to an abrupt end as well. Given the situation on the ground, then, asking Rwandans about ethnicity was both unnecessary and probably, if not plainly, unethical.

As is described in part 2, one way of describing rural Rwandan society is to separate the "people from up" from the "people from down." This is only one way in which Rwandans regularly refer to potent class differences. These differences tend to be identified as dualities, such as the "High People" and the "Very Low People" (or even the "Ignorant People") (Sommers 2006a: 85), and are apparent to Rwandans in many ways. A taxi driver in Kigali, for example, related the difference between people with different mobile phone number prefixes. A person with a mobile number beginning with the 0830 prefix signifies that "Wewe ni Bosi kabisa" ("you are absolutely a Boss"), while any prefix beginning with 03 "ni mbaya" ("is bad"). The prefix 03, the taxi driver explained, is a common one for a houseboy or house girl. Such a phone is given to a servant in order to receive their employer's calls. A boss, the driver explained, thus answers a phone by saying "hello," while a servant answers a phone by saying "yes, Boss!" Another common differentiation separating people is signified by their preference of beer. It is widely accepted that those who drink Amstel beer (which is more expensive and considered high quality) are wealthy and influential people, while those who drink Primus (which is cheaper and is thought to be of lower quality than Amstel) are not.

Not all differences in Rwanda are dualistic. There are identities determined by region. A decade ago, nicknames for "old caseload" refugee returnees were used to identify which of the four neighboring countries they had returned from. The nicknames, together with a fifth for genocide survivors, are now banned in Rwanda.[34] Bert Ingelaere and An Ansoms cite six distinct categories of rural Rwandans identified by Rwandan government studies:[35]

- *Abakire* (The Rich). Those with significant amounts of farmland, livestock, and cash savings. They employ agricultural workers, have servants, are educated, send their children to school, and "can solve any problem as they know many people" (Ingelaere 2007: 12).
- *Abakungu* (The Rich without Money). Those with food security, some livestock, good soils, and cash.
- *Abakene Bufashije* (The Poor with Means). "Poor with a bit more land, few animals, besides subsistence production they have a small income to satisfy a few other needs" (Ansoms 2009: 57).
- *Abakene* (The Poor). Those having land but unable to produce a surplus to sell. They may have limited livestock (perhaps one goat), no savings, and often work for others.
- *Abatindi* (The Vulnerable). The "very poor" (ibid.), with limited land and low harvests, and no animals; they work for others.
- *Abatindi Nyakujya* (The Most Vulnerable). The completely destitute, with no land and no animals. They beg or work for others, are "not respected, discriminated, and look like 'fools'" (ibid.). "There is nobody who can help them" (Ingelaere 2007: 12).[36]

These six Rwandan gradations of difference in rural Rwanda vividly illuminate just how difficult life is for nearly all those who live there. Even the second-highest category—The Rich without Money—are merely stable. The bottom four of the six constitute some dimension of impoverishment, with absolute, abject poverty as the lowest level. These are indications of a nation in which "inequality is high by international[,] including African[,] standards" (World Bank 2008: 5) and is increasing.[37] Ansoms's conclusion from her research on the Rwandan government's agricultural policies is startling: instead of being "pro-poor" (as the government promotes them), the policies actually "focus on maximum output and growth, without regard for equitable wealth distribution." The result is a rural sector plagued by socioeconomic inequalities that are worsening, which "may even increase conflict risk by enlarging the mass of rural poor with few if any employment chances outside the rural sector" (2008: 25). The situation of Rwanda's urban youth, virtually unresearched to date, is detailed in part 3.

HIV/AIDS. Trying to gauge the magnitude of the HIV/AIDS situation in Rwanda results in confusion. Data on genocide victims suggested that HIV/AIDS rates within the Rwandan population were high. It was estimated that a quarter of a million Rwandan women were raped during the genocide and that, among the survivors, 70 percent were infected with HIV (Amnesty International 2004: 3). While that figure is of course not representative of the entire Rwandan population, it indicated that HIV/AIDS infection was a serious concern in Rwandan society. A sense of the seriousness of the situation was suggested by subsequent statistics, such as, in 2003, the Rwanda AIDS Control Programme's estimate that "at least 13 percent" of Rwandans were infected with HIV/AIDS (IRIN 2003). The confusion surfaced when a 2005 national survey reported, somewhat remarkably, that the HIV/AIDS infection rate among adults in Rwanda was 3 percent (Institut National de la Statistique du Rwanda and ORC Macro 2006: xxix), while the 13 percent figure persisted in two forms: as the infection rates for urban dwellers in Rwanda (OZ Architecture et al. 2006: 54), and for Rwandan youth (Ministry of Public Service and Labour 2005: 27).

In contrast, the 2005 national survey also stated that "among 15–24 year-olds, the [HIV] prevalence in Kigali is 3.4 percent" (Institut National de la Statistique du Rwanda and ORC Macro 2006: xxix). Since findings from this research, particularly among urban youth (many of whom would fall within this age range), strongly pointed to a significantly higher prevalence rate, two comments are necessary regarding the methodology of the national survey. First, the design of the 2005 survey included only what the authors considered "ordinary households" in their sample. While this category is not defined, the lifestyles of nearly all urban youth and many rural youth in the sample for this book would seem to exclude them from belonging to households that might be considered "ordinary" in the 2005 survey. Second, the severe social stigma against being labeled as HIV positive, as uniformly reported in research for this book, would probably prevent loads of youth from participating in the HIV testing that the 2005 survey provided to members of the sample (7, 8). In other words, the national survey appears to contain a self-selecting sample. This issue is revisited in chapter 9.

Decentralization. Government decentralization in Rwanda is creating administrative reforms and increasing the level of authority and responsibility at lower levels of the government. It is informed and inspired by the following declaration in *Rwanda Vision 2020*: "People's participation at the grassroots level will be promoted through the decentralisation process, whereby local communities will be empowered in the decision making process, enabling them to address the issues, which affect them, the most" (Ministry of Finance and Economic Planning 2000: 12). The subsequent reforms have been characteristically expansive, rapid, and intriguing. A component of the decentralization process is to make the performance contracts (known as *imihigo*) of many government officials—including President Kagame—publicly available. Government efforts, ever determined, include frank assessments of the strengths and weaknesses of decentralization. On the plus side, the government noted that there has been "a visible improvement in the participation of women and civil society in local governance and socioeconomic reforms through the decentralization process." On the minus side, the speed of the reforms "has contributed to an imbalance between stakeholders' expectations created by decentralization policies and real capacities at [the] local level to deliver" (Ministry of Local Government, Good Governance, Community Development, and Social Affairs 2007: 10, 11).[38] While such challenges with decentralization, and the fact that the Rwandan government is attempting an array of major reforms at the same time, might be put down to bumps on a learning curve, Ingelaere suggests otherwise. His research suggests that the decentralization process is "an ambitious and internally coherent national ideology and vision [that] is translated to the local level where measures are taken by coercion irrespective of 'real-world' considerations. . . . [In addition,] local authorities often demand a lot of investments [from] the population, often enforced through a system of fines" (Ingelaere 2007: 38). While the issues of fines and regulations will emerge as important issues in subsequent chapters, it is also the case that the apparent competence and diligence of government officials with which the research team interacted was noteworthy.

Regulated Trade. Youth and adults alike explained that obtaining government permits to sell goods in a particular place legally (in a market or along a street) was, from their experience, difficult or impossible. The reason given was that it took funds, and perhaps connections, to obtain such a space. Most had neither. Most also reported not to have other avenues for making some sort of a living. As a result, in Kigali, one of the most common forms of economic activity for urban youth was to try to make money by hawking their goods on foot and without a permit. They knew that this "unorganized commerce" was illegal and invited intercessions by members of the Local Defense Force (LDF; a volunteer corps of government security officers) or policemen. What has ensued is a kind of economic cat and mouse involving people trying to hawk goods without getting caught and government officials on the lookout for precisely this sort of economic behavior.

The National Youth Council (NYC). The task of locally elected National Youth Council members is vast: to support and promote youth development in Rwanda. They all work as volunteers (except those working at the Executive Secretariat level in Kigali) with limited budgets. Their challenges in rural and urban Rwanda are examined in chapters 3 and 6, respectively.

Youth Organizations. One of this book's findings is that few youth who were surveyed reported to be receiving development support from government or nongovernment sources. Given the fragile state of nongovernment youth organizations in Rwanda, that was not surprising. The research team surveyed twenty-eight nongovernment youth organizations in Rwanda in 2007. The survey mainly revealed tiny agencies carrying out training activities that attempted to engage directly with Rwandan youth in vocational, agricultural, literacy, life skills, HIV/AIDS prevention, and civic educational concerns. Many of the youth organizations appeared to be led by unemployed male university graduates based in Kigali. Outreach, activities, and budgets were mostly minimal. Few programs had been evaluated, so the impact of these programs was impossible to assess.

Education. Boosting the education sector, naturally enough, is a critical component for Rwanda's transformation "from an agrarian to a knowledge-based economy" (Ministry of Finance and Economic Planning 2000: 9). "There is clearly a need to educate and train people at all levels: primary, secondary and tertiary," the government's Vision 2020 proclaims, "with special attention paid to the quality of education." There will also be "major emphasis" placed on vocational and technical training targeted at secondary school graduates and "various sectors of society" including youth. The document also states that a skilled labor force is needed not only to spur the nation's economic transformation but to develop secondary and tertiary schooling as well (13).

The results thus far have been mixed. Although tuition for primary schools is nearly free, the United Kingdom's Department for International Development (DfID) states that almost 95 percent of Rwandan children enroll in primary school but only half complete it (DfID 2009).[39] Secondary school statistics are much worse. The Rwandan government's Economic Development and Poverty Reduction Strategy for 2008–12 states that "only a small fraction of children enter or complete secondary education" and that secondary-level enrollment disparities between the richest and poorest households is greater than at the primary level—and is increasing (Republic of Rwanda 2007: 23). One can clearly see the steep enrollment triangle (not uncommon in developing countries) between the three education levels. The start of primary school includes nearly all children of that age. It drops to half by the end of primary school. Then enrollment collapses: to 10 percent for secondary school-age children for secondary school and 3.2 percent for the tertiary level (ibid.).

The investment statistics help explain why school experiences for most Rwandan children and youth are so limited and why Rwanda's education system, in terms of access and equity, is unbalanced. Nearly half of the national education budget (48.2 percent) is spent on primary education. A ranking of such expenses positions Rwanda as twenty-seventh out of 110 countries (NationMaster n.d.). However, 16.7 percent of the government's education budget goes to secondary school. Only one country in 107 reserves a smaller proportion of its education budget for secondary education. The proportion jumps markedly for tertiary investment: to 34.7 percent of all government spending on education. This level of investment is remarkably high: only three countries in 108 invest a greater proportion (NationMaster n.d.). The Rwandan government seems mainly intent on full enrollment for Rwandan children in primary school while allocating truly significant amounts of its reserve for relatively few students at its universities. The vast education gap in the middle—concerning secondary-school-age youth—applies to vocational education as well. The government states that "it is a matter of concern that not only were there no more professional and technical training centres in 2006 than in 2000, but that several of the existing centres are not adequately equipped and fully operational." Meanwhile, and "of greatest concern," is the fact that "population growth is higher than planned" (Republic of Rwanda 2007: 33). With more students on the way, the situation is unlikely to get easier.

The loaded, overlapping issues of ethnic identification and history play significant roles in Rwanda's educational environment, particularly for its youth. There is an official government version of history, featuring a general condemnation of ethnicity, an assertion that Belgian colonialists imported it, and the view that ethnic identification has been used in Rwanda to kill people of certain ethnicities (mainly Tutsi) (Freedman et al. 2008: 674–75).[40] Challenges to the government version are not permitted. The government's intent is "to instill a single national history in the minds of all Rwandans," "foster social cohesion," and bolster national unity and reconciliation across society (Hodgkin 2006: 205). The postgenocide moratorium on teaching history in Rwandan schools has slowly begun to ease. Warnings and alarm have been sounded about what amounts to a policy of state control over memories that include genocide. The warnings are worth reflecting upon. Marian Hodgkin challenges an assumption that she contends is pervasive in the international donor community that "formal education is inherently positive and harmless" before attacking donor support for the Rwandan government, as donors "rarely mention the moratorium on the teaching of history" and instead tend to "focus on positive developments" (206). More recently, following a facilitated process with Rwandan educators and government officials in which reintroducing history into Rwandan secondary schools was discussed, the Rwandan government "publicly embraced the importance of teaching history, as well as the adoption of new teaching methodologies" (Freedman et al. 2008: 686). That said, the leaders of that study also found that the government's "policy of denying the reality of ethnicity and the inability to discuss ethnicity comfortably make it hard for everyday citizens to process what happened during the genocide and to talk about lingering fears and dangers" (685).

Meanwhile, although teaching history in Rwanda's formal schools is moving slowly, the government's version of history has been a featured part of a controversial nonformal education program called *ingando*, or "solidarity camps" (Mgbako 2005: 202). *Ingando*'s underlying purpose is under debate. The Rwandan government view is that they "demystify and break down barriers between people by freeing free expression" (Musoni 2007: 10), "promote patriotism," and lead to "a Genocide ideology-free society" (Buhigiro 2009). *Ingando*'s purpose is also considered "reeducation" (Freedman et al. 2008: 674; Moore 2009) and "political indoctrination" (Mgbako 2005: 224). The government plans to have every Rwandan adult "attend *ingando* at some point during his or her life" (209). Among the groups that have thus far attended *ingando* solidarity camps are former *génocidaires,* former combatants during the civil war, genocide and the warfare in DRC as part of their preparation for returning to civilian life (209), and secondary-school graduates who will enter a university in Rwanda (203). Several university-educated Rwandans and international agency officials privately reported during our interview process that the *Ingando* curriculum version for incoming university students differed in at least one way: it included teaching them how to use a gun.

Just in case extreme violence erupts again. Rwanda's continued war footing does not make sense unless fear of genocide is taken into account. The existential terror of annihilation is haunting and can take a long while to recede. With the government's tight grip over Rwandan society, the country often feels in lockdown. Despite many signs of progress and a booming economy, Rwanda's legacy of encompassing, bloodcurdling violence remains while its poverty, inequality, land scarcity, urbanization, social controls, and youthfulness are manifest. What most youth will do with their lives is unclear, even to them. As this book details, the difficulties of becoming an adult in Rwanda, or simply surviving, fuel alarming degrees of desperation, fatalism, and entrapment for many youth.

One can thus sense, gazing through the gauze of government mandates on history, identity, housing, and land, that the Rwandan ground underfoot may not be quite as stable as is so glowingly announced. The positive pronouncements—which are, unquestionably, broadcast effusively and often—contain an air of unreality. As Stephen Buckingham wrote in an article titled "Kigali—Miracle City,"

> Most visitors to Rwanda now cannot believe that this was the country which just fourteen years ago was coming slowly out of the swiftest and most cruel genocide of modern times. The country still harboured the smell of death and a hopelessness which most people said was here for eternity.
>
> But the miracle happened. It did not strike like a light from heaven, as Saul was struck on the road to Damascus and then became Paul. The miracle came from the faith, resilience and determination of the Rwandese people themselves and their leaders to say "No—Never again." (2008: 24)

And yet, in a country where peace, stability, and security are repetitively touted, an evening walk with a World Bank official from his Kigali office to a nearby (fancy) restaurant featured an eerie passage through a wealthy residential area noticeably lacking people on the streets. Except when we passed an armed soldier standing sentry outside a gated house. Alongside him were an older woman and an adolescent boy. The three were silent as we approached. The woman and boy looked startled and frightened to see us. Earlier that evening, a Rwandan research associate and I had to walk into town from a poor Kigali neighborhood because the taxi we had arranged to pick us up did not come. That wasn't the first time, either: drivers are afraid to enter that area after five in the evening, we were learning.

Walking past a market at dusk, in search of a taxi stand, my Rwandan colleague related that several male youth were calling out to us, threateningly asking in Kinyarwanda what the *umzungu* (the white man—me) had in his bag. My colleague was absolutely terrified. Nothing happened.

Doing Research in Rwanda

The Passive Voice

Prior to starting field research for this book in September 2006, I learned of a field research endeavor that had ended abruptly perhaps two years earlier, with Rwandan government officials detaining research assistants and giving the lead researcher (a foreigner) twenty-four hours to leave the country.

The response by foreign researchers and international agency officials who mentioned this episode to me was illuminating. No one blamed, or even mildly criticized, the Rwandan government for what had happened. To everyone who explained why the government had shut down the research effort, the fault lay—entirely—with the lead researcher. The reason they uniformly supplied was that the researcher had done things that researchers cannot do in Rwanda, and because of this, it would now be harder to conduct research in the country. The perspective reminded me of how children of an abusive parent might reproach one another when mom or dad got mad. The fault would be with the child who upset mom or dad, since the children accepted and worked within whatever environment the parent had created. Similarly, in the collective version of events that I received, the Rwandan government was beyond reproach, while researchers had to avoid upsetting it.

The need to be careful while carrying out research in Rwanda extended to writing the initial draft of this chapter. It was informative yet dull: detailed, technical, cautiously written, and loaded with verbs in the passive voice. Reading it again months after I had completed the draft, I realized why I had written it that way. I had internalized the restrictive environment within which I had carried out the field research in Rwanda, keeping that watchful government peering over my shoulder as I wrote. In a way, I realized, I had become "stuck," too: I wrote the draft anticipating government criticism. As the findings from the research created a picture of Rwandan youth lives that was, for the most part, difficult if not desperate, I sensed that I would be disparaged for detailing it. Some Rwanda experts had thought that I would be unable to carry out the research at all (they were wrong). A few also predicted that government sources would deliver ad hominem attacks once the book was published and criticize the methods as not being representative of Rwandan youth concerns (I hope they will be wrong about this). To be sure, postgenocide Rwanda is not a place where qualitative research has thrived. It has proven difficult to convince people in Rwanda that research featuring extended, probing, open-ended interviews with 530 people is a significant sample. This is not surprising: quantitative research about specific issues in Rwanda is far more common.

My use of the passive voice in the first draft of this chapter is worthy of comment. While conducting field research in Dar es Salaam, Tanzania, with urban youth and Burundi refugees residing there illegally in 1990–92, I noticed how often Tanzanians and refugees alike frequently resorted to the passive voice. Over time, I learned that the passive voice was an ingrained precautionary way of expressing oneself in Kiswahili. Things "happened" ("vitu vimetokea"). This was not merely a response to extensive government surveillance. It was also a general method for self-protection. I vividly recall, for example, arriving on the scene of an automobile accident. "What happened?" policemen demanded of witnesses. The onlookers' responses all featured the passive voice. Many repeated the same phrase: "Sijui! Gari imegongwa!" ("I don't know! The car was hit!"). Tanzanians discussing this with me afterward explained: identifying a particular person as responsible for the accident would result in the person making the statement being taken to the police station. That was a place that most Tanzanians and refugees sought to avoid at all costs. It might also invite trouble from the person you had fingered as responsible for the accident.[1]

Reliance on the passive voice is a way to shield oneself from being held responsible for particular actions. Using verbs in the passive voice creates a world in which actions simply take place and accountability is hard to pin down. Rwandans are as expert at describing actions in the passive voice as Tanzanians, and so, I realized while rereading the first draft of this chapter, am I. Even when I was back in the United States and writing about research methods, I found I had internalized my anticipation of criticism of the findings, particularly those from the Rwandan government.

The next section of this chapter considers the research context. The last section largely contains what was present in that first chapter draft: a description of the framework, mechanics, and logistics of doing qualitative research in the tightly controlled environment of today's Rwanda. What mainly differs in this published version is that I have endeavored to change to active voice most of the instances of passive voice.

Notes on the Research Context

ISSUES AND CONCERNS

The following story illustrates how interviews with Rwandan youth could begin and illuminates the sorts of issues and concerns that youth and other Rwandans have. After I asked three female youth if they would consent to a group interview while they worked a small farm plot together, the three young women conversed in Kinyarwanda to consider the request. Passersby, noting the peculiarity of seeing a white man in their remote valley, stopped to watch. As my field researcher-translator and I silently awaited the young women's response, several people stood or sat just above us, along the path above the plot. As the three female youth continued their deliberations, two old women initiated a discussion through my translator about a pressing issue they wanted to share with me, a stranger they evidently hoped could help them.

The women related a story of local injustice. One explained that a community association had received permission to farm on a government plot of land at the bottom of the valley, just below us. The association had begun to work the land "before the genocide" and regularly paid taxes to the government in exchange for raising crops on it. According to the two women, a wealthy man who hails from the area (but lives elsewhere) recently swiped the land. "The association is off the land," one of the women explained. "We were forced out and he took it."

Who was this man? The second woman shared her version of why her association had lost access to the government farm plot: "That man studies and went to school. He is smarter than we are. He went to the university. He paid more money to the government and was more educated than [we] were." The discussion became heated and engaged others. "Our hunger is because of him," one of the female youth said. "He's responsible for our hunger." "We can't do anything in response," the second older woman added, to which the female youth asked rhetorically, "Can you accuse the government [of corruption]? No, you can't accuse the government."

Another female youth joined in. "How can we accuse the government if we're only farmers? We can go to prison if we do." The second older woman then explained that "you need to be educated to go to the authorities. How can you compete with someone who has more money and education than you do? That man is bigger than you, so he has a bigger head. But we didn't do anything wrong." Other examples of corruption and nepotism surfaced in this exchange, including an angry denunciation by the older woman who had initiated the discussion: "When white people send support here, only the educated people get the support." Two female youth raised the question of culpability. "It's the educated people doing this," one stated. "No, it's the government authorities," another countered. The second older woman added, "the government is ordering us to go to the *umudugudu* [the housing area at the top of the hill], and I can't afford to live there."

And then the five women—two older women and three female youth—stopped short. Talking of corruption, fear of retribution from well-educated Rwandans and government authorities, and pressure to meet government mandates in the hearing of a white foreigner and his Rwandan colleague, they suddenly realized that all they had related could be dangerous for them. What if I were to write down their names and report them to the authorities? Could the two interlopers be trusted?

In the end, the women agreed to be interviewed. I explained two key elements of our research protocol: that we never write down anyone's name, and that their contributions were both completely voluntary and would be kept confidential. These protocols also meant that I could not report to the authorities this specific story of alleged corruption (whether it was true or not I could not, of course, verify, nor did we ever raise the issue again). A description of part of an ordinary day of fieldwork in rural Rwanda appears in box 2.1.

LOCAL SUPPORT AND PRECAUTIONS

Conducting research in Rwanda requires meticulous planning. During my initial visit to Rwanda for this fieldwork, and together with World Bank officials who were supporting the logistics of the research, I sought to acquire a letter of introduction from a government minister. All four of the researchers on the team could then present photocopies of the letter when entering a district or sector and introducing ourselves to government authorities there. Indeed, throughout the entire field research period, the research team consulted with World Bank and Rwandan government officials for advice, insights, logistical

BOX 2.1

Fieldwork in Rwanda: A Sketch of One Day

The road is before us, and it's predatory. Just below a tiny town we find clay soup, which we successfully slide through this morning. There's a rutted area next, and villagers wait alongside, hoping, just perhaps, that we'll get stuck (so we pay them to help push us out). Then there are a series of log bridges over rushing waters. Most are in pretty good shape, but one is getting worse by the day, particularly since our worn, four-wheel-drive Toyota diesel Land Cruiser is daily passing over it. One morning we grab large stones to fill some gaps between the logs. We cross carefully but get across fine. I wonder how many more days we'll be able to cross this bridge safely.

Getting out of the car to move rocks or help direct Alexi, who's driving our car, I attract crowds and a stream of remarks. Evidently whites aren't often seen in these parts. The road is inaccessible during both rainy seasons, which means that the area is cut off half of the year. Children gather and want to shake my hand. Older people gawk and test my Kinyarwanda. Sometimes I take pictures, which amuses most, particularly the kids. They are dressed in trousers, T-shirts, and skirts that are dirty and torn. They are barefoot. As with children elsewhere in the developing world, they often act with the poise and grace of tiny adults.

Finally, we hit our destination. Eugide goes down his path for the day, and Alexi drives Mathias [pseudonyms are used throughout this text] and me farther up the road. One research method we're using is to go down the same path every day for several days, so people become accustomed to seeing us in their area. This hopefully allows people to relax and open up over time. It seems to be working, as some of the people we interview relate that the talk of their community in recent evenings is the visits of the researchers.

It's Mathias's turn to accompany me. He'll translate for me today. He rotates with Alexi and Eugide. We get out of the car. I put a bag of peanuts and a packet of cookies into my bag with my pens, notebooks, maps, and camera stuff, grab my umbrella and a water bottle, and head off with Mathias down the hill. It rained the night before, so it's slippery. This is our third day here, on the same path, and our return is news. Rwandans can report news to neighbors by yelling across valleys and down hills. There's no way we can surprise anyone: here we come. Calls announcing our arrival can be heard on the hillside. Our path is steep. The views of the valley and mountains are beautiful.

We meet a young blind man along the path. We greet and pass him, and then I change my mind—the team has interviewed few handicapped youth, so this is an opportunity. We return to ask if we can interview him. He's surprised, and he accepts. He's waiting to attend a Pentecostal church meeting. He walked for several hours to get to this place for the meeting. It begins to rain. An onlooking couple welcomes us into their unfinished house. They are poor, and the roof is made of banana leaves, which provides precious little protection from the elements. The couple joins the interview. Perhaps ten children look on.

The rain increases, and I invite one boy to hold my umbrella while I ask questions and take notes. Mathias opens his umbrella, too. Lines of water are pouring down from above. "This is how we live," the wife says. I acknowledge it, but there's not much else to say.

The interview lasts something like two hours. We finish, we're all a bit weary, and Mathias and I go outside, thank everyone for their time, and head farther down the hill. We run across Anatole. He had joined Alexi and me the day before, insisting on carrying my bag and water bottle. He's wearing a huge smile, thoroughly elated to see us, and we're soon joined by Domascene, his friend. Domascene had also joined us on the previous day. Every time I mention Anatole's name, he shouts, "Hello!" with delight. He is fascinated by the interviews, and was a terrific interviewee himself the day before. Being our escorts seems to have made these two young men temporary celebrities in their neighborhood. I ask if that's true, and they nod and grin.

We go to the local community leader's house, Dieudonné. He's thirty, married with two young children. He's also a former soldier. He is, in addition, very much in love. In the sitting room of his home, which we enter, he has painted two overlapping blue hearts, over which he has written "love" in English. There are Kinyarwanda phrases on the wall, too. When his wife enters, I say, "your husband really loves you." She giggles and answers, "badly!"

A crowd of neighbors gather. Dieudonné's wife brings out a mat and other women join her on it. There are people in the sitting room, and others peering in from outside. Children sidle up near me and stare. So much is fascinating: the hair on my arms, my rushed scribbling of notes, my clothes and boots.

We start the interview, and Dieudonné turns out to be very quiet. This allows others to join in with their own comments. I break out the cookies and pass them around; the cookies provide me with an energy boost and often help break down any discomfort people may feel. Most have never been interviewed before, and many youth relate that no one beyond their friends has ever asked them their views before the interviews by our team. They usually have much to say. The interview in Dieudonné's house is long and lively. I take photos of Dieudonné and his wife in front of Dieudonné's mural and then show them the digital photos. They're delighted. Dieudonné says "it's a miracle" to have me in his house. He explains that no other white person has ever visited him, and it is, in local culture, an honor. Other houses that we've visited in previous days have inspired similar statements.

Leaving Dieudonné's house and yard requires an escort. The act of escorting a person from one's home is captured in a verb in Kiswahili ("kusindikiza") and in Kinyarwanda. Perhaps twenty people walk us to the main path. Dieudonné's wife gives me three eggs from their hen, each carefully wrapped in the pages of someone's school exercise book. The farewells are heartfelt.

Mathias, Anatole, Domascene, and I start climbing the steep hill. As we do, Anatole points to a ramshackle house that we pass. It's the house of a single woman who is expecting her third child. I ask Mathias to return to ask her for an interview tomorrow, as her story is the sort that we want to include in our research. (He did, and later reported that some of the questions turned out to be painful for her to answer. In such cases, none of us probe.)

We pass a small house that, earlier in the day, we had promised to visit. We want to include the views of adults concerning the lives of youth in our research, and there seem to be a number of older men and women there that day. We immediately find out why: they're brewing banana beer in the small sitting room. Drinking hasn't begun yet, so our visit sets up a short and theatrical interview, with men and women, and, as always, children, crowded around us. Mathias and I sit on a bench, while everyone else stands except for the young woman straining the fermented banana beer across from us. The vat looks like a small dugout canoe. The smell is pungent.

There are too many people to have a lengthy interview. We also have to meet Alexi and the car way, way up the hill soon. So I cut the interview short. The crowd follows us outside, and there, next to a cow in their small pen, is the grandmother.

Like many older women, she has short, close-cropped hair. She wears a worn dress and wants to talk to me. "It's too late for me," she says, "But please help these youth." She gently strokes the shoulder of one of her grandsons standing next to her. "They need so much help," she says. Tears begin to brim and then fall from her eyes, and she repeats the word "nuko" several times. It means "that's the way it is." It's an extremely moving moment (and not what takes place most days in the field), and she puts her arms out toward me. We embrace, and then she hugs Mathias. The kids gather around, and they all want to shake my hand. I explain that the research is intended to provide support to youth in Rwanda, adding that I cannot say whether the assistance will reach the youth in her family. But, Mathias and I state, we hope so. She nods, and an awkward moment befalls us. Finally, with an escort to the main path and more farewells, we leave.

Up the path, there's a gathering of toddlers. I think they may be seeing a white person for the first time, as they shriek in terror at the sight of me. This is not the first time has this happened to me. There's nothing to do except trudge onward. No one among us can console them, including Mathias. Anatole and Domascene think it's hilarious.

I'd promised Anatole the day before that I would photograph his house. So we have to pause at his house. His friends and siblings, whom we interviewed the day before, are all there, and they're happy to see me again. The handshakes are vigorous and the smiles are huge. Anatole's house is tiny but cool: he has a kind of bunk bed, with a mosquito net, a radio, and a speaker that is aimed into a hanging gourd. I guess he likes the resulting echoing sound. He smiles with delight at the photos, and I take more pictures and show them to him. He seems overjoyed. Everyone wants to see the photos. It's like a party, but we have to leave. So, after many, many more handshakes and another departure escort, we're off again up the hill.

This is a revised and abridged version of Sommers 2008.

support (including, most thankfully, an introduction letter from the Ministry of Youth, Culture, and Sports that was shared with government authorities during field research), and any issues of particular concern to them.

The wording of the introduction letter itself required research. The initial terms of reference penned by World Bank officials in Washington, D.C., was first shared with World Bank and other international and local officials I knew in Kigali. Some key words had to be removed. It was thought improper, for example, to mention that counterpart research was taking place in Burundi (Rwandan government officials would be displeased that the two countries were being compared); to describe Rwanda as a postconflict nation (officials viewed Rwanda in terms of its development progress, not by the civil war and genocide that took place over a decade previously); and to refer to undereducated or at-risk Rwandan youth as "marginalized" (the term may infer that the government is exclusive and seeks to marginalize youth, whereas the government strove for the opposite).

The description I developed, with heavy input from others, was that the research sought to discover the views of Rwandan youth and use them to provide policy recommendations. This may appear to be obvious and too simple. The context suggested otherwise. The approach the book employs—using poor youth views to inform policy—runs counter to what normally occurs in Rwanda and, in my experience, a great many other countries. As is described in chapter 3, educated people (such as, in general, government officials above the lowest, *umudugudu*, level) normally assume that poor, undereducated people, including most youth, require direction, instruction, motivation, encouragement, sensitization, and mobilization. This assumption informs the approach that most government officials take toward members of the poor and undereducated Rwandan majority: with their advanced education, higher level officials and other elites are able to make informed decisions about issues that concern poor and poorly educated people.

Yet nearly all government officials supported and were intrigued by the novel research and policy approach we employed. Entering each district and sector, researchers introduced the research and its approach to the relevant district and sector authorities. Usually they were expecting us, as we would normally telephone beforehand to set up a meeting. During the initial meeting, the researchers introduced themselves and briefly reviewed the research objectives and methods. Virtually every local official we approached went out of his way to welcome the research team, offer logistical assistance, and agree to be interviewed themselves. Research team members also offered to share general findings with sector officials before leaving the officials' area, an invitation that was always accepted. All such meetings took place with men. The people we generally met were the head of their respective government level (all but *umudugudu* officials have offices and staff). While the sector and district offices typically included women personnel, every government official with whom we met at the *umudugudu*, cell, sector, and district levels were men. The lone exception was National Youth Council membership at the cell and sector levels, which included some female youth representation. However, to preserve the anonymity of the officials interviewed, I use the gender-neutral and plural "they" and "their" throughout this book.

The interviews with officials were substantive. It was significant that no cell or sector officials were surprised by the main findings the team shared at the end of our research period in their respective areas. Instead, they confirmed that all of the main research findings were both relevant and significant. Executive secretaries (i.e., the highest-level sector official; sector residents regarded them as extremely powerful) of rural sectors, for example, were well aware of the significance of housing to youth and how difficult it was for them to build a house. Indeed, some confessed that they were unsure just how the government was going to accomplish the prominent national government objective of having everyone on *imidugudu* in rural Rwanda by 2020. Officials were equally aware of the low demand among most poor youth for secondary education and the perils that poor urban youth generally faced (see part 3). Reflecting on the frankness of these interviews after the field research had ended, I wondered whether officials were using my interviews with them to communicate their concerns discretely up the bureaucratic ladder. As I describe in chapter 3, officials tended toward caution when relating troubling information; some said that they did not report to their superiors any information that did not support policy objectives. Instead, it appeared that some sector officials chose to share disquieting information about policy implementation challenges with me, since the research was designed never to reveal sources of interview data. In retrospect, my sense is that this was quite often the case.

Reactions to the research findings were, in general, vastly different at the district and national government levels. The generally low demand for education and the striving for roofing (in rural areas) and survival (in urban areas) surprised many of them. I eventually purchased a roof tile and displayed it at higher-level government meetings about our rural youth findings, to help highlight the prominence of housing in the research. Some officials were defensive about some of the findings, usually resorting to recitations of how policies were to be instituted. Probably the most prominent example of the surprise and pushback from district- and national-level officials concerned housing in rural areas. Many of the higher-level officials asserted that getting rural youth to build houses on *imidugudu* was occurring with little or no resistance or difficulty. However, this was not what the research revealed (see part 2).

The prominence of the housing issue, and the generally low priority that poor youth necessarily placed on education, inspired me to write and circulate in 2006 to Rwandan government and international agency officials a short preliminary report containing research findings. The study team also participated in a meeting involving government and nongovernment officials in January 2007, hosted by l'Institut de Documentation et de Recherché sur la Paix (IDRP) in Kigali, that addressed the findings and possible implications arising from the preliminary report.

Higher-level Rwandan government officials were not the only ones surprised by the research findings. They were joined by most international-donor, United Nations, and nongovernment officials during presentations of findings in Kigali and various locales in the United States and Europe. The fact that the research findings suggest a different experience and perspective of contemporary Rwanda than is commonly depicted in publications about Rwanda appeared to startle some officials. It also inspired some to share stories privately with me about reactions to other reports that ran counter to prevailing views of Rwanda's challenges and progress in Kigali and beyond. In several of these confidential conversations, I was told that international agencies might alter or simply not release reports that might upset Rwandan officials.

But the tendency toward precaution (or, perhaps, risk aversion) could be much more pronounced as well. One UN official, for example, said that a Rwandan colleague in their office in Europe had begged them not to e-mail a report to them that raised questions about an aspect of Rwandan government policy, presumably because it just might be intercepted by Rwandan authorities or its affiliates. A professor at a European university revealed that a Rwandan student had asked the professor to lock up the student's paper on Rwanda in case other Rwandan students somehow read it and reported its contents to Rwandan government officials. A student from southern Africa related how Rwandan students based in her country limited the information that they shared with their relatives inside Rwanda, in case government officials there read their e-mails and tapped their phones. An American working with a Rwandan nongovernment organization told me that their first meeting in

Kigali featured warnings to be very careful what they wrote in e-mails or said on telephones.

Were stories of self-censorship, precaution, and government surveillance such as these true, or were they examples of exaggeration or unjustified paranoia? Was it necessary, to share still other examples, for a former international nongovernmental organization (NGO) official based in Kigali to misspell deliberately the names of high-level Rwandan officials in e-mails to the official's headquarter office to ward off the possibility that Rwandan officials might read them? Were the heads snapping sideways at adjacent restaurant tables in Kigali, which I observed several times when someone in my dinner party asked me about my research findings, a sign that my conversations were being eavesdropped? Or was I myself a little paranoid about mere expressions of curiosity? Was the same Rwandan man reading a thin Rwandan newspaper in three consecutive restaurants where I held meetings one afternoon in Kigali spying on me (when I asked the waitress in the third restaurant to offer him a beer from me, the man abruptly left)? Were the intermittent, high-pitched squeaks during certain mobile phone calls signs that the calls were being surveilled? Was it really necessary for Rwandans to warn me that I must always begin presentations to Rwandan officials with findings that were upbeat and never use words like "disastrous" while describing any aspect of the situation of Rwandan youth?

While it was impossible to determine reliable answers to such questions, the sequence of stories on this subject collectively suggest a picture of pronounced risk aversion, worry, and suspicion with regard to the perceived sensitivities of and possible actions undertaken by the Rwandan government. Although this environment did not directly impact the interview process—responses to our questions were, on the whole, strikingly forthcoming and illuminating—it most certainly inspired the research team to maintain vigilance and precaution about research protocols. An example of this is illustrated in a contrast between conducting research in Burundi and Rwanda. While carrying out extensive field evaluation work in rural Burundi, I sometimes used the following method to help put at ease people I was about to interview. I would occasionally tell people in a combination of Kiswahili and Kirundi, that "Mimi ni umuzungu umunyarucari" ("I'm a destitute white man."). Many Burundians responded with a mixture of astonishment and delight. It was unusual to hear a foreigner speak Kiswahili or Kirundi, and what I was suggesting was—to them—so preposterous as to be hilarious. Most would respond by explaining that no white man was destitute (instead, they were all fabulously wealthy and powerful). The fact that a white man was making this claim inspired laughter—and helped foster a relaxed atmosphere for extended interviews.

Compare my use of this gentle and useful ploy in Burundi to the response I received in Rwanda. The corollary phrase in Kinyarwanda for destitute white man—"umuzungu umutindi"—was generally met with uncomfortable surprise. With some Rwandan officials, the reference tended to invoke a bit of alarm. "You just said a bad word"—"umutindi," which means "destitute"), a Rwandan official warned me once in the early stages of field research. The characterization was illuminating. While there certainly were Rwandans who were poor, the idea that a Rwandan was destitute might be interpreted as a criticism of the government. As a result, while Rwandans the research team interviewed in the field regularly and casually made reference to Rwandans who were "umutindi," I dropped use of the word at the outset of interviews or during conversations with ordinary Rwandans and Rwandan officials.

Methodological Details

RESEARCH OVERVIEW

This research endeavor arose from an interest at the World Bank in the situation of youth in Central Africa (here narrowly defined as Burundi and Rwanda), and the policy and practice implications that derive from their situation. I developed the general research framework—particularly the site and sample selection techniques, and the questionnaire—in collaboration with Peter Uvin (a Central Africa expert and former colleague), who led the Burundian youth component of this effort, and World Bank officials either supervising this effort or variously engaged on issues and activities connected to Burundian and Rwandan youth. The highly similar structures of our youth research work allowed us to compare findings from the two countries (I discuss the most significant contrasts in chapter 9).

This book features interviews with Rwandan male and female youth ages fourteen to thirty-five—Rwanda's government definition for youth—as well as adults and government officials. The interviews took place in 2006–7.[2] I made extensive efforts to develop a research sample that reasonably represented the broad outlines of Rwandan youth demographics. Accordingly, while the research team included educated and reasonably successful Rwandan youth in the sample, most youth we interviewed were poor, unemployed or underemployed, and lacked any education beyond primary school. In addition, I placed a high research priority on issues of gender.

Across the fieldwork period, members of the research team interviewed Rwandan government officials at the national, district, sector, cell, and *umudugudu* levels of government, in addition to members of donor agencies and NGOs, including World Bank officials, about issues relating to youth (I carried out most of these interviews). These interview sessions included invitations for officials to respond to preliminary findings and share their suggestions on how to address youth challenges. The exchanges were fruitful.

The fieldwork for this book began on November 10, 2006. It took place in four rural sectors (in Muhanga, Rulindo, and Gicumbi Districts) and two urban sectors (both in Gasabo District, Kigali). The field research team was comprised of four researchers (three field researchers and myself). We spent a total of approximately eight weeks in the rural areas and four weeks in the urban areas.[3]

There are constraints on virtually every research endeavor. The primary constraint to the Rwandan youth research was limited time. The general re-

EST
NORD
OUEST
SUD
VILLE DE KIGALE

KILOMETERS
0
30
60

N

Districts of Rwanda (Courtesy of USAID)

sponse was to emphasize high-quality, in-depth, qualitative interviews with a reasonably representative sample of youth, the techniques of which, including site and sample selection, I detail below.

A second constraint arose from the qualitative nature of the interviews. They featured asking youth and adults questions from a written questionnaire (see box 2.3). I designed the questions to be as neutral and nonleading as possible; collectively, they invited each youth to become analysts of their own societies and situations. They encouraged youth and adults to describe the situations of youth in their areas, the adulthood expectations that influence youth lives and the people and entities that provide assistance to youth, and their own views of peace, development, governance, security, and social and gender relations, as well as other subjects. The research team also asked youth about their plans for improving their people and entities. The interview approach sparked consistently useful, and usually lengthy, discussions with youth and adults. However, in the drive to get youth and adults to speak with confidence and authority about their views, it also allowed them to *not* mention issues that they preferred not to raise. Too often, Rwandan youth and adults would not volunteer information about such issues. As a result, I added a few supplementary interview questions (see the Interview Techniques section of this chapter) so that the research team could gather people's views about important issues such as education and HIV/AIDS.

There were other issues that the research was unable to address with specific questions. One was alcohol abuse, which youth, adults, and officials rarely mentioned during interviews. And yet, from the bottom of valleys to hilltop roadsides, from the tiniest economic outposts to sprawling Kigali neighborhoods, there are bars in Rwanda. Most have throngs of male youth in or near them. Banana beer brewing is an important economic activity (particularly for poor women) and an integral component of Rwandan culture. Members of our research team were regularly approached in market areas by inebriated young men, emboldened enough by alcohol to approach strangers, even a white one.

A few government officials, and small numbers of youth and adult citizens, referred to the attractions and downsides of beer drinking during interviews. The issue also surfaced in earlier field research with rural Rwandan youth (Sommers 2006a). One can certainly understand why female youth and adult women, in particular, might not bring it up with researchers. Perhaps it is so commonplace for Rwandan men to drink that they didn't think of mentioning it. Perhaps women chose not to discuss the domestic violence that they suffered when the man or men in their life beat them. Alcohol can help fuel youth fatalism, too, as the stories of drunk male youth visiting prostitutes and shunning condom use in part 3 suggest.

THE APPROACH

Site Selection. Selecting field research sites for this book began with the team coordinating potential sites with Peter Uvin's counterpart research in Burundi.[4] We decided to select one rural area that was located close to each country's capital (Kigali and Bujumbura) and had had an extensive experience of political violence. The other area we chose was to be located farther from the capital and had had a similarly extensive experience with political violence. To facilitate selecting the four rural areas (two per country), we endeavored to include any relevant prior experience that either Peter or myself had had in our respective study countries, or any connections to agencies that could help facilitate our research in particular rural areas.

One purpose of our selection criteria was to determine whether, with the experience of violence as a shared characteristic, proximity to the capital had an impact in how youth were devising plans for their future: if you live closer to the capital, might that impact how you develop a trajectory for yourself? The areas we selected were Bubanza and Ngozi Provinces in Burundi (Bubanza is very near Bujumbura, the capital of Burundi), and Muhanga, Rulindo, and Gicumbi Districts in Rwanda.[5] I held discussions with district-level officials to identify two sectors accessible to main roads (and thus, to urban areas) and two sectors that were unusually remote and largely inaccessible. As a result of these discussions, I selected two "accessible" sectors (Mushishiro in Muhanga District and Kisaro in Rulindo District) and two "remote" sectors (Nyabinoni in Muhanga District and Muko in Gicumbi District).

That we settled on three rural districts instead of two in Rwanda requires explanation. I selected Muhanga District, in the Southern Province, because it was located near Kigali and had suffered extensive violence during the civil war and, especially, during the genocide period (1990–94). It was also the site of more recent violence from what are called infiltrators from the DRC. In addition, I wanted to include research sites in the Northern Province, since I had conducted field research there in the past and still had useful contacts in and contextual knowledge of the area.[6] To maintain a consistently northeastern representation in the sample, I combined Kisaro Sector in Rulindo District with Muko Sector of Gicumbi District, both of which are reasonably close to the main northeastern town of Byumba. Muko and Kisaro Sectors are part of the same traditional cultural area (Urukiga). The Nyabinoni and Muko Sectors in Muhanga District are both part of the traditional cultural area known as Nduga.

I chose the urban field research sites according to a similar criteria: one "downtown" area with proximity to markets and services, and one that was (for an urban area) fairly remote. I chose two sites. One was in Nyamabuye Cell, Gatsata Sector, Gasabo District, which I selected because it is close to main roads and a large and important market (Nyabugogo), as well as the fact that it was a new, densely populated and rapidly expanding area containing large numbers of rural–urban youth migrants.[7] I chose the second urban site because it was located farther from main roads and large markets. It is a peri-urban area, where many residents farm small plots as well as work (or search for work). This research site was in Nyabisindu Cell, Remera Sector, Gasabo District.[8] As with the selection of rural research sites, I consulted local government officials for suggestions on where to carry out urban research. And as with the rural research work, I followed their recommendations.

The two urban cells and four rural sectors were each subdivided into two smaller groupings. The intention was to carry out research both in sections of each cell or sector that were relatively remote and in sections that were relatively accessible. However, it was not always easy to identify such sections. For example, in Nyabinoni Sector, Muhanga District, which was the most remote rural sector visited, it became difficult to distinguish which cells were more remote and which were more accessible. The entire sector, the team learned, was entirely remote. The distinctions were similarly difficult to identify in the urban cells. Regardless, all selected rural cells and urban *umudugudu* were located far enough apart to avoid overlap between interview teams (box 2.2).

Sample Selection. Field research interviews divided into two sets. The principal set consisted of 398 qualitative interviews with youth and adults that featured the researchers (myself and three Rwandan colleagues) asking virtually the same set of questions to everyone. We wanted half of all interviews to be with male youth and a quarter with female youth, with the final quarter comprised of an equal distribution of male and female adults. These targets reflected our primary emphasis on learning about youth views and, within this group, a secondary emphasis on masculinity. The interviews with adults aimed to gauge and incorporate their views of today's youth and to investigate the degree to

Field Research Sites

1. *"Remote" Rural Sectors*
   Nyabinoni Sector, Muhanga District
   Muko Sector, Gicumbi District

2. *"Accessible" Rural Sectors*
   Mushishiro Sector, Muhanga District
   Kisaro Sector, Rulindo District

3. *Urban Cells*
   Nyamabuye Cell, Gatsata Sector, Gasabo District (Urban)
   Nyabisindu Cell, Remera Sector, Gasabo District (Peri-Urban)

which youth life today differed from their experience as youth a generation earlier. We also wanted most of the youth we interviewed to reasonably represent the youth majority (that is, poor youth with limited education). We were successful in approaching these targets (see Sample Selection Results later in this chapter).

The second interview set consisted of interviews with 132 government and nongovernment officials. The topics covered in these interviews ranged more widely and had a more informal format. The accent on informality aimed to allow key contextual issues to surface during interviews and invite those who were interviewed to share their responses to preliminary findings. I prioritized interviews with the primary government officials from the cells, sectors, and districts where the research took place, with National Youth Council (NYC) officials at the cell, sector, and national levels, and with Kigali City Council officials. I also interviewed Rwandan government officials at the lowest (*umudugudu*) and the ministry levels, World Bank and other donor agency officials, and members of NGOs (including UN agencies). I consulted World Bank officials frequently. In the end, the research team interviewed forty government officials and thirty-three donor and local and international NGO officials, conducted a dozen meetings with NYC members in all sectors where the research took place (with a total of fifty-nine NYC officials), and carried out formal briefings with government, NGO and donor agency officials on several occasions.

No visit to any field research site was undertaken until research team members first met, in succession, with government officials at the district, sector, and cell levels. Research team members interviewed *umudugudu*-level officials over the course of rural site work.

The research team employed snowball sampling techniques, which involved returning to the same hillside or urban neighborhood, so that people in that location become increasingly familiar with the researchers. The word gets out that researchers are interviewing youth. Directly and indirectly, "you get handed from informant to informant and the sampling frame grows with each interview" (Bernard 2006: 193). A particular strength of this sampling method is that it fosters relationships based on trust. Establishing trust is essential when interviewing youth, particularly with those who are economically disadvantaged and have a low social status.

To implement this trust-building sampling technique, research team members walked on the same pathways down rural hills or through urban neighborhoods within the selected sites for several days in succession. To avoid the possibility of any organization influencing what respondents said, the researchers did not meet with youth or adults at or near government facilities, churches, offices, etc. Once this process began in a particular field site, researchers relied on their expanding familiarity with community residents (particularly those that were interviewed), and their growing knowledge of local context, to proactively identify other youth and adults to invite to be interviewed.

Each day, researchers spoke to youth and adults during their walks into the field and explained why they were there.[9] The interviews always began by reading a script that explained the purpose of the research and stressed that any participation was voluntary (no pressure to participate was ever applied) and confidential (no names were ever recorded; each respondent was assigned a code). As the interview neared conclusion, the researchers invited respondents to ask us questions. To gain a general background of each person whom we interviewed, the interviews ended with the researchers asking specific data profile questions regarding respondents' age, gender, education level, marital status, profession, and a series of questions designed to identify their economic status. I detail the determination process later in this chapter.

Emphasizing that interviews are voluntary and confidential is an established practice of social science research. The protection that people receive from these protocols is designed to allow them both to decide whether to participate and what to share. Hopefully, it will encourage them to speak freely. The frank discussions that took place during the interviews for this book strongly suggest that people did just that. The Rwandan context makes such protocols particularly important, given the government's broad definition of, and forceful stance toward, dissent (see chapter 9 for examples of this). Such a situation can transform a seemingly innocuous comment into something provocative and risky. The appendix, which I discuss in chapter 3, sheds light on the watchful, controlling environment that permeates everyday Rwanda. Rwanda has lots of stated rules and regulations, and lots of unstated dos and don'ts. Accordingly, the research team never tape-recorded any interviews, since authorities might try to trace the source of audio recordings if they apprehended them. In addition, quotations from interviews in this book are accompanied with neither the specific source of a quotation nor the exact location or date. What I do often provide is pertinent profile data, such as the age, gender, and economic status of those interviewed.

The 398 interviews with youth and adults were either carried out individually, or, more often, in what might be called unstructured peer groups. All youth and adult interviews were organized informally, and the peer groups arose from two or more youth or adults agreeing to be interviewed together. Most of these interview groups were small; two to four people. Very occasionally, they expanded to perhaps six or eight. Larger group interviews were avoided. Structured, planned focus groups were also avoided because my prior research experience was that the most influential members of such groups either dominate discussion or influence the responses of less powerful focus group members. Determining the representativeness of such groups is thus difficult.[10]

In significant contrast, the peer group interview sessions tended to feature open, relaxed exchanges and debates among respondents. Such sessions were also difficult to avoid, since the researchers were quite often the first, or among the first, researchers to carry out interviews in the visited communities. The interviews that took place were both voluntary and attracted the attention of others. Hence, unstructured interview groups became the norm, and individual interviews the exception.

At least twice a week the researchers checked their profile data to gauge whether they were reasonably meeting the interview targets (that is, approximately 50 percent male youth, 25 percent female youth, 25 percent adults; and mostly poor youth with no postprimary education). The researchers would then attempt to adjust their interview sample in subsequent days.

Sample Selection Results. Employing snowball sampling techniques is always an imperfect process. The researchers employed every reasonable effort to approximate the research targets already outlined. However, because the interview process was voluntary, it was not possible, and indeed we considered it unethical, to impose our target goals: if an interview session attracted large numbers of male or female youth, for example, the new contributors were included. The results from the sample process detail the final research sample that the researchers obtained.

We roughly achieved our goal of a research sample containing 75 percent youth. That said, our efforts to include more adults was hampered by the unwillingness of some to agree to an interview. This was particularly difficult in urban areas, where nearly all adults initially stated their requirement of being paid, and therefore wound up not being interviewed. There were also few available adults to interview. The dominance of youth in Kigali's population helps explain this. In fact, some contended that the ratio of youth in some sectors was even higher than the city council estimate that Kigali's population was two-thirds youth: as high as 85 percent of the total population, a NYC official reported. There were also fewer adult women available to interview in urban areas than adult men.

Since the research team's policy was to do only voluntary interviews (in no case was anyone paid or pressed to talk to us), we were forced to accept constraints on reaching our target of 25 percent adult respondents in our interview sample. The final numbers of youth and adults sampled are given in table 2.1.

As the gender breakdown in table 2.2 shows, interviewing sufficient numbers of female youth (a quarter of the total sample and a third of all youth) and female adults (a random amount—no gender targets were devised for adult interviews) was reasonably, but not optimally, achieved.

The research roughly broke down into a month in each of three locations, as given in table 2.3: rural remote sectors, rural accessible sectors, and urban areas. Despite this equal breakdown of time in the field, we interviewed significantly more urban youth than youth in either the "remote rural" or "accessible rural" venues. This was largely due to the fact that interviews with urban youth were shorter (see the Interview Techniques section that follows for an explanation of why this occurred), and they also generally answered fewer follow-up questions. In most cases, the primary reason for this was that the interviews took time away from their search for work (and money). While the official Rwandan government age range for youth is fourteen through thirty-five, the

TABLE 2.1

Research Sample by Designation
(Male Youth, Female Youth, or Adult)

Interview Subjects	Number Interviewed	Percent of Interviewed
Male youth	242	61
Female youth	93	23
Adults	63	16
Total	398	100

TABLE 2.2

Research Sample by Gender

Interview Subjects	Number Interviewed	Percent of Interviewed
Male youth	242	72
Female youth	93	28
Youth Total	335	100
Male adults	46	73
Female adults	17	27
Total adults	63	100

research sample, as denoted in table 2.4, tended to attract few youth under the age of eighteen.

There are six primary school grades in the current Rwandan education system (the prior system had eight primary school grades). A graduate is called a "P6" (a person who completed the sixth grade level), while those from P1 through P5 are considered to have "dropped out" and never completed primary school. Most Rwandan youth never advance beyond primary school, which is reflected in the research sample (table 2.5), in which approximately three in four youth attended only primary school and the ratio of postprimary educated youth to those with no schooling whatsoever was less than two to one.

Devising the economic status of youth who were interviewed was necessarily inexact. Each researcher made the final determination, as based on the

TABLE 2.3

Research Sample by Location

Interview Location	Number of People Interviewed	Percent of People Interviewed
Remote rural sectors*	110	27.6
Accessible rural sectors†	123	31.0
Urban cells	165	41.4
Total	398	100.0

* "Remote rural sectors" combines Nyabinoni Sector in Muhanga District and Muko Sector in Gicumbi District.

† "Accessible rural sectors" combines Mushushiro Sector in Muhanga District and Kisaro Sector in Rulindo District.

TABLE 2.4

Youth Research Sample by Age

Age	Number of Youth Interviewed	Percent of Youth Interviewed
14–17	11	3
18–24	213	64
25–35	111	33
Total	335	100

TABLE 2.5

Youth Research Sample by Education Attainment

Education Level	Number of Youth Interviewed	Percent of Youth Interviewed
No primary schooling	28	8.4
Some primary schooling (P1P5)	134	40.0
Primary schooling only (completed P6)	116	34.6
Some secondary schooling	49	14.6
Some vocational schooling	2	0.6
No response	6	1.8
Total	335	100.0

respondent's answers to profile questions regarding their profession, whether they worked as laborers for others (and the kind of labor they performed), whether they ever hired labor, and the kind of possessions they owned (such as farm animals and household property). The research team devised and then revised the criteria for the four categories (destitute, poor, nonpoor, and wealthy) over time.[11] Our general definitions were:

- A "destitute" person had no farm animals or other significant possessions, lived in a poor dwelling (such as a mud house with a thatched roof), had extremely limited nonfarm income, and was either landless or owned very little land.
- A poor person was somewhere above the designation for destitute but was certainly not "nonpoor" (see below).
- A "nonpoor" person owned land, hired laborers, and lived in a reasonably comfortable permanent structure (such as cement walls and floor and a roof made either of iron sheets or roof tiles).
- A "wealthy" person had clearly identifiable indications of wealth and comfort, such as a mobile phone, a car, an expansive house, and/or a staff of household assistants.

The sample results mirror the broad economic impoverishment of Rwandan youth: more than four in five youth in the sample (84.5 percent) were either destitute or poor (table 2.6).

As is illuminated in research with both rural and urban youth, the delays in and difficulties of getting married in Rwanda are considerable. The presence of approximately two in three Rwandan youth in the research sample who were single helps dramatize this challenge, as shown in table 2.7. But in addition, the interview data made clear that most of those who said they were married most likely had married informally (that is, they decided to live together without a legal wedding ceremony). References to formal (legal) marriages—the sort that helped a youth gain recognition as an adult—were exceedingly rare. Youth who had achieved the goal of formal marriage, in other words, were most probably a very small proportion of those youth who said they were married.

Interview Techniques. My three Rwandan colleagues adjusted the preliminary set of open-ended questions before translating them from English into Kinyarwanda with painstaking care. We subsequently field-tested and further adjusted our questions over time.

TABLE 2.6

Youth Research Sample by Economic Status

Economic Status	Number of Youth Interviewed	Percent of Youth Interviewed
Destitute	170	50.75
Poor	113	33.75
Nonpoor	37	11.00
Wealthy	6	1.80
Unclassified	9	2.70
Total	335	100.00

TABLE 2.7

Youth Research Sample by Marital Status

Marital Status	Number of Youth Interviewed	Percent of Youth Interviewed
Married (formally and informally)	87	26.0
Unmarried	220	65.6
Widowed	3	0.9
Engaged	1	0.3
Unclassified (did not answer)	24	7.2
Total	335	100.0

The twenty questions that emerged from this process are provided in box 2.3. With input from other research team members, I made four major alterations to the core question set, most of them during the initial weeks of fieldwork, late in 2006:

1. Some of the original twenty questions didn't stimulate much useful discussion during interviews. After perhaps three weeks, we stopped asking questions 14–17 often.

2. The research team devised follow-up questions to gather additional information about important issues that surfaced during interviews. A prominent example was to understand, in depth, repeated references to expectations on male youth to build houses as a critical step towards becoming a man. Together with research team members, I developed questions to

BOX 2.3

The Twenty Original Research Questions

[Starting the Interview]

1. How do you spend your time on a normal day? Do the weekly requirements that you have (like *umuganda, gacaca,* meetings with government leaders, night patrol, and so on) affect your normal days?*

2. How is your life different from the life of your parents (adults)?

Development/Future

3. Now, please tell me about the young men/women in your area. What is their situation?

4. Are there organizations who support young men/women like you?

5. If you suddenly were the district mayor and you were in charge of this district, what is the first thing you would change? What are the other things?

Personal Plans

6. Do you have a plan for improving your situation?

7. Who might help you with your plan, so that you may find success?

8. If you achieve your success, will you also achieve the "good life"? What is the "good life"?

9. [For rural youth] What is interesting about staying here, where you live?

What if you compare life here to life in the city? (Which city?)

[For urban youth] What is interesting about living in Kigali? What if you compare life here with life in rural areas?

Youth/General

10. What do/did your parents expect you to be?

11. If you can't meet their expectations, what happens?

12. How do you choose whom to marry?

13. By the way, I'm confused by what people mean by 'youth.' Can you explain to me what a youth is?

Relations/Dignity

14. Who listens to you?

15. Who treats you well (with respect, dignity)? Who does not treat you well? Why?

16. When you have a problem, who helps you?

17. Who do you admire?

Security/Peace

18. Can you tell me about the security situation here?

19. Can you tell me about the social relations here?

20. When someone talks about "peace," what does it mean to you?

* I added this follow-up question after youth made it clear that there were actually very few "normal" days in their lives, since particular days of most weeks are reserved for specific events, including community work/umuganda, gacaca court proceedings, meetings called by government officials, and night patrols by male youth in their communities.

understand the details of house-building challenges, such as the cost and status of different roof materials (roof tiles or iron sheets, both costly, were preferable, while roofs made of banana leafs were a sign of poverty, low social status, and even desperation).

3. I inserted questions into the rural youth question set about education because few youth respondents were raising the issue in their responses, particularly to the question of future plans (question 6 in box 2.3). This finding was in direct contrast to Burundian youth responses to the same question. In Burundi, youth highlighted the significance of education as a key feature of their future plans. In response, I added a set of questions for rural Rwandans, the most important of which were the following:

> Some youth go to secondary or vocational school, and some do not. What is the difference between youth who go to these schools and youth who never go? Is it different for male youth and female youth?

4. Although many adults raised the significance of HIV/AIDS during interviews, most youth did not. In response, and after we had concluded our rural research, one research team member returned to a rural sector for an additional week to interview more youth and adults. He included new questions about the HIV/AIDS situation, and why youth do not normally volunteer information about this issue, during his interviews. We retained the questions on HIV/AIDS when we conducted interviews with urban youth.

Rural youth generally made time to be interviewed for fairly prolonged periods (1–2 hours). This was not often the case with urban youth. In Kigali, youth (and adults) who agreed to be interviewed often would become restless after a half or three-quarters of an hour, since they generally had something to do (usually related to searching for money or food). As a result, the research team had to shorten its question list for urban residents to focus on questions considered higher priority (questions 1–4, 6–7, 9–11, 18–20; i.e., omitting questions 5, 8, and 12–17).

Interviews with nongovernment and government officials were intentionally wide-ranging. The research team included only four questions (box 2.4) from the original set of twenty during interviews.

Analysis: Trends, Correlations, and Comparisons. Together with student research assistants (who worked under my supervision), I analyzed all interviews

Four Questions That We Asked Officials

1. Please tell me about the young men/women in your area. What is their situation?

2. Are there organizations here that support youth?

3. Can you tell me about the security situation here?

4. Can you tell me about the social relations here?

with youth, adults, and officials to identify the primary shared trends and themes that arose. We employed comparative analysis to explore differences between youth according to significant characteristics, such as economic status (destitute, poor, nonpoor, wealthy), gender, location (remote or accessible rural areas, urban or rural, urban or peri-urban areas, etc.), age, and educational achievement. We also organized the interviews with youth and adults by their responses to particular questions. Then, we divided the responses to each question according to the main themes that arose. In cases of particular relevance, we made correlations to the profile data to reveal any shared characteristics of those who gave similar responses to the same questions. An example of this was to identify which youth (by gender, by economic status, etc.) responded to question 6 ("Do you have a plan for improving your situation?") by stating that they had no plan. The significance of such responses are highlighted in subsequent pages of this book.

PART TWO

Fear of Failure

RURAL YOUTH LIVES

People who live up, near the sector office, are developed.
Female youth, age twenty-two

People living closer to the sector are closer to development. But down here, we are very far from it. We don't know what's happening up there.
Male youth, age twenty-nine

Those living at the bottom are far from development.
Adult man, age thirty-eight

Youth at the top are well informed. They are aware of everything. They are different.
Male youth, age twenty-five

If you have money, you can live at the top of the hill. If you don't have money, you live at the bottom of the hill. It's always been like that.
Male youth, age twenty-eight

CHAPTER THREE

Living in a Vertical World

RURAL YOUTH AND THE GOVERNMENT

Most main roads in rural Rwanda run atop the high ridges of the famed mille collines (thousand hills). The roadways are home to minibuses, trucks, cars, taxis, motorcycles, bicycles, and the large, high-status, four-wheel-drive vehicles of influential Rwandans and internationals. Up on these roads, the vistas are often extraordinary: high, rolling hills and a patchwork of rectangular farm plots interspersed with clumps of banana trees running across deep valleys that, in the mornings of rainy seasons, are thick with mist. One can sense, atop these beautiful hills, why exiled Rwandans yearned for decades to return home.

Peering closer, however, another Rwanda comes into view. Much of the Rwandan countryside is missing something common to that in many other countries: woodland. Advancing deforestation and erosion is wreaking havoc on Rwandan farmland, making already steep inclines ever steeper. Some farm

Rwanda's hills and mountains are justly renowned
for their breathtaking grandeur.

plots seem to be heading straight downhill, at an angle more vertical than ski slopes. Many of the trees one sees are thin, their surroundings foraged, heavily, for anything that might be burned to cook food. These are the signs of a rural area that continues to thicken with ever more people. Underneath the pretty picture, in other words, lies a deepening drama and the site of difficult lives led amid struggle and poverty. It is here where most of Rwanda's huge youth population strains to stabilize and hopefully advance their lives.

The Rwandan countryside is spatially and socially vertical. In addition to lives being led at the top of or below high hills, the research found frequent references to differences between people from "down" and those from "up;" people from the "country" (in the valleys and on hillsides) and people living in the "city" on top; those who are "ignorant" below, and those who are "developed" above. And so on: the characterizations of life "below" and "above" depict locations of perceived social difference, and where Rwanda has long toiled (in valleys and on hillsides) and where it eventually must go (along main roads; frequently atop hills). This is not just a symbolic difference but a cornerstone of government policy, which wants Rwandans to move "up" in terms of development and, often, location, to live along roadways in organized *imidugudu* housing settlements. There, the benefits of development are expected to be readily available, as the current mix of farms and homes evolves into modern, untraditional farmland featuring the latest techniques and strategies for efficient land use and productive crop yields.

The tension between traditional lifestyles and those promising the advantages of modern life informs a large part of the story that unfolds in this part of the book. Most rural Rwandan youth live away from main roads. Although male youth are expected to build houses as a prerequisite for marriage and manhood, it is a struggle for a young man to find enough funds to build his own house. Traditionally, houses are built on farmland that sons inherit from their fathers. But in addition to the plummeting size of inherited land and expanding landlessness, there is the problem of where a young man's house is built, as all new homes, by law, are supposed to be constructed on *imidugudu*.

As with any profound lifestyle change, there are challenges arising from this requirement, which helps set the scene for struggles over how male and female youth advance in their lives, and how, and how fast, rural Rwanda adapts to the twin pressures of increasing population and decreasing land holdings. Life in rural Rwanda may look timeless and traditional. But it is not: it is instead the site where the challenges of a land-bound people, and a government, are playing out, as they try to devise viable ways to survive and move forward.

The three chapters in this part are based on findings and analysis drawn from extensive interviews with 196 rural youth (142 male youth, 54 female youth), as well as interviews with thirty-seven adults, and officials at all four levels of government in rural Rwanda: district, sector, cell, and *umudugudu*. These include interviews with NYC officials at the sector and cell levels.

Pressure: Government Reform in Rural Rwanda

In 2001, a Rwandan government official responsible for district-level youth activities recalled a provincial meeting about the problem of land scarcity. The official said that when district officials were asked how they planned to address the issue in their districts, "the collective response was, 'There's no way out'" (Sommers 2006a: 91).

Admitting to a lack of options, and expressions of entrapment, in response to the difficult straits facing rural Rwanda no longer seems acceptable. The government has created a way forward, the centerpiece of which is decentralization. Annual contracts between the president of Rwanda and district mayors are signed documents whose contents are made public. District officials openly talked about the expectations outlined in the contracts, and one district mayor displayed, with considerable pride, his signed contract with President Kagame. The official also explained that "even the president has a performance contract." The new, decentralized arrangement has also increased pressure on government officials, particularly those at the higher levels. As one district official explained, "every district official has a performance contract, with indicators and objectives. It's to be reviewed every three months. If you're not meeting your indicators and objectives, you're asked to leave [your job]." Pressure on land and on people was found to be a dominant theme in rural Rwanda. There was pressure on government officials to produce and pressure on youth to become adults, while land scarcity appeared to apply pressure on just about everyone by significantly narrowing options for advancement.

While pressures on youth are examined in later chapters, this chapter draws mainly on interviews with government officials at district, sector, cell and *umudugudu* levels in rural Rwanda who function with both increased responsibility and authority as well as enhanced expectations on them.

Contours of the Rural Youth Challenge

Research for this book revealed a predominant interest shared by government officials and youth: how to get the government "close to" youth. Many rural youth expressed their interest in getting the government "close to us," as I describe in chapter 4. Government officials also expressed an interest in increasing mutual understanding and appreciation between youth and government officials. A prominent district official, for example, described plans in his district to hire local youth to improve roads and bridges and terrace farm plots. He considered all of these activities "small projects." The official then explained the underlying purpose of such projects: "Giving youth something to do would build a very good ground for the district to get close to our youth and tell them what they can do to benefit their future lives."

Three important themes arise from this official's comment. First, it sheds light on the ways in which government officials were found to view youth, including that most require direction. Second, the implied purposes of getting closer to youth is to build trust (or credibility) with them in order to have them accept useful instruction from the officials. Dialogue with youth is not suggested here, and this well-intentioned but directive stance was strongly reflected in interviews with other officials in rural areas, too.

Third, the comment reveals an interest in devising strategies to support youth. The research found this interest to be widespread among the officials we interviewed. The plans involved not just employment and gathering youth in associations and cooperatives but formal and vocational education as well. At the same time, it became apparent during the research phase that few of the identified options appeared to be viable. The research found, for example, that the two main education options were available to hardly any rural youth in the research sample in part because they did not qualify for postprimary schooling. Many youth never finish primary school, a tendency illuminated by the research sample: 43.7 percent of male youth and 63 percent of female youth in the sample did not complete primary school. At the same time, graduating from primary school did not necessarily lead to enrollment in a secondary or vocational school: around a third of male and female youth in the research sample for rural Rwanda (35.2 percent and 27.7 percent, respectively) completed primary school and went no further.

Common reasons for not continuing in school after graduating from primary school included examination scores that were too low to qualify for secondary school. Another was that many families could not afford to pay secondary or vocational school fees. A third reason, particularly for vocational schooling, was that few schools existed and gaining access to them was difficult. A fourth reason was that many youth contended that they would be unable to attend either kind of school even if they had the opportunity. Their reason was tied to socially mandated requirements that had to be met before youth would be fully accepted as adult men and women, an issue that is detailed in chapter 5. In all, only 18.3 percent of male youth in the research sample for rural Rwanda either had attended secondary school or were current students, while 1.4 percent of male youth had attended a vocational school or were current students. Meanwhile, only 7.4 percent of the female youth sample were found to have secondary education experience. None had vocational school experience.

Other data on the profile of youth in the research sample helped shed light on challenges confronting rural youth. Over three in four male youth (76 percent) and four in five female youth (85 percent) were either destitute or poor. Over half of male youth (54.6 percent) stated their profession as simply "digging," while another 8.5 percent listed "digging" plus some sort of small jobs (which would include "digging" on the lands of others for pay).

The use of a verb in response to a question about a person's occupation ("I dig" and "digging" were the most common forms of this response) is illuminating because it suggests that youth saw farming not as an occupation as much as a basic activity. The same cannot be said for other occupations, which youth stated as nouns. While the proportion of male youth who mentioned specific jobs was unquestionably in the minority, the diversity of mentioned trades was wide. It included traders, mechanics, taxi drivers, houseboys, and shop sellers. More skilled jobs were represented as well (teacher, hair cutter, economist, executive, and welder).

No such diversity presented itself in responses from female youth. Well over four-fifths of the female youth sample (85.2 percent) listed their occupation as "digging," with another 7.4 percent mentioning "digging" as well as a small job. Only three of the fifty-four female youth respondents supplied other responses: one was a student, one a teacher, and one a government official. The data strongly suggest that while options for the majority of youth were meager, and mainly amounted to farming and nothing else, the range of possible off-farm occupations was far greater for male than female youth. For both male and female youth, there was a strong correlation between working solely as a farmer and being either destitute or poor: an indication that the potential for upward economic mobility, however small, improved if one had at least some off-farm work. And opportunities for advancement—again, however, small—nonetheless appeared to be greater for male youth than for female youth.

Less than a third of youth in the rural sample said they were married (28.9 percent of male youth, 35.2 percent of female youth; 30.6 percent, total). All sixty of these youth were at least twenty-one years of age. Since Rwandan law prohibits marriage before age twenty-one, the finding suggests that Rwandan youth abide by this law. However, the interview data tells a completely different story. Youth, adults, and government officials reported that informal marriages (where a young couple lives together without a wedding or legal sanction) were the norm and formal marriages were the rarity. Many also reported that some youth under age twenty-one marry informally. Just how many of the sixty youth who had said they were married (or had been: there were two widows and a widower among the sixty) were members of informal unions was impossible to gauge. But it is probable that most of them were. It was also highly likely that some of the rural youth in our sample under age twenty-one were married—but, given Rwandan law, exclusively in informal marriage arrangements.

How Government Officials View Youth

In a sequence of interviews with government officials about rural youth, from the district to the cell levels, a number of common themes concerning youth emerged. Before I describe these themes, two sets of government officials, whose views are not represented here, require comment. The views of NYC members are not included because a later section in this chapter, titled Rural Youth, Risk Aversion, and the National Youth Council, features their roles and views regarding rural youth. The second set of official are *umudugudu* officials. They occupy the lowest and least powerful level of officials in the entire government structure. They reside within communities, and they do not seem to be viewed by community residents as particularly fearsome or influential people. Nor do *umudugudu* leaders who were interviewed see themselves in this way. Instead, they appeared to view their role in government as that of one who carries out tasks and completes statistical reports for higher government levels.

While *umudugudu* officials lack stature and influence in the government system, they evidently have, by far, the highest level of credibility among rural

Rwandans. Interviews with *umudugudu* leaders typically took place in their homes (none seemed to have offices) with neighbors and family members present. Some are reportedly chosen for their post simply because they are men with a high education level relative to others in the vicinity. One such official told me that he was one of the few in his community who could read and write well (he had completed primary school but had never attended secondary school). Because the requirements for *umudugudu* officials are the lowest of all government levels, such officials in rural areas have a distinctive profile: lesser educated, accessible, and unusually credible.

What follows are seven prominent, broadly shared themes about youth that arose from interviews with government officials at the district, sector, and cell levels in the rural areas we visited:

1. *The main problem confronting youth is poverty.* A dominant theme that government officials expressed was that youth were hampered by impoverishment more than anything else. Expressions of empathy were commonplace. Some related poverty to simple misfortune. As a cell leader stated, "the main problem for youth in this cell is poverty due to the weather." If periods of rainfall were more predictable, then youth would face fewer problems in their lives.

2. *Youth won't take advice.* One source of frustration for officials was their impression that youth resisted their advice. As a cell-level official remarked, "The most difficult thing to do is to make youth do something. When I talk to youth, I call them and tell them what to do. I also teach them, but when they leave, some say that they won't put the teaching into practice." The directive nature of the official's interaction with youth is unmistakable. While not all officials interacted with youth in this way, the tendency was strong for officials to describe interactions as dominated by instruction and orders (instead of dialogue, for example).

   Some officials equated youth resistance to what they contended was well-informed advice to the belief that uneducated youth resist change. This perspective communicated the idea that people lacking much education or broad experience had a narrow information base and a too-conservative nature. It was not uncommon for officials to characterize uneducated youth as "ignorant." A cell leader tied his definition of an ignorant person directly to someone who was stubbornly set in their ways; someone who is "not able to cope or adapt to a new situation." A person with this sort of character was regularly thought to have, the cell leader continued, a "lack of understanding" about how the benefits of change "will come to them." The idea of poor and poorly educated youth lacking "understanding" of new developments was a common theme during interviews with officials. Such a mindset, another cell leader asserted, was problematic for Rwanda's development, since "it will be difficult for ignorant youth to cope with Vision 2020."

3. *Youth are unproductive with their time.* This view appeared to be largely directed at unemployed male youth who congregate in market areas, such as those near sector offices. They seemed to be unhappily idle and were a clear source of frustration for many officials. As a district-level official stated, "youth don't exploit [opportunities] that are available to them." Instead, the official explained, they venture into bars. "Most of the time they are drinking," he said. "Local beer is very cheap, and the boys waste too much time drinking beer."

A sector official addressed the same sort of male youth in a manner that communicated both frustration and disregard: "Those who come to the sector center don't like to work. They like to play pool and watch videos and wander around and go to Gitarama [the nation's second-largest city, in Southern Province] or Kigali. I don't like that. Here, we like people who like to work, because if people don't work, they will eventually become thieves." The apparent lack of a work ethic for those youth looking for work, or perhaps loitering or socializing, in centers, inspired an official from another sector to remark that "the biggest challenge is that youth don't work. That is a fact. You can go into centers and find youth doing nothing. So they need sensitization and mobilization. We must sensitize them to work so they can achieve what is asked by government policies."

4. *Youth won't collaborate.* A central tension between youth and government officials is that the government wants youth to "come together" to form registered associations and cooperatives to develop money-making projects. In particular, government officials and youth regularly mentioned associations as a government remedy for youth.

In contrast, cooperatives were rarely discussed, most likely because they were newer, fairly unfamiliar even to some government officials, and were obviously out of reach for most youth. The one government official who described how cooperatives worked highlighted this last reason to explain why they had yet to take off. Cooperatives raise money to allow groups with income-generating projects to secure bank loans, he explained. Cooperative members must raise 60 percent of the collateral for these loans. The official explained that if the cooperative "presents its project to the national bank, the government of Rwanda can provide the remaining 40 percent of the collateral." The main problem, he explained, lay in the challenge for youth to raise enough funds to cover their share. As the official asked, "Where will youth get the 60 percent in the first place when most are very poor?"

The government accent on collective endeavors for youth was emphatic. The problem was that most youth either couldn't or wouldn't join them. The chief reasons that officials provided were that youth didn't trust each other and didn't see the benefits of collaborative work. As a district official explained, "Youth don't trust each other and they can't [work] together." These were not small concerns, since government officials contended that the best way for youth to improve their lot was to work toward collective solutions. At the same time, however, the issue of low trust levels extends far beyond the youth cohort: a national survey in Rwanda found that "The weak level of trust within the community constitutes an obstacle to community development" (Desmarais 2004: 25).

Despite evidently high levels of distrust within communities, many officials nonetheless expressed frustration about the resistance of youth to accept their advice and join associations. As a cell-level official remarked, "Most youth don't join associations. It's because of their mentality, which is to not see the importance of putting people together. In part, it is like ignorance. It's frustrating to work with youth." Another source of frustration, widely mentioned by officials, was that they were impatient, something a sector-level official explained in the following way: "The first thing that youth want is a direct benefit: if you work today, you get a profit immediately. But associations have processes where youth have to work for a while and then share the profits later on."

5. *Rural youth want to migrate to town.* The restlessness and impatience of youth was expressed, in the minds of some Rwandan officials who were interviewed, as an aspiration toward urban migration. As a district-level official remarked, "Youth want a soft life. They want town life. There is rural–urban migration now. But the government can change it to urban–rural migration by putting some of the same facilities in villages already present in urban areas, such as electricity, running water, recreation centers, good schools, and hospitals. Putting these things in villages can put youth back in villages." There is little evidence in Africa to support the contention that urban youth with rural backgrounds ever return to live in the countryside (Ogbu and Ikiara 1995: 54), regardless of investments made there or govern-

ment attempts to force urban migrants to return to rural areas (Sommers 2003: 3; Sommers 2010: 321). Nonetheless, severe land scarcities and exploding urban growth may invite a concerted campaign to initiate urban youth returns (forced returns from Kigali thus far appear to be sporadic). As the same official noted, "The government has the right to move people back to rural areas. You cannot defeat your government. It's not about democracy, it's about having an organized plan. District governments have the responsibility to help youth in rural areas so they don't come to town. But the problem is that helping them will be very expensive."

6. *Youth need education.* One district official explained his government's "strong accent on education for youth" with the following simple reason: "because there's no land." More education was a widely mentioned answer, or partial answer, to youth problems. Yet officials are also aware of the evident, and significant, constraints on the emphasis on education. Another district official, for example, explained the circumstances and results arising from the presence of so many school drop-outs: "A lot of youth drop out of primary school, especially boys, . . . because of poverty. After they drop out, they look for a job, and the work they seek requires strength. Also, the government has emphasized girls having the same rights as boys. So you see more girls than boys in school. By the time the boys become youth, they see no future. They have no education, no qualifications, and they become desperate." A third district official bluntly asserted another serious constraint on the education remedy: "Most youth can't get into secondary school."

7. *Youth leaders represent the views of the youth majority.* This contention forms the foundation for the government's strong reliance on the NYC to deal with and address youth concerns, and then represent their views and priorities in government venues. As one district mayor noted, "the NYC is in charge of organizing youth. The projects come to us from the sector level, and then they are discussed." A cell leader supported this view: the NYC provides youth with "representatives and youth committees." It is through these government structures, the official explained, that "the youth can be helped."

Taking these seven tendencies together, one is left with a strong sense of officials viewing youth as young people who must be guided, shaped, led, influenced, directed, and persuaded. An equally strong theme is the steady resistance of youth to accepting their instructions, orders, guidance, remedies, and advice. The conflicting tendencies suggest that officials seek to assert their wisdom, authority, and credibility with youth much more than dialogue with them. Given the considerable shortcomings that the poor youth majority are thought to have, officials see their primary role, during interactions with youth, as speaking to them, while seeing the main role of youth, during such exchanges, as listening.

"It's Policy": Decentralization Challenges

Easily the most sweeping current Rwandan government reform affecting rural areas in recent years has been decentralization. It was well underway when the research team reached the countryside in November 2006, and was, in fact, in the process of implementing the performance contracts already mentioned for the cell and *umudugudu* levels of government. These reforms were found to influence youth lives heavily, and it is for this reason that some description of decentralization, as it was being practiced in rural areas, is necessary.

An in-depth case of decentralization in one particular sector described by the executive of one sector and with documentation provided by him, illuminates how decentralization was taking shape in the countryside. While the following is not comprehensive, it provides a sense of the local intent, design, and application of decentralization in rural Rwanda.

The sector executive displayed a combination of vigor, commitment, discipline, and vision when speaking about his sector's plans for the future. Sitting in his office in a remote corner of Rwanda, in a sector with a main road reportedly so bad that no vehicle could drive on it for half of every year, where there was no electricity, virtually no telephone reception, few schools of any kind, a longstanding reputation for poor education, a high rate of school drop-outs, and reportedly not one soccer field in the entire sector, the official listed his ambitious plans for the sector.[1] There would be, he stated, Internet in all the primary schools and a fully repaired road by the following year. The sector would very soon have a vocational school, two secondary schools, and two "good" primary schools. The primary schools would soon have telephones, as well.

Other changes in the sector were much closer to being realized. Together with leaders at the cell and *umudugudu* levels, sector officials maintained files on every household in the entire sector, a sizable endeavor in a sector of eighteen thousand people. The contents of the household form revealed the kind of concerns that local Rwandan government offices, increasingly, are highlighting. It was highly detailed and contains what the official called "everything that people are supposed to be doing." The list included such things as having an established compost area, a clean latrine, and a clean yard. People should also wear clean clothes. The official also explained the role of officials in this task in the following way: "To lead poor, uneducated people is very difficult. We go and meet people in their houses to sensitize them. We have a file of every house in the sector. It tells them what is to be done [by them]. It also encourages them to change, and their progress is recorded in the file of each house in the sector." Officials regularly made reference to "sensitizing" people, particularly when describing the implementation of decentralization reforms, to characterize how they interacted with what they regularly referred to as "the population" (*abanyagihugu*). The sector executive illustrated this approach with the comment that "the most important thing is to sensitize the population. For example, I have to explain to them why you can't drink from a traditional straw [long, hollow reeds]. And why it is better to drink bottled water." The official did not suggest what poor Rwandans should do if they could not afford to purchase bottled water regularly.

A product of Rwanda's decentralization effort is the widespread introduction of regulations (often termed "obligations") and fines at local levels. The methods aim to reform and regulate the behavior of Rwandan citizens. They were mainly directed at members of the poor, undereducated Rwandan majority. It is a method that has attracted considerable attention and was regularly referred to by youth and adults during interviews. A description of the phenomenon was reported by "Albert B." in a Rwandan newspaper: "Wear shoes, be clean, use a mosquito net: those are a few of the numerous obligations recently put into action in Rwanda. The locally elected authorities have recently signed performance contracts with the government, and are putting pressure on the population, including those without means, to respect the new obligations" (B. 2006, translation). In a revealing passage of the article, B. noted how government leaders at the district and sector levels responded to new and daunting objectives. The newly elected leaders "have effectively agreed in front of the President of the Republic to improve the socioeconomic situation of their populations." Accordingly, the performance contracts that the President and the elected officials have signed list "the objectives that [the officials] need to reach and how much time they have to reach them."

To meet these objectives, B. wrote, "the promises of the leaders have become constraints" for "the population" (B. 2006). Parents are expected to provide their children with shoes and uniforms so they can go to school. The list of obligations included constructing toilets, a compost pit, a table for dry-ing dishes . . . a cooking stove, wearing clean clothes after leaving the farm plot, and paying into the national health insurance program. "For a family of seven," the writer noted, "the annual cost of the main measures is more than two hundred [U.S.] dollars," which was "more than the annual revenue of an average Rwandan." The author also reported that in Bugesera, people "hid in the bush when they saw officials making their rounds" to hand out fines. B. quoted one government official who explained the rationale for this action: "By changing mentality with force, one can see changes in the population, slowly, even with proud people in the population." In other words, creating regulations and levying fines for noncompliance successfully forces behavior changes, even if, in the short term, it might negatively impact poor people.

The article revealed a harsh edge to the application of the regulations and fines. In contrast, local officials said in our interviews that sometimes they were lax in imposing fines: they might give people warnings before levying fines. They also knew that people borrowed sandals from others before enter- ing public areas such as markets and government office compounds, since being barefoot in such places had become illegal. At the same time, there was a strong sense from government officials that assigning regulations and fines was succeeding in changing citizen behavior. An instance of this was proudly recounted by the sector executive mentioned just above. The official described three steps that swiftly improved attendance at primary schools: "First, I went to school and got the names of all of the school drop-outs. Then I met with the heads of *imidugudu* and cells. Second, we announced fines for parents of children who were not in school. The fine was 1,000 francs per child [$1.85]. It would be given to any person who reported that the child was not in school. It's a kind of reward. Third, we registered all the students in a school attendance list, which teachers announced every day in school." It was notable that many adults and youth who were interviewed viewed these sorts of regulations as ultimately useful. The problem lay in how severe the fines were, and how draconian their application was. At the same time, other regulations—regarding housing and the local production of roof tiles—were the cause of far more comment, criticism, and concern from rural Rwandan youth and adults. These issues are considered in chapter 5.

The Rwandan government's tendency to attempt to force changes in citi- zen behavior by administrating and enforcing specified behavior changes is illuminated by a document given to the research team by the sector executive (see the appendix, Bet/Wager [Performance Contracts] on the *Umudugudu* Level). The executive explained that the document came from the Ministry

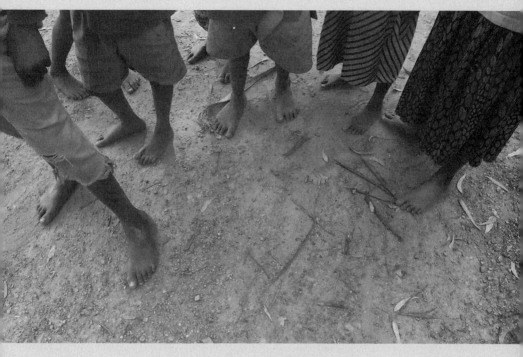

Although walking and working in bare feet is commonplace in Rwanda, government regulations prohibit people from entering public areas without shoes or sandals.

of Local Government, which is charged with leading the national decentralization effort. Its purpose was to provide *umudugudu* leaders with what the official insisted were mere "suggestions," and not "obligations," to help them devise their performance contracts. The process took place during the field research period (November to December 2006).

The document, which is printed as a table rather than in narrative form, provides a compelling, on-the-ground vision for the implementation of government decentralization. It is characteristically detailed and thoroughgoing, covering five areas of "good governance," thirty objectives, and sixty-eight strategies for officials to implement the objectives. The good-governance categories were security, ideology, development, social affairs, and justice (including "opposing the culture of false claims"). The objectives included eradicating (fighting) infiltration [i.e., ending attacks by the "infiltrators"—former Rwandan *génocidaires* still lodged in eastern DRC], bringing people to love their country (patriotism), promoting a hygienic culture, improving production and eradicating poverty, and fighting injustice. The strategies include identifying individuals who enter and leave the village to help fight infiltration, participating in all government programs to help promote patriotism, publicly blaming those harboring what is known in Rwanda as "divisionism" to help eradicate genocidal ideology and its roots, and having neighbors visit each other to help promote mutual assistance. For the "caring about youth welfare" objective, there were four specific strategies: sensitizing (raising awareness) about patriotism, creating jobs, getting youth to join associations, and preventing HIV/AIDS.

It is a long list. While the sector official repeatedly insisted that the Ministry of Local Government document contained mere suggestions to help *umudugudu* leaders discuss performance contract issues during meetings with citizens, the document's explicit detail and implicit expectations raised questions about the extent to which other ideas might surface during meetings. An *umudugudu* leader, for example, intimated that he was obliged to follow all of the suggestions. A cell leader's comment about how cell and *umudugudu* officials operated suggested that the impact of their suggestions to sector officials might be minimal. Such officials, the cell official stated, "don't want the government to know their failures and that they don't do their jobs well."

This is an instructive comment for the purposes of this book in two ways. First, it supports an impression, detailed by a former senior government official, that "there are two kinds of government officials." The two lowest government levels—*umudugudu* and cell—have leaders "that are from the sector, the local area." Cell leaders have more education than the *umudugudu* leaders, the former official explained. On the other hand, sector leaders are university educated and are not from the local area (some, in fact, told me that they had grown up in Uganda as refugees). Having identified differences between government levels according to origin and education (or class), the former official then raised the following question: "Do they trust each other?" In the estimation of the cell leader cited just above, *umudugudu-* and cell-level officials were not part of what he termed "the government," whereas the sector-, district-, and national-level officials, by implication, were. In contrast, and with reference to knowledge of the local situation, the research illuminated a different cutoff point in rural areas. Interviews with government officials at various levels shed light on a pronounced difference between officials at the district and the sector levels regarding knowledge of poor youth views. In general, sector-, cell-, and *umudugudu*-level officials were familiar with many of the key findings the research team shared with them, while district-level officials were significantly less aware of them.

This finding relates to a second way that the cell leader's comment is helpful: shedding light on how the Rwandan government evaluates the accountability of its officials. There was considerable discussion, during interviews with officials at the district, sector, and cell levels, about their need to meet the objectives outlined in their performance contracts. Assigning fines for parents who did not send their children to primary school was an example of a tool to help them meet the objective of improving primary school enrollment.

While officials were clear in our interviews about what many of their performance objectives were, much less clear was what they did with information that directly challenged performance objectives. There were strong indications that many kept it to themselves. Several officials at lower government levels quietly related that they simply did not tell their superiors about many of the difficulties they faced. Some hinted at the possibility that officials who admitted to higher-ups that they were having trouble meeting established government objectives might be replaced: officials are supposed to solve problems and meet government objectives. If they can't do the job, then, evidently, someone else would be given a chance. One sector official, for example, explained that the reports that he and other sector officials send "up" the government chain highlighted achievements that supported government objectives. They did not, however, often relay information that conflicted with them. Difficulties in getting youth to build houses on *imidugudu* or to join associations, faltering AIDS prevention efforts, and difficulties in limiting deforestation were among the persistent challenges that officials identified. The partial information that higher government levels are reportedly receiving invites distorted, and overly positive, assessments of actual realities. Such reports would support the impression that solid advances are being made toward the achievement of national policy objectives. But it may not be true.

The two reported exceptions to this tendency both came from sector officials. One said that he once asked his superior, the district mayor, how he should address the challenge of getting youth to build houses on *imidugudu* housing plots. The mayor only said, "it's policy." The sector official took the mayor's implication to be that he needed to find a solution himself—the policy would not change. Referring to the same challenge, another sector official declared that "if it would have been possible, everyone in Rwanda would already be living in [*imidugudu*]." The official then related how higher-level government officials resisted his explanations of local obstacles to the national government's housing policy: "The people planning all those policies [like the housing policy] don't realize the difficulty and realities in the field. When I explain these realities to them, the authorities defend their position and insist that the *imidugudu* housing policy is feasible." It is notable that even a sector official would refer to his government superiors (by implication, those at district and national levels) as "the authorities." The comment supports a collective sense that local government officials view those above them as "authorities" or "the government," even though they are part of a dramatic government decentralization activity. In contrast, the youth and adults we interviewed viewed sector officials—not district officials—as wielding tremendous power and influence. They also viewed cell-level officials as powerful. They did not view *umudugudu* officials as "authorities" and did not consider them particularly influential. Few youth ever mentioned district-level authorities, who were not present in their sectors. In rural Rwanda, the "secteri" is king.

The study team investigated the influence of ongoing decentralization reforms because of their evident impact on youth lives, particularly in the form of numerous new regulations (or obligations) and fines that were significantly affecting poor Rwandans, youth among them. The setting of development priorities at district levels, with substantial contributions from lower government levels, demonstrated that decentralized reforms were expanding responsibility and contributions to governance from lower government levels. Decentralization has also expanded accountability, and it is in this context that one could sense government officials, from district to *umudugudu* levels, being under considerable pressure to deliver on objectives that officials themselves, particularly those at the district and sector levels, helped to devise. At the same time, passing along challenging information to higher authority levels appears to have been the exception, not the rule.

Despite clear changes wrought by decentralization reforms, one is nonetheless left with the impression of a system still reliant on centralized ways. This may have surfaced from a tendency to employ a bureaucratic logic based on centralization—the form that is both familiar and immediately available—when carrying out decentralization reforms, as earlier observed in Ethiopia (Sommers 1996). During the initial phase of decentralization, this may in fact be unavoidable: the tendency to look "up" at the more powerful levels of the system may be hard to avoid. At the same time, it was apparent that the higher government levels had retained greater levels of influence over those operating beneath them. In short, while the national Rwandan government had decentralized responsibility and accountability to lower government levels, it had yet to reduce much of its power and influence.

Indeed, the opposite may well be the case. The powerful Ministry of Local Government drew up the translated document in the appendix and had it disseminated to the lowest-level officials in the land. The document seemed to be a highly effective means for communicating national government priorities to most Rwandans. There was no indication from this effort that the contents of the document were really "suggestions," as a sector official had insisted. It certainly would be safer for *umudugudu* officials to follow and not challenge any of the contents, particularly given intimations that doing so might result in dismissal. In this and perhaps many other ways, the decentralization process appears to provide the national government with opportunities to expand, rather than transfer or devolve, its power and influence.

Rural Youth, Risk Aversion, and the National Youth Council

Local government officials interviewed in rural Rwanda generally viewed youth as exhibiting unproductive and unhelpful behavior. Their difficulties with youth might be described in the following fashion: the government wants youth to change their behavior in prescribed ways, whereas youth want the government to help them solve specific problems. The tension between government officials pressing for behavior change and youth seeking substantive support left them in a standoff. This is illustrated in the response of youth to what is, by far, the most frequently touted government remedy for youth: persuading them to join associations. As a cell leader remarked, "I don't think youth are afraid to tell the government about their problems. But they always get the same answer: join an association." The fact that most rural youth, particularly those lacking much education, refuse to join associations is a problem that is largely the responsibility of the elected officials of the NYC who operate at district, sector, and cell levels in Rwanda. Since creating youth associations is a central NYC responsibility, some description of them, drawn from interviews with government officials working in rural areas, is useful here.

A critical card in the government's hand is that associations can apply to get government land, including plots with rich soil at the bottom of valleys, to grow additional crops that can then be shared among association members. Since most Rwandans are desperately short of land, with a great many landless or nearly so, the incentive for joining associations is viewed as a viable and available way to induce youth to work together and benefit economically. The difficulties of getting youth to join associations appears to be a nationwide concern, most particularly for youth who are poor and undereducated. One reason that youth wouldn't join associations, some reported, was because they were afraid of being taken advantage of by association leaders (most of whom are comparatively well educated). That "associations have no internal regulations," as a sector-level official explained, seems to allow opportunities for misuse and corruption.

The sector official added that government emphasis on encouraging youth to join associations continued even though the government had evaluated associations "and discovered that associations do not produce benefits for most members." Hence the push to transform associations into cooperatives, he stated, and the government's interest in following the cooperative model established in Kenya. Officials also related that the financial requirements for joining a cooperative precluded the involvement of most youth. Distrusting educated youth may also play a part in their hesitance. Taken together, youth appear at least somewhat justified in their hesitance to join associations and cooperatives.

This stands in stark contrast to the popularity of *ibimina* (informal savings associations) among many poor youth. *Ibimina* membership requires regular contributions of capital (in rural areas, it tended to be monthly, while in ur-ban areas it tended to be weekly). The returns to each member were identical, and each member waited for their turn to receive their share. For example, if ten members each contributed 1,000 francs ($1.85) every month, then each member would receive 10,000 francs ($18.52) when it was their month to re-ceive it. Youth reported that *ibimina* were reliable, since the monetary penalty for dropping out was considerable, requiring, for example, repayment with livestock or a portion of land. It did not appear to happen often. Some also reported that the poorest youth could not participate in an *ibimina* because they could not afford the required installments.

The popularity of *ibimina* among poor—but not destitute—youth provided dramatic evidence of a widespread interest in accessing enough capital to make small investments, such as purchasing seeds for planting beans that could be stored or sold, or livestock that could be raised for food and bred. But *ibimina* also represented an apparent trend toward risk-averse investment strategies among poor Rwandans generally. Some youth and adults we interviewed explained the rationale of buying livestock as a reliable and established means of improving household wealth. A goat or a cow (goats were more popular only because they cost less to purchase and feed) could be used for milk, meat, and animal husbandry: the owner of a female goat, for example, would share the doe's offspring with the owner of the buck that sired it.

This tendency appears to be either misunderstood or underappreciated by many government officials. The national *ubudehe* (local collective action) program gives grants to groups of household heads and lets each group decide how to use the grant (most youth could not participate directly in the program because they were not heads of households).[2] The tendency of many poor household heads was to divide up the sum equally and distribute shares to each member. The approach is the same for *ibimina* members: shares are invested individually, not collectively. But from the view of one sector executive, this general tendency was a sign of Rwandans being able "to see only the present." Using the example of recent *ubudehe* deliberations by members of one community in his sector, the official related the following account. The members divided the amount of the grant into equal amounts per household, the official recalled. Then each household took their portion to buy "a pig or a goat." He explained that the *ubudehe* members "don't see the future." The official said that members could have invested the total amount to artificially inseminate cows. But the members, he said, would have none of it. Those sorts of new, progressive ideas, he stated, "can't work" because "people want an immediate profit." In this case, what could be viewed as a risk-averse investment strategy by poor farmers or an inclination against collective investment, was instead discounted by a powerful local government official as a simple failure to embrace development.

Analysis of interview data for this book found that government underappreciation of (or intolerance for) risk-averse strategies, and the hesitance of many rural Rwandans to work collectively, were central causes for the widespread lack of popularity of associations and cooperatives among poor Rwandans (distrust of educated Rwandans was a third cause). It also underscored the unusually difficult starting point that NYC officials assumed, particularly given the persistent impression that the NYC, in the rural Rwandan sectors we visited, barely functioned.

NYC officials are elected youth volunteers. Meeting after meeting with NYC officials revealed to the research team that they were poorly trained, overwhelmed, and undersupported. Their morale was low, they admitted to accomplishing little, and their credibility among youth was in short supply. As one NYC leader commented, "the youth are complaining about us, and they are right." Because NYC officials lack training, one cell-level NYC official commented that "we don't have advice to give these youth."

One group of NYC officials from sector and cell levels described the various activities they engaged in. They had tried to set up "anti-AIDS" clubs at cell levels, but the clubs collapsed due to lack of financial support. Next came gathering youth to perform drama and songs, but again, the lack of financial support led to failure. A third effort centered on having NYC officials hold literacy classes for illiterate youth and adults. But as one of the three officials who were involved in this effort recalled, "after a while, the other two [NYC officials] got jobs and I was left alone to do the work. I couldn't stand it." That effort failed as well. Officials mentioned having organized sports competitions. Soccer (for male youth) and volleyball (for female youth) were the most popular choices for sports, and all NYC groups that the research team met with strongly endorsed these activities. The universal problem was obtaining and maintaining equipment: the balls wore out and were never replaced. NYC officials mentioned only one effort that partially succeeded: working with other government officials to let youth know about new government policies. The officials recalled that, soon after announcing the new state health insurance plan, some youth began paying into it.

NYC officials were generally educated male and female youth (mostly male youth in the four sectors that were visited). Their ages ranged from twenty to thirty. Those at the sector level tended to have some degree of secondary or vocational school accomplishment, although very few were graduates. Those at the cell level generally had lower levels of educational accomplishment. Many had no postprimary school experience. There were no officials with university education experience.

The young officials' records of fairly good educational accomplishment (relative to nearly all other youth in the local area) undoubtedly aided their election as NYC officials. Their education also appeared to play a factor in their efforts to recruit other youth to work with them or even to attend NYC meetings. Officials related that, for the most part, other educated youth attended their meetings and joined their activities, while undereducated youth did not. The following example of efforts by one group of sector and cell leaders reveals the tendency for NYC officials to engage with small numbers of youth—mainly those with similar backgrounds of reasonable educational accomplishment. It also sheds light on the very low levels of communication and interaction between youth leaders and members of the poor, undereducated youth majority.

NYC officials explained that they had met with youth following an *umuganda* (collective work project). The *umuganda*, they explained, had been explicitly called for youth. The purpose was to repair the main road on the top of the hill. *Umuganda* activities, officials had repeatedly informed the research team, are compulsory, and fines are meted out for those who do not participate. Nonetheless, out of perhaps ten thousand youth in the sector (by our estimate; the NYC officials had no idea how many youth lived in their sector), they reported that only two hundred attended the *umuganda* and then met with NYC leaders afterward. Which youth attended? Not married youth, because, as one official explained, "they don't consider themselves as youth." While the national government defines "youth" as everyone in Rwanda from ages fourteen to thirty-five, the research team found that a popular definition of "youth" covered only those who were single.

The list of youth present at the NYC meeting narrowed further. The majority of those attending, NYC leaders explained, were "educated youth" (i.e., those with at least one year of postprimary schooling) and those living "at the top of the hill." A sector official summed up participation tendencies in the following way: "People on the top are the majority of those attending *umuganda* and our youth meetings." As with other NYC leaders, it did not appear that many of these officials had ever visited areas far from the road, where most rural Rwandans, including most youth, live. One sector official shared what appeared to be her only adventure away from the hilltop: "Once, I went to the valley. It was a very remote area, there was no road, and people there didn't know about cars. I asked myself, 'Is this possible?' When people in the valley learn the importance of roads, I'd say next time they're called for *umuganda* they'd be willing to participate." There is evidence from this revealing comment that youth in valleys don't participate in *umuganda* either because they didn't hear about the *umuganda* or because *umuganda* activities take place on hilltops and are not seen to benefit the people who don't live there. At any rate, most youth, at least in this sector, did not participate in activities even when it was compulsory. The leaders discounted such disinterest in their meetings, or in *umuganda* as, in the words of an NYC official at the sector level, "not having an understanding of [new] information or programs."

A pattern emerged in our interviews with officials in rural Rwanda. NYC officials are normally reasonably educated, unmarried youth. They periodically "call" or "inform" youth in their cell or sector to attend meetings to discuss matters such as AIDS awareness, but mostly to discuss the importance of forming associations. Most youth in their cells and sectors don't attend. Some youth reported that they weren't informed of meetings. Others said the meetings were of no use to them. Regardless of the reason, attendance was low and the few attendees were mainly youth with precisely the same general background as the NYC leaders: unmarried, educated youth living on or near main roads.

There was no question that NYC officials had low credibility with most youth we interviewed, in large part because they had such a poor record of achievement: most government-registered youth associations in the visited sectors were not operational, reportedly because they lacked funds, facilities, or equipment (e.g., the two youth associations in the sector just discussed existed in name only). But one could also sense a significant class distance between NYC officials and the vast numbers of poor youth living on hillsides and down in valleys.

The evidence the research team gathered, in short, strongly suggested that the NYC had minimal impact in all of the rural Rwandan areas we visited. The assumption that NYC officials represented youth majority views proved inaccurate. In the end, expecting young, largely unskilled and untrained volunteer officials to influence youth lives positively was far too much to expect.

Low Horizons

Entering a rural sector begins, appropriately enough, at the sector office. There, the government leaders who manage and administrate sectoral policies preside. Just outside, civilians and lower-level officials can often be seen waiting for meetings or audiences with officials. Nearby the offices are, quite often, other government buildings, such as clinics, meeting rooms, and a police station. Schools and massive, colonial-era Catholic churches are usually in the vicinity. There may be some public-water taps; there may even be electricity. There is also commerce: sector offices and their environs tend to mark the economic center of the sector, and here is where shops, restaurants, and bars are usually located. In these areas one begins to see male youth in large numbers, strolling along roads, bantering in hair salons, and, nearly always, waiting. They are unemployed, and they are looking for jobs that do not involve farming. Many are educated beyond the postprimary school level and, as a result, are not expected to farm.

Moving away from the sector's center, along the main roads, are occasional village centers with dwellings, churches, and shops. These areas are generally much smaller than the markets and institutions near the sector offices. Between these villages, increasingly, are *imidugudu* housing settlements. Here one can see a feature of Rwanda's planned future, where people live in identical houses, or nearly so. The housing settlements tend to be long, narrow, and compact, and they snake their way along roadways. While all Rwandans are expected to live in *imidugudu* at some point, these are nowadays mainly homes for teachers, bureaucrats, and other educated and reasonably successful folk.

It is astride or beneath Rwanda's hills where most people live, and the differences between the hilltops and valleys are stark. "Roads" beneath the hilltops are no more than footpaths. Electricity rarely exists, nor do, for the most part, public-water taps. Children work and play and are regularly in view of older youth. Houses are surrounded by large compounds with family members, crops, and perhaps a cow or goat. Voices can be heard from great distances, and people communicate with shouts just as some up on the tarmac use mobile phones. My initial ventures into valleys routinely invited stares and exclamations, such as the following from a destitute thirty-four-year-old female youth I passed while she was digging with a hoe: "*Wazungu* [here, "white people"] usually only sit at the top of the hill and take suggestions from educated people. We didn't think someone like you could ever come down to talk to us—we're so dirty and poor." The notoriety of white visitors in valleys invited the recounting of stories, such as one about a portly German gent who once came to Byumba and walked into a deep valley—and then couldn't climb back up. It took six local men and a stretcher to haul him back to the road.

Down at the bottom, beside rivers or streams coursing through them, are public lands that are generally reserved for associations. This is prime farmland, rich in nutrients, and it may be the only place where crops can be irrigated during dry seasons. It is also very far away from the hum of the sector's center, on their hilltop perches where government offices can be seen. References to differences between hilltops and valleys were so frequent that I added a new follow-up question to our questionnaire: "Is there a difference between living at the top of the hill and living at the bottom of the hill?"

More than two-thirds of the ninety-three respondents to this question (67.7 percent) contended that there were numerous advantages to living at the top of the hill, particularly near the sector office. People living at the top were better informed and less isolated. They had better access to health care and off-farm employment. They had easier access to sector officials, who were widely seen as powerful and influential. The valleys, in contrast, were remote, many observed. News of job opportunities or government-led meetings rarely reached people living below the hills. Distributions of useful goods, such as crop seeds, often reach people living in valleys only indirectly, trickling down after distributions have already taken place at higher elevations.

Heavy rains erode farmland and destroy houses in valleys. A common phrase that government officials employed to describe people living in the valleys was that they lacked "understanding" and "development," references both to the lower education levels and to the assumed backwardness of people residing in valleys. These terms were also ways to describe social difference: those with salaries and more education tend to live at or near the hilltops, whereas those who work on the land with little education tend to live below.

While none of the respondents who had not attended school saw any advantage to living in valleys, more than a quarter of all respondents (28 percent) viewed living "down" or "below" as advantageous, and their explanations are revealing. One male youth, aged thirty-one, believed that "people living at the bottom of the hill don't have many advantages. But they have one: they have water." He was referring to the difficulties that people living at the tops of hills face without pumped water (it remains uncommon in most rural sectors, including those the research team visited). Water on some hilltops has become a commodity that porters can sell. Limited available water on hilltops also means that girls and women, who traditionally fetch water, have to haul water much farther than their counterparts living closer to valley streams and springs. Most of Rwanda's hills are steep and deep, making the task of carrying water tiring and time consuming.

A handful of youth and adults who were interviewed believed that while erosion was a problem not faced by people at the tops of hills, those at the very bottom benefited because, as a female youth of thirty-three noted, "erosion adds good soil" to a person's land in valleys. An adult man of forty-six attributed the advantages of living on his valley farm to his hesitance to live on an *umudugudu* beside hilltop roads: "They [the authorities] are asking us to come up to the *umudugudu*. But the land [up there] is infertile, and you can't plant bananas there. In terms of fighting erosion, people on the *umudugudu* have less problems. But people in the valley have opportunities: our lands are stable and fertile." This man's description mixes housing policy and farming work, a common tendency among respondents expressing hesitance about moving to the *umudugudu*. The housing policy implies that farmers will commute from their roadside homes down to their farms in valleys. One can understand that this would be difficult for some to appreciate, since Rwandan farmers traditionally live beside or near their farms.

A final advantage of valley living observed by a few respondents was the distance from powerful authorities living atop hills (sector officials, but sometimes cell officials as well). A male youth of twenty-two, for example, explained that "when you live close to the authorities, you are always being watched and asked to participate in everything. You are also the first to be fined if you do not participate. So it is not good to [live] close to the authorities." Living in valleys and away from government offices allows people to opt out of participating in compulsory activities, of which there are many: *gacaca* meetings and *umuganda* work are typically weekly activities, and participation is compulsory. But some people living in valleys reported that they do not hear about requests to attend meetings or participate in activities. Living in the remoter parts of a cell or sector also provided people with a handy excuse: you could avoid participation merely by later reporting, if ever asked, that you did not hear about a particular meeting or activity in time. A female youth of twenty-three

Clear signs of erosion on this hillside are present in the lower right quadrant.

provided the following example: "People who are up there [on the hilltop] are quickly informed when there is news or programs from the sector or in town. But down here, sometimes we find out about events a week after they happened. So people up there can't escape attending *gacaca* meetings, but here in the valleys there are people who have yet to attend one." Here one can detect the quiet resistance to government expectations that many Rwandans practice. While the extent of such practices was impossible to measure, it was evident that some Rwandans found advantages to living outside the purview of those on hilltops. Living in valleys and on hillsides, in other words, could be extraordinarily difficult. But it also offered some discrete advantages.

The remainder of this chapter describes youth life in rural Rwanda, largely away from the hilltops, where most of the nation's youth reside.

Digging, Eating, and No More Education

Some youth go to school, some go for vocational training, and some dig. The unlucky ones dig.

Female youth, age twenty-one

I do what my arms can do. They can dig and fetch grass for the cows.

Female youth, age twenty

In this area, young men start by digging for others. It's the only profession they have. If you can't dig for someone, you become a dog.

Male youth, age twenty-seven

I haven't dug since I dropped out of school. My father digs, my mother digs, my grandfather digs; all of them dig. But when I look at them, I see that they have achieved nothing.

Male youth, age twenty

We are too down to go farther down.

Male youth, age twenty-six

We are poor for life. There is no way out.

Male youth, age twenty-six

More than anywhere else, life for most of Rwanda's rural youth takes place at the end of a hoe. Nearly all youth had at least one foot in farm work. Most had both. Of 105 responses to the question, "How do you spend your time on a normal day?" nearly every youth mentioned digging as a daily activity. Indeed, "digging" was a core activity for 82 percent of respondents, and some of the remaining 18 percent mentioned that they also "dug" for their families or those who had hired them. Digging was the reference point for most discussions about rural youth as well. It is the main thing that most youth do.

Youth were found to dig on family land, on their own land (if they had any), on land held by associations, on land which they rented to grow crops, and on land owned by others that they worked on for either 200 or 300 francs per day (200 francs, or $0.37, was more common than the higher figure). Male youth did most of the paid work. Female youth performed many more household chores (although some male youth mentioned that they also fetched water). Male youth also stated that they socialized much more often than female youth, particularly in the evenings, when some ended up in bars. Female youth work days were generally longer.

We soon added a follow-up question, "Do the weekly requirements that you have affect your normal days?" (part of question 1 in box 2.3) because many respondents were stumped by the notion of a "normal" day. This was because most days of the week contained regular required activities. For a people reliant on farming for survival, these other activities extracted a significant chunk of their time. Typically, one day a week was reserved for attending *gacaca* trials and a second day for performing *umuganda* activities. Some youth and adults reported that they were regularly absent from both of these compulsory activities. There were also meetings with government officials on issues such as HIV/AIDS prevention and new decentralization measures. Respondents said that such meetings generally took place on a third day each week. Some youth listed a fourth day that was not reserved for digging: Sunday, when many if not most rural Rwandans attend church and then socialize or simply rest.

On the average, that left only three days each week during which rural Rwandans could devote their time to digging or other work activities. Government or community-related activities might not take up an entire day, but people may be required to walk significant distances to a meeting, a trial, or an *umuganda* work site. More than half of sixty-five respondents to the follow-up question (55.5 percent) stated that the weekly requirements reduced their productivity. Over a third (37 percent) contended that the requirements had no substantial negative impact on their productive capacities. The remainder (7.5 percent) merely explained that the requirements were obligations, and they had to respect government orders (as well as avoid possible fines for not participating).

Significantly, only one youth mentioned school as part of a normal day. Despite the fact that secondary and vocational schools were rare or nonexistent

Three female youth "dig" together. Two of their children
are also present at right: an infant in the arms of a male youth,
and one sitting on the grass.

Two male youth take a break from digging, for which they are paid 200 francs ($0.37) a day. With considerable pride, the youth in the foreground asked that his cap and radio be included in the portrait.

in the visited areas (vocational schools in particular), and the fact that some youth may have been too old to attend school, the near-complete absence of education in the lives of rural youth was nonetheless striking.

The impact of the absence of education on youth lives was suggested by responses to a question about future plans ("Do you have a plan for improving your situation?"). Of ninety-nine youth responses, a sizable proportion (44.5 percent) described some sort of future plan, while an identical proportion of youth stated that, while they had a plan, they lacked the means to implement it. The remaining respondents (11 percent) said that they had no plan whatsoever.

The responses from the last group of youth are chilling. They strongly suggested lives inflected with hopelessness and aiming at mere survival. A twenty-seven-year-old female youth simply stated that, "when I work, it's only for food. I don't progress." A thirty-year-old female youth explained, "when you don't have any means, you can't think of improvement." As a consequence, she added, "I don't plan anything." A male youth of twenty-two explained that "I just live day by day and praise God that I'm still alive. That's all." Nearly two-thirds of this last group of respondents (63.5 percent) were single, and nearly three-quarters (73 percent) were destitute.

As for those youth who said they had plans to improve their situation, most of the responses were more like hopes or aspirations than viable strategies. Most plans lacked detail, and few of the youth lacking financial support expressed any way of attracting it. Youth also mentioned barriers to achieving their plans. There were difficulties in getting loans (and paying them back), saving money, and finding sponsors of any kind. Many raised youth associations as a possible source of support, although some expressed significant skepticism, and even scorn, about being unable to afford the membership fees, to trust others (particularly educated association leaders), or to see evidence of successful associations. The prominence of farm work in the future plans of many rural youth is aptly illustrated by a twenty-one-year-old male youth who said, "my plan is to keep on digging to save money." This may not be a surprising finding for young people with farming backgrounds. Yet it remains significant because most rural youth continue to rely so heavily on land, which is increasingly scarce in Rwanda. Extensive reliance on this dwindling resource was the predominant economic theme in the rural youth research.

With this in mind, it was equally significant that very few youth mentioned education at all or any kind of training when describing their future plans. Only 12 percent of rural youth who communicated a personal plan said that education was part of their future. A mere 5 percent mentioned training. The proportions were even smaller among youth in the urban sample (detailed in part 3), where just 5.5 percent of respondents mentioned education or training as a component of their future plans.

Perhaps these proportions are a collective expression of realism. After all, only one in ten primary school graduates attend secondary school (Save the Children UK 2007: 2), and far fewer attend vocational schools, which, as of this writing, scarcely exist in Rwanda. Yet the collective finding proved to be a surprising, even startling, discovery. The contrast with research findings in Burundi was dramatic. There, a very large proportion of both youth and adults responded to the identical question about future plans by highlighting formal or vocational education as a core component of their future. The difference surprised many Rwandan officials at the district and national government levels, in addition to international officials with whom I shared the findings. For many, it was unforeseen in the midst of a major expansion of child and youth access to education in Rwanda. I address the stark differences in findings between the Rwandan and Burundian youth research in chapter 9.

The infrequent mention of education in Rwandan youth responses is connected to the widespread contention among respondents that postprimary education and training—even apprenticeships or other means of learning a new trade—were entitlements available to few youth. The research suggests that the demand for education and training is low among what might be assumed is their primary target group: the lesser-educated youth majority. This may be viewed as an alarming and potentially tragic finding. Yet most youth we interviewed appeared to have taken a different view, which is, evidently, to accept the reality that entrance into a secondary school, a vocational school, or even into a training program, will never be available to them. Life may be easier for them to deal with, in other words, if they simply accept the limitations on them.

Since youth rarely mentioned schooling of any kind during the initial fieldwork period, we were able to gather most comments about education only after we inserted specific follow-up questions about it.[1] The responses reveal, generally in stark, blunt terms, that education was for others—not for most of the youth who were interviewed. "People who don't go to school are ignorant and people who go are not," a male youth of twenty-two succinctly stated. "The youth who go to secondary school always have the advantage," a male youth of twenty-one said. "Those who don't go to those schools can't cope with life these days," another male youth of the same age announced. "Life is becoming more and more difficult for them," he continued, "and that is the only difference." Still another said, "The ones who go [to secondary or vocational school] step forward. The ones who don't are simple diggers." A thirty-one-year-old male youth said, "educated people can go far in society, and have a better life, but the uneducated cannot." A destitute female youth of twenty-three listed three ways that educated and uneducated youth have what she termed "different situations":[2] "The educated share knowledge, and when there are small projects, they are the first to get them due to their advantages. Second, their lifestyle is different from ours: they are clean and smart because it has been their style for a long time. When an educated youth comes from digging, he washes and puts on clean clothes. Third, educated youth express themselves freely. They are not afraid like us." Such views do not depict a society in which substantial advancement is viewed as possible by the poor majority. Nearly two in three (65 percent) of the sixty-three respondents to the follow-up question of differences between youth who go to vocational or secondary school and those who don't detailed their perceptions of a vast gulf between youth who received and did not receive this education. The educated youth minority live in an entirely separate world from the uneducated youth majority—or so it seemed from the responses of most youth. As a destitute twenty-four-year-old male youth observed, "how could an educated person become uneducated, or an uneducated person become educated? It's impossible to change your situation."

To better understand this gulf, it is instructive to examine how respondents described the situation of youth in their areas. While some believed that upward (and downward) mobility was possible, the imprint of expectation was shallow, and the realm of possibility rarely included education. Twenty-one of twenty-six rural respondents (81 percent) who directly addressed follow-up questions relating to social mobility felt that it was possible to move up or down in society.[3] One might "move up" in a variety of ways, such as developing savings and capital over time, obtaining good harvests, migrating to a city, or marrying a rich person. But none of the respondents mentioned a better education as a means of doing so. The idea for most uneducated youth seemed to be that one has to first accept one's plight, and then sculpt a life as best as one can. It is a life lived within narrow expectations and limited possibilities, where realism dominates and imagination seems to be the reserve of the more fortunate. It is, in short, a life based on regrettable fate: you either have the advantages of education, or you don't, and most don't.

The rationale of many uneducated youth seemed to entail the idea that accepting one's low position in society limited frustration. Educated people may be able to reach higher and accomplish more, but they will likely have a harder time when they encounter difficulties. A poor male youth of twenty-one, who never completed primary school, illustrated this apparent tendency: "Imagine a person who finishes school but can't get a job afterwards. It's worse for him than for us because we don't have high expectations in life. Educated people expect many things after they're done with [secondary or vocational] school, so when they can't get a job, they become *inzererezi* [wanderers] because of their frustration." As is examined in chapter 5, getting into secondary school appears to increase chances for social humiliation if one is unemployed, or even worse, fails to complete their secondary education. Failure at the cusp of advancing carries a heavy social cost.

Here one can sense lowered expectations as a risk-averse life strategy. The impression is strengthened by findings from responses to the question, "If you achieve your success, will you also achieve the 'good life'? What is the 'good life'?" (question 8 in box 2.3). Nearly all of the respondents equated achievement of their plan with attaining the "good life." The definitions of what constitutes the good life, however, are much more revealing. Overwhelmingly, most respondents (69 percent of sixty-four responses) viewed the good life as meeting the most elemental of needs—having water, food, shelter, health, and basic commodities like soap—and not much more.

Indeed, what is remarkable is just how little most youth expected of life. This is reflected by comments about having "something to eat" after returning from a day of digging, as mentioned by a female youth of thirty-two, or the idea of eating twice a day when a single daily meal is the norm, as expressed by a male youth of twenty-one. The idea of having enough food, or of at least eating something every day, was a central component of two-thirds of all definitions of a good life among respondents.

Having some food (and avoiding hunger) was also central to respondent definitions of peace.[4] One of the central tenants expressed by respondents was that hunger invites insecurity. It might create thieves ("when you don't eat, you become a thief") who might rob you ("security is when you don't fear for your crops or animals getting stolen"). The connection between averting hunger—for oneself and for others in one's community—and improving one's safety and health was a dominant theme. Meeting such minimal needs proved central to the thinking of virtually every respondent, not just youth. As a fifty-one-year-old woman said, "For me, peace is when I'm alive, I have food, I'm healthy, and I'm safe in my house. What else can I expect?" A male youth of twenty-four defined peace even more simply: "peace is when a person can eat as much as he wants."

Indications of everyday difficulty surfaced in other ways, as well. Responses to a question about social relations revealed sources of tension within rural communities.[5] Of the sixty responses that could be trended, almost half (48.3 percent) said that, although relations were generally acceptable, significant problems existed. A somewhat smaller proportion of respondents (38.3 percent) emphasized negative dimensions in their social lives. The remaining eight stated that social relations in their communities were essentially fine. Among the examples of positive relations provided by these eight respondents were intermarriage between ethnic groups and instances of people assisting others. The answers of this last group were uniformly short and general, which could suggest a hesitance to discuss an issue as potentially sensitive as social relations in an interview.

The potential sensitivity of the subject did not limit most respondents, however. The collective view of the majority (86.6 percent of the total) suggested tense community environments. There was mention of theft, distrust, fear, poisoning, suspicion, frustration, hatred, jealousy, selfishness, witchcraft, domestic violence, violent fights in bars, conflicts caused by accusations during *gacaca* proceedings, corruption, death threats, inequality, and a lack of compassion for others, particularly for those less fortunate (such as the landless). Land conflicts involving neighbors and relatives were mentioned with more regularity than any other issue. A destitute male youth of nineteen illustrated the too-common Rwandan cocktail of land scarcity and extreme poverty: "Social relations here are very bad. Due to the small amounts of land that most people have, neighbors are always in conflict. They may also become enemies and end up poisoning each other. I think the main reason that very few people here have good relations with others is poverty. When you start improving your situation, others get hungry and jealous. They look for ways to destabilize you." The social environment described here is bleak and potentially explosive, and it supports our findings that many rural Rwandans see their lives as desperate and unstable. Surely endemic poverty and tightening land holdings can inspire such outlooks. Yet it is instructive to examine another theme that arose only in answers from the largest group (i.e., the nearly half who stated both positive and negative aspects of social relations in their communities): the involvement of local leaders in dispute resolution, particularly regarding land conflicts.

The descriptions of "local authorities" and "grassroots leaders" collectively evoke a corps of public servants acting swiftly and decisively. As a destitute twenty-five-year-old male youth noted, "Social relations are good here, although small problems can arise. But when they do, people go to leaders, who solve them. The promoter of the conflict is punished and things keep going." Some respondents hailed their local leaders for creating solutions that did not call for appeals to higher-level officials or the courts. This stated reluctance to take land and other conflicts before the formal justice system is supported by prior research on dispute resolution preferences in rural Rwanda. Earlier research had found that poor farmers who were interviewed viewed the justice system as "slow, expensive, and frequently unjust" (Sommers and McClintock 2003: 54). Resolutions to communal conflicts that higher-level officials meted out were also "thought to be arbitrary, unpredictable, or subject to influence from one side or the other" by members of the rural poor. The study also found that local leaders were "overwhelmed with disputes and responsibilities" (ibid.). While it was unclear from research for this book whether the style of dispute resolution that low-level government leaders employed was effective, the rise of regulations and fines that have emerged as a product of Rwandan decentralization points to firm and fast decision making and harsh consequences for the parties judged as guilty.

The reputation for decisive action by Rwandan officials did not appear to dim their awareness of the dire straits that most Rwandan youth face. Youth's and civilian adults' descriptions of the general situation of youth (in response to question 3 in box 2.3) broadly correlated with the views of government officials. Whether civilian or government official, the assessments generally began with mention of severe difficulty. However, civilian respondents provided much more detail. Youth and adults described youth as isolated, left behind, in a bad situation, enmeshed in poverty and ignorance, and lacking land, jobs, education, and access to money. Almost two in five of the seventy-four respondents (39 percent) referred to difficulties relating to livelihoods of some sort (land, employment, associations, and urban migration). Urban migration was also connected to the most prevalent response (40.5 percent of respondents): getting married, building a house, or acquiring roofing to build a house. Marriage and housing were expressed as interconnected concerns, since building a house is a cultural prerequisite to marriage, and neither male nor female youth can be considered adults until they are married. This issue is examined in chapter 5, together with urban migration, which was primarily described as an outlet either for those searching for funds to build a house (in order to get married) or for those hoping to escape the expectation of marriage. Fifteen percent of respondents highlighted social relations as central to the youth situation, which included issues such as the need for youth recreation and the failure of youth to emulate or learn from their parents.

Echoing the virtual absence of education as a central youth concern highlighted earlier, only four (5.5 percent) respondents even mentioned education in relation to the youth situation. All of them related education to failure of some sort: one about a vocational school graduate who couldn't find work, another about students leaving school and migrating to Kigali, and two about parents lacking enough money to pay for secondary school fees, which caused their children to drop out.

Given the generally desperate situation facing most youth, who is helping them (question 4 in box 2.3)? over half of respondents (57 percent of 144 respondents) said that while there were organizations, associations, or cooperatives in their immediate area, none were targeting youth. That did not mean that some youth were not involved: respondents noted that some youth may qualify for programs such as those that targeted orphans or those infected with HIV/AIDS. But many respondents made clear their view that most youth were not benefiting from projects or assistance being provided. Nearly one in five respondents (19.5 percent) said that there were no organizations, associations, or cooperatives of any kind operating in their area. Slightly more (23.5 percent) said that there was some sort of organization working with youth—mainly either an NGO or a youth association. Yet most of these organizations, respondents said, were plagued by some sort of problem, such as corruption involving leaders, a lack of land to operate on, failed administration, or some other sign of ineffectiveness.

If assistance was sorely lacking for nearly all poor rural youth in the surveyed areas, expectation was not. In response to the question, "Who might help you with your plan, so that you may find success?" (question 7 in box 2.3), over a third of the eighty-two respondents (34 percent) explicitly stated that the government should assist youth. Many mentioned the influence and predominance of the government over rural life. A male youth of twenty-five, for example, contended that "the government is above everything, and everything passes through the government." Therefore, it was logical that the government should extend assistance to him. Adults expressed similar sentiments, including one fifty-nine-year-old man who commented that "the government should help us. The government is our parent. They should find a solution for us." An additional 8.5 percent stated that associations should help them achieve success, which is a government-supported approach. Another 8.5 percent of respondents mentioned a bank loan, while 10 percent suggested development projects from an NGO or donor organization; 6 percent of respondents said that either family members or friends would assist them.

The gender dimensions of rural youth expectations of the government are illuminating. Exactly half of male youth respondents stated that either the government or associations can or should help them, compared to 23 percent of female respondents. The expression of distance of most female youth from government support, real or expected, is starkly suggested by these data.

This finding on distance is further supported by a closer look at the final third of respondents (33 percent) who, instead of identifying possible sources of support for their plans, were entirely bereft of ideas. More than half of this group expressed no hope for improvement; that "only God" could assist them. The others explained that they didn't know of anyone who could help them. Which youth responded in this way? Close to half of all female youth respondents (45.5 percent) were part of this group (as well as 29 percent of all male youth respondents). Taken together, responses to this question suggest that, among the poor, undereducated youth majority, male youth are far more likely to have an expectation that the government, in some form, might assist them. In dramatic contrast, few female youth shared this confidence, and nearly half expressed a view that no supports below God were available to them.

The research sample for this question response is too small here to do more than suggest a desperate situation for female youth. At the same time, the findings indicating distance and despair in female youth lives were expressed in other ways, and with more substantial data to support them. Accordingly, particularly significant aspects of female youth life in Rwanda are highlighted in chapters 5 and 8.

"If I Were the Mayor"

The responses to the question, "If you suddenly were the district mayor and you were in charge of this district, what is the first thing you would change?" (question 5 in box 2.3), sheds further light on many of the issues that have arisen thus far in part 2 and foreshadows others that are detailed in chapter 5. The question's invitation to respondents to imagine themselves as a high-ranking government authority empowered most to assess gaps and weaknesses in government provision and to identify priorities in their lives and their communities. In many cases, responses to the question also highlighted the nature of interactions between government officials and ordinary Rwandans.

The question's emphasis on imagination was revealing even when it did not work. A minority of respondents (5 percent) were overwhelmed by the question. It was clear that these male and female youth were unable to even imagine themselves as powerful leaders. "I can't know [what it would be like to be the Mayor] because living in the countryside makes you unable to think," a poor male youth of twenty-two explained. "I won't be capable" to answer the question, a poor male youth of thirty stated. "What could I do as mayor if I didn't go to school?" a destitute twenty-three-year-old female youth asked. "I didn't even go for one year of primary school." Their inability to answer the question suggests that one viable survival strategy among poor and destitute Rwandan youth is to accept their lowly status and expect little from life, a theme that aligns with evidence that many rural and urban Rwandan youth sought to stabilize their situation, however lowly, instead of trying to move "up" in society.

Nonetheless, most of those who were asked to imagine themselves as the district mayor were able to do so. Their responses provided two kinds of information. First, they highlighted what respondents felt should be addressed first by someone in that position. Second, they illuminated what they believed was the best way to accomplish them.

Five categories of emphasis arose from the 123 people (62.5 percent of whom were male youth, 25.2 percent were female youth, and 12.25 percent were adults) who answered the question about what they would do if they were the mayor. Nearly a third of respondents emphasized some sort of economic development (such as poverty reduction, enhancing agricultural production, or improving access to water) as their priority. "I'd start by improving farm production by having farmers use new and modern techniques," one female youth stated. "I'd advocate to the higher authorities to give more animals" to people, so they could improve their ability to fertilize their farm plots, a poor female youth of twenty-three explained. The compost fertilizer that livestock would provide to farmers was essential, she continued, because "our lands are getting tired." This youth's explanation suggests a view that even a district mayor was not all that powerful. Despite decentralization reforms that were well underway when the field research was undertaken, reference to the hierarchical structure of the Rwandan government and the belief that the highest reaches of the structure retained the lion's share of the state's power, were recurring themes.

The second most common category of response (26 percent of all respondents) referred not to economic development generally but to addressing the particular needs of youth. Quite unlike respondents to the first category, which contained only slightly more male than female youth (eighteen versus fifteen), the overwhelming majority of respondents in the second category (83 percent) were male youth. This may be explained by the fact that, as we remember, the Rwandan government defines youth as everyone between the ages fourteen and thirty-five, although its reference point in Rwandan culture remains almost entirely a male youth concern. Many male youth, in other words, probably sought to speak about their needs, which mainly meant providing them with economic support and development projects (in contrast, only one of 123 respondents, a poor female youth of twenty, highlighted addressing the needs of women). Certainly the frequent references to danger and threat among many of the respondents in this category referred to male youth concerns. The collective message regarding this point is clear: if leaders don't start prioritizing youth needs soon, many male youth may be forced to resort to crime and violence. This sentiment is reflected in the following three comments. Addressing youth issues "can help build the country," a destitute male youth of twenty-three noted, "but youth can also destroy the country" if their issues are left "unsolved." Another male youth warned that improving the youth situation was crucial because, he asked ominously, "don't you realize that youth were involved in the war to a big extent?" A third male youth put it simply: "when youth are not taken care of, they become bandits." In all, seven respondents (5.7 percent) mentioned security issues prominently, such as pervasive banditry or general violence in their area.

A mere 10 percent of respondents (twelve of 123, or 9.75 percent) highlighted education in some way. Only two of the respondents even mentioned vocational education, yet another indication of its near-complete unavailability to nearly all Rwandan youth. The starting point for many responses highlighted enticing youth into some sort of formal school or, perhaps, into literacy classes. Another theme shed light on why some youth don't go to school or dropped out early: the excessively poor quality of rural schools. A forty-three-year-old adult male said that if he were the mayor, "I'd ask myself why, when you go to a secondary or primary school in this district, you can't even find one teacher there. I have one son who was in P4 [the fourth year of primary school]. He told me he never saw a teacher in his class. How long are we going to be patient? We think it is a problem of teachers who are useless." An adult woman of forty-five added that even when teachers are in class, "your child can get to P6 [the final primary school grade] without knowing how to read." As a result, if she were mayor, she would emphasize school inspections "to find out if teachers are drinking all day long." Youth dropped out of school, the two adults implied, at least partly because going to school was a waste of time.

The remaining two categories highlighted working to change attitudes in different ways. Some prioritized "changing the mentality" of the "population" if they were leaders (9.75 percent of all respondents). If these respondents were mayors, they would encourage ordinary citizens to "work together," join associations, or create group economic projects (the details of such projects were always vague, largely, it appears, because there are so few successful examples); precisely the sort of approach that current leaders expressed during interviews. More common (17 percent of respondents) was, effectively, a sharp criticism not of farmers who lacked motivation but, instead, on leaders whose methods were deficient. Frequent themes included that current leaders were corrupt, impassive, or largely absent. "I'd change all these leaders because they are doing nothing for me," a destitute nineteen-year-old male youth stated.

To gauge the attitudes of respondents to leaders and citizens more deeply, all responses were analyzed a second time to reveal what they highlighted about leader-citizen interactions. This second cut at responses was smaller than the first. Eighty-two of the original 123 respondents (two in three) expressed a clear emphasis about the attitudes of either leaders or citizens.

The results divided into four categories. Just over a third of respondents (34 percent) said that they would treat youth and others in rural communities in essentially the same way their current leaders already do. These responses were characterized by words such as "sensitizing," "encouraging," "urging," or "mobilizing" youth to carry out certain actions, such as getting them to "fight against HIV/AIDS," "to dig," and, especially, to join associations. Employing the same tactics to change citizen behavior that existing leaders use might be explained in two ways. First, cajoling and otherwise pressuring people to act in specific ways may be how people envision the role of leaders. Accordingly, they would act in the very same way if they were leaders themselves. Another possible explanation is that telling or encouraging people to do something may be the only way to change their behavior.

The remaining two-thirds of respondents had other ideas. Over one in four respondents (27 percent) highlighted the need for government leaders to "move closer to the people." The act of "getting closer to the population"—a phrase that regularly arose in interviews with youth, adults and officials alike—was here defined in a different way than government officials. Instead of providing encouragement and/or pressure to get people to somehow change their ways, most of these respondents emphasized direct engagement and discussion with, and listening to, citizens. "I would meet with the population and ask them for advice on how to better organize their lives," a poor male youth of twenty-six stated. "If I were the mayor of this district, I'd start by visiting the population in my district and talk to them, and listen to them and their problems."

Another common response (21 percent) was to emphasize injustice in some way. These responses highlighted that leaders disrespected and took advantage of ordinary citizens. There were references to teachers who "drink the whole day," leaders who take funds intended for development support and "put them in their stomach," educated people who "take advantage of others," the meting of unreasonable fines on citizens (such as for not participating in mandatory *umuganda* activities), and the "suppression of the rights of youth." Several respondents also mentioned that youth who are ignored by leaders have no choice but to turn to banditry.

The final response category (18 percent of respondents) emphasized the importance of advocating for the poor with higher-level government officials and international donor agencies to gain development funds for the respondents' areas. The collective sense by two-thirds of respondents was that current leaders generally overlooked, disregarded, and even exploited them. A related concern was fear of leaders, something that two respondents, in particular, highlighted. A female youth of twenty-seven stated that, if she were the district mayor, she would "try to diminish the distance between leaders and the population, so that the population wouldn't be scared when they're in front of the authorities." A male youth of twenty-two went still further, indicating how some poor Rwandans regard their leaders: as powerful and distant—and themselves as children, hoping for attention:

> We think getting a leader is like getting a parent. Once, our executive secretary [the head of the sector] came here and everyone ran away. Later he asked people why they ran away. He was told that everyone thought that he was like the other leaders. He told his staff not to traumatize the population. He is the one who gave us back our tranquility. This would also be one of my priorities.

All these guys here can't afford to marry a woman because they can't build a house. Male and female youth are failing to get married.

Male youth, age twenty-four

The roof tile problem is so big. I started a house but it fell down. What can I do?

Male youth, age twenty-two

Youth are marrying late these days because they can't afford to buy *mabati* [iron roofing sheets] for their houses. If a youth builds a house with a banana leaf roof instead, he's humiliated.

Adult man, age forty-five

There are no youth able to marry in my *umudugudu*, even when they are old enough to do so. This is due to the lack of roof tiles. This leads to boys meeting girls in the bush. The girls get pregnant, and there are children born outside of marriage. I can say this about girls here: they are not getting legally married.

Umudugudu-level government official

CHAPTER FIVE

Striving for Adulthood

Rural Rwanda is a tough place to come of age. The pressure on youth to meet social expectations is great, and the consequences of failing are harsh. The hard edge of what appears to be an inflexible part of Rwandan culture is illuminated by the following quote from an executive secretary of a rural sector: "You can't become a man without building a house. To be a woman, you have to marry. If a woman produces children without a husband, then she's a prostitute. And if she reaches twenty-eight years old without getting married, then she will be rejected by youth society. She will become an old lady and not a woman." As this chapter describes, findings from the research demonstrated that a majority of unmarried male youth are striving to build houses and most female youth are waiting to get married in a socially acceptable union.

The odds against most youth achieving these goals weigh heavily against them. For female youth, the window of opportunity for marrying (and obtaining social recognition as a woman) is exceedingly narrow. From the start, many young Rwandan women will never be able to marry, since there may be as many as 12 percent more women than men in Rwanda (Ministry of Youth, Culture, and Sports n.d.: 9), and the prohibition against polygamy (until recently a common occurrence in rural Rwanda, particularly in northern areas) is strongly enforced. In addition, Rwandan authorities are unwavering about the minimum legal marriage age of twenty-one. In addition, while the executive secretary quoted above stated that a female youth must marry by age twenty-eight, many of the Rwandan men and women I informally asked about this point stated that age twenty-eight was much too high for a rural Rwandan female. As one man explained, "Even a twenty-five-year-old [female youth] is too old for most young men." In other words, a female youth may have as few as four years to marry legally. But the availability of eligible husbands is seriously limited by much more than the fact that there are fewer Rwandan men than Rwandan women. A male youth must build a house before he can prepare for a proper marriage to a female youth. Few male youth who were interviewed believed that they would be able to ever complete their houses.

The challenge of male and female adulthood usually begins, and too often ends, with discussions of roofing. The fallout from this issue was remarkably significant: without finding the means to build a roof, male youth cannot build their house. If they cannot build their house, then male and female youth will find it difficult if not impossible to ever enter a formal marriage, which means marrying in a way that society would approve (that is, in a large sanctioned wedding). If youth cannot marry in such a way, frustration, humiliation, and perhaps ruin ensue. To youth and adults in rural areas, the lack of roofing connected, ultimately, to informal, live-in marriages, illegitimate children, urban migration, education, crime, prostitution, AIDS, and to a particularly perilous fate: becoming an *inzererezi* (wanderer), which is, essentially, to be homeless and thus a social outcast. The downward spiral that youth face, and their difficult quest for adulthood, was detailed by an *umudugudu* leader we interviewed in a rural area:

> The situation of the youth here is bad. They are desperate. They have no hope that their situation will ever change. The only thing they can do is dig until they get rid of that life and migrate. They have given up on the idea of getting [formally] married because they can't afford that. They can't build their own houses because the price of roof tiles is too high for them.

So we've got a problem here. When [male] youth are unemployed, with no occupation, they wander, they smoke marijuana and end up having sex with girls [female youth]. Girls are probably desperate, too. They know that they can't find husbands. Since they are also poor, they can't say no when a boy [male youth] or even an adult man comes to them and wants to have sex in exchange for money. People are hungry now, too.

The quest for housing was found to be the dominant preoccupation of most rural youth. The social imperative was similarly clear: many male youth reported that they "had no choice" but to strive to work and save for the distant but essential goal: completing a roof. The need to build a house was so great that many youth worked instead of attending school (many viewed attending secondary school as particularly problematic, as we see later in this chapter) in order to work and save money to purchase roofing materials instead.

To understand why so many youth, and male youth in particular, relentlessly worked toward a goal—getting enough roofing to construct a house—that they knew they would probably fail to achieve, it is useful to first understand some of the basic elements of house building and its relation to manhood in rural Rwanda.

Roofing as a Measure of Manhood

Two male youth (according to the Rwandan government's definition of youth)—one thirty-two years old, the other thirty-five—explained their housing situation in terms of roof tiles. "I have five hundred roof tiles on my house," the younger youth said. His house was not even half complete: he needed "seven hundred more" to finish the entire roof. Then he said, "I'm not going to make it because I don't have enough land to dig on." The meager dimensions of his land—100 meters by 50 meters for his entire farm plot—illustrates the extreme difficulty that many Rwandan farmers face to survive, much less finding enough money for roofing. The older youth had slightly more tiles: 550. He said that he needed six hundred more to complete his roof. Both youth covered the untiled areas of their roofs with a combination of banana leaves and grass. These sections of each house leaked whenever it rained.

The two youth then explained how manhood was measured by roof tiles in their community. They said that there were three kinds of people living there: *umutindi* (a destitute person, or, in the words of one of the youth, "someone who is very, very poor"); *umukene* (someone who is poor but not destitute); and wealthy people. No doubt unaware of the six wealth categories of people that Rwandan government studies had determined (as described in chapter 1), these youth used house roofs to determine economic class. An *umutindi*, the youth explained, will get somewhere between two hundred and five hundred roof tiles in their entire lifetimes, one youth explained. Such a house "is very small and in bad shape." An *umukene* "can have up to eight hundred roof tiles," he added. While one of the youth explained that "You can know whether a person is *umutindi* or *umukene* by seeing how their house is built," it was likely that neither an *umutindi* nor an *umukene* would ever live in a house with a roof made entirely of tiles—an *umukene* would have more tiles, but still not enough for a completely tiled roof.

The consequence for *umutindi* and *umukene* men, they said, was humiliation. "Most men are embarrassed by their houses," one of the youth explained. An *umutindi* is especially embarrassed, he added, "because the house isn't big enough for his family, and it doesn't have enough roof tiles." Indeed, merely being called *umutindi* is the mark of failure: "if someone calls you that," one youth explained, "you feel humiliated and very inferior compared to the wealthy people."

The problem with such humiliation, both male youth said, is that it is difficult to escape. The thirty-five-year-old youth explained the pressures on male youth in his community:

> The problem is that you need a house big enough for your family. But then you don't have enough roof tiles to cover it. So you have to work hard to find the remaining roof tiles. A youth from a wealthy family doesn't have to work hard to get roof tiles, but a poor youth will find it hard to get enough.
>
> These poor youth will keep trying: you have to store up your roof tiles until you have enough. They keep trying because there's no other way out. Even though very few youth ever get enough roof tiles, they have to try. Wealthy men will make fun of you if you don't have enough roof tiles.

The obligation of male youth to construct houses, the threat of failing to become a socially recognized man, and the abuse that one may never be able to escape, were prominent themes during interviews with male youth in rural Rwanda.

As a result, there was much talk about roofing during discussions with male youth in particular (roofing is the most expensive component of a Rwandan house; see the Housing section in chapter 1). Many Rwandans reported dur-

A common sight in rural Rwanda: the unfinished house. Tiles cover no more than a third of the roof. New tiles will be added as they are purchased. Hopefully, no one will steal any tiles. Such thefts usually happen at night, while residents are asleep. The remainder of the roof is a thatch of banana leaves, which are both leaky and signify struggle and embarrassment for the house's residents. Technically, this house may be illegal: all new houses are supposed to be built on *imidugudu*. A second unfinished house, with its own collection of tiles, is in the background.

ing interviews that clay roof tiles were the easiest to accumulate and were generally the most preferable roofing option in the sites that were visited (as opposed to iron sheeting). Roof tiles can be bought one or two at a time, when someone has enough cash to purchase them. They also last longer than other roofing materials: a man of fifty-two proudly displayed his roof made of tiles that were, he said, older than he was. Most youth buy tiles that are produced in rural areas that have the right sort of soil to make them (some amount of clay is required). Tiles produced by a factory on the outskirts of Kigali cost several times more than the locally made version and are far out of the price range of most male youth.

As noted in chapter 1, another suitable roofing option is also commonplace in other parts of Africa: *mabati* (iron sheets). While this option is found on some rural roofs in Rwanda (it was, for example, the primary roofing used for houses constructed with government or international agency funds following the 1994 genocide), our research revealed at least four difficulties relating to *mabati*. First, iron sheets do not last as long as tiles—the sheeting eventually rusts and leaks. Second, their cost is high: the reported price for one iron sheet was 4,500 to 5,000 francs ($8.33–$9.26). One roof may require five or ten sheets to complete, or perhaps much more. Third, in a theme that was widespread in rural and urban Rwanda, many youth have difficulty saving money. Before a reasonable amount is gathered, other temptations, such as beer or marijuana, may arise. Contributing to family needs might be required, as well. Finding a proper place to store the money is yet another challenge. The fourth reason for favoring tiles over iron sheets is perhaps the most important of all. As he accumulates roofing tiles, a male youth can install the tiles atop his future house, where they are visible, or he can display them atop another dwelling. This display stands as a public demonstration of his progression toward manhood. Displaying iron sheets is a less attractive option for many youth because it takes so long to save enough to buy one.

A third roofing option—banana leaves—was widely viewed as the roof of desperation.[1] Living in a house with a banana leaf roof was a public signal that those living there were destitute. It could also severely reduce male youth prospects of getting married. A twenty-nine-year-old male youth explained his situation: "I live in a house with a banana leaf roof. I can still marry someone, but the problem is my house. There's no girl who could accept to live in a house like this." There were exceptions to this; others reported that, on occasion, a female youth might decide to marry a male youth living under a banana leaf roof. But female youth who would accept such an offer would view doing so as a last resort; their only chance of getting married (and only of the live-in variety). Informal marriage or not, living in a house with a banana leaf roof was universally viewed as a kind of tragedy. One male youth of eighteen succinctly described the result: "If there are no roof tiles, you have to build your roof with banana leaves. It's no good—you only do it because there's no other way. When it rains, you get wet. And everyone is really laughing at you if you have one. They laugh at you and won't even give you water because you're a nobody." The inability of even being offered water from others suggests that those living under banana leaf roofs are social outcasts. While this may have been somewhat of an exaggeration (if only because the roofing was so common in some of the visited areas), the statement nonetheless highlighted the high degree of embarrassment, humiliation, and difficulty that beset those living in houses with banana leaf roofs.

In one of the visited areas, the advent of local roof tile production in 2000 had eliminated banana leaves as a roofing option. A group of adult women in that area described what had happened. Prior to 2000, there were three kinds of banana trees growing in there. Two of them—*umukenye*, which grew on hillsides, and *ubukangaga*, which grew in river valleys—were used for roofing and other household products such as seating for chairs. A third type of banana tree, *inshinge*, was grown both for cooking bananas (*igitoke*) and for brewing two kinds of beer (*rwarwa* and *umutobe*). Locally produced roof tiles initially sold for 5 francs ($0.009) each. Demand for this relatively inexpensive, high-quality product soared in the local area. With farmland at a premium in their heavily populated area, a land use change was made. Banana trees that had been used for roofing were removed. The *ubukangaga* trees in the valley were the last to be cut down. As one woman recalled, "after youth here found out about roof tiles, people stopped growing" banana trees to make roofing. "You can't find those trees here anymore." The woman added that replanting the trees in the area probably wouldn't work because the soil's fertility had declined. "The soil around here has been used too much," she said. "Those trees wouldn't grow here now."

Without this third choice, and with roof tile prices soaring (as is explained in the Two Regulations section that follows), a new housing option arose: house rental. As one woman described, "The youth today are suffering. They don't build houses at all. So if they want to marry, they have to rent a house in town. There are maybe four or five in this area who can do this. The rest have given up. If they can't get money to rent a house in the center, they don't get married."

The severe difficulties that youth face in marrying is one of the reasons most respondents to the question, "How is your life different from the life of your parents (adults)?" (question 2 in box 2.3), suggested that youth lives in today's Rwanda are far more difficult than when their parents were youth—the question essentially invited respondents to contrast life for youth before and after the genocide, which a few respondents explicitly highlighted. A poor male youth, for example, stated that when his parents were his age, roof tiles cost 2 francs, not the 50 to 70 francs ($0.09–$0.13) they cost at the time of the interview (late 2006). In addition, by the time his parents were eighteen years of age, "they were married, but in our time you may even reach fifty without getting married." Nearly two-thirds of the sixty-seven responses that could be trended (forty-one, or 61 percent) painted a picture of a rapidly deteriorating situation for Rwanda's youth. In addition to the difficulty in getting married, the most prominent themes related to issues of land.

Soil fertility is far worse these days, many stated. There was reference to the fact that, with land allotments so small and in demand by today's youth, there's little chance for most people to let any land lay fallow for a season (so that the land "can recuperate its energy," as a female youth of twenty-four described it). A young man of twenty-three, for example, noted that the inability of many male youth to inherit land meant that they had to live at home and give half of their earned money (from digging the land of others) to their parents. "You live like that until you get old and die," he concluded. Others described a state of sheer desperation for many of today's rural Rwandan youth. A generation ago, when land (as well as livestock and food) was more plentiful, a male youth of thirty-five recalled, his grandfather had the ability to take time off from farming to help his father get started as a farmer. Yet today, the youth said, "All I have is from my hands. Nowadays, youth are on their own." A woman of forty-five suggested that landlessness is also causing some rural youth in contemporary Rwanda to "steal food crops from others," which they do "not because of habit but because of hunger."

Two respondents described an additional factor that contributed, in their view, to what amounts to a state of prolonged, if not permanent, landlessness for an expanding proportion of rural youth. It arises from a government mandate that daughters have equal access to inherited land. As a result, a young man of twenty-four explained that since his parents had twelve children, "they had to divide their land into twelve parts. You can imagine how that looks now [that is, a dozen tiny parcels of land]. But it's a regulation: boys and girls today are equals!" This "regulation," which two male youth mentioned, is actually the landmark 1999 Law on Matrimonial Regimes, Liberalities, and Successions, which established, "for the first time, women's right to inherit land" (Powley 2006: 11). The legislation is an indication of the Rwandan government's commitment to the promotion of gender equity. Potentially, this is an extremely important measure for women, including those who are divorced: the law aims to ensure that such women do not become landless. Reportedly, however, the law also reduced the size of inherited land parcels for sons and daughters. Some male youth contended that the law further constrained the promise of land for a male youth seeking to start his life as an adult. The challenges for female youth were even more serious. Just what becomes of the land a married woman has inherited from her parents was uncertain. Since a woman is expected to leave her parents' house to live with her new husband, it was often unclear what became of any land parcel she may have inherited from her father. Our interviewers heard stories of land that daughters inherited from their fathers that their siblings farmed on (largely brothers, it appeared), since she was not around to use her inherited land. Elizabeth Powley highlights further challenges to the implementation of the 1999 law. Regarding land that women inherit not from their fathers but from their husbands, she observes that

> many rural Rwandan women have not been able to access their rights [to inherited land]. An estimated 60 percent of Rwandan women enter into nonformal [or informal] partnerships and, without a legal marriage, have no claim on their husband's land for themselves or their children. Even among those that are married, some don't know what they are entitled to, others are blocked by male relatives or prevailing cultural norms, and still others do not have the resources to pursue their rights in court or with the local authorities. (2006: 13)

Slightly more than a quarter of respondents (27 percent) weighed the benefits of youth life between the current and previous youth generations and found some advantages in youth lives today.[2] Among the stated benefits of youth life in the current era was more "development," a vague term referring to an array of improvements, including infrastructural advances: more and better roads, more schools and clinics, and the availability of electricity and piped water for some people in rural areas. Another highlighted benefit for youth today is their increased access to medical insurance and education (and far less illiteracy). A woman of sixty-two also highlighted the advantage of freedom of movement in comparison to earlier times (under the previous

Passing a thin stand of trees alongside a steep valley path, a female youth poses for a photograph as light rain falls.

regime). When she was a youth, she recalled, "no one could go to Kigali. But now, boys are moving around and even to Kigali to look for money. They are developed now, and are free to move."

Yet even for these respondents, mention of the downsides of life in present times in comparison to the prior generation was striking. There is far more poverty today than in the past, several noted, including a destitute male youth of seventeen, who explained that a generation ago, "there was no poverty. But now people are getting poorer and poorer." The benefits of national health insurance were balanced against the fact that, as a male youth of twenty-six noted, his parents' generation "were more healthy because they didn't have this AIDS." A man of forty-seven highlighted a contrast that other respondents in this category also addressed: the fact that, while contemporary Rwanda provides youth with access to some advantages of "development," the prior generation had far more personal assets. Today, he said, "We have development, we have this [national] health insurance. But [a generation ago,] youth had more properties than today. They had more land, food, and other things, but no development." The collective sense of impending disaster and a rapidly declining standard of life for Rwanda's rural youth had as much to do with their limited access to land in comparison to prior generations as difficulties in building houses. While the two issues are related, the housing difficulties for rural youth arose from more than the size of a young person's land holding. Indeed, the housing situation in all of the rural areas visited by the research team was critical when the team entered the field in November 2006. We now examine the reasons for what amounts to a housing crisis in rural Rwanda.

Two Regulations

The reduction of the quest for manhood to roof tiles—as exemplified by this quote from one man, "youth nowadays cannot marry because they can't afford to pay for roof tiles"—is tied to a key regulation restricting roof tile production. The result was an increase in the cost of roof tiles, which was a near-constant theme of our interviews in rural Rwanda. Yet the statement is also somewhat misleading because it does not address another housing challenge for youth: their location. The two government regulations have effectively, if unintentionally, made the male youth quest for housing significantly more difficult.

Rwanda's roof tile market has been directly affected by the introduction in 2005 of a regulation that sharply limited their traditional production. The rationale for the regulation was sound: traditional methods for hardening the tiles require significant quantities of firewood. Indeed, thick smoke pours out of the brick kilns and ground pits for hours while tiles are being fired. The regulation itself, which prevented the cutting of trees without government approval (many respondents referred to it as the regulation that "protected the environment"), appeared to aid important reforestation efforts. But it devastated the roof tile market. The availability of locally made tiles plummeted, and their scarcity caused significant price increases. In every location that we visited, the roof tile price had at least tripled over the previous few months.

An alternative method for producing roof tiles was discussed in two of the four rural areas visited. In both of these areas, roof tile production had, officially, ceased, which left many male youth and adults unemployed. The new method employed peat to fire tile ovens. It was unfamiliar to everyone whom we interviewed, including government officials, and it required new machinery and technical training that, it was widely reported, were unavailable. According to a government official at the cell level, permission to secure the training and machinery was also needed from a national government office in Kigali—but it was difficult to obtain. Frustration ran particularly high because the difficulties of obtaining roof tiles combined with high local unemployment. Local government officials had no viable solutions to provide to citizens. They were also frustrated.

The second regulation that directly and negatively affected youth efforts to construct houses was, as we saw in chapter 1, the established national policy mandating that all new houses should be built in *imidugudu* housing areas. An executive secretary of a rural sector explained the policy and the challenges of implementation. "The government policy is that everybody should live in the *imidugudu*," he explained. "Youth constructing new houses will be directed to an *umudugudu*, and by 2030, the government vision is to have 80 percent of the population living on *imidugudu*." The official then shared three reasons for this rural housing policy: improved land management ("If people live in the same place, then farmland can be managed more effectively); fewer ruined houses due to mudslides, since most *imidugudu* housing schemes are located on the tops of hills alongside roads; and improved infrastructure: "When people live close together, they can get close to electricity, health centers and schools." The official could not see any disadvantages to the living on an *imidugudu*.

Problems abound in transforming this policy into reality, the largest of which

With a finished house in the background, a group of rural youth eagerly pose for a portrait at the side of a dirt road. The female youth in the center wears a traditional Rwandan hairstyle. The youth on the far right is wearing a symbol of status: a hip-hop T-shirt. From his remote countryside location, the shirt broadcasts his interest in and connection to global youth culture.

is the policy's profoundly negative impact on youth house building. Among the difficulties that officials reported regarding policy implementation were

- The standard dimension of an *imidugudu* house. A youth may only be able to afford to build a very small house consisting of "one simple room," an executive secretary of one rural sector explained. Such a house, he said, might require five iron sheets to roof. But the minimum required dimension of an *imidugudu* house is six times that size. "In general they have three rooms: two to three bedrooms and one sitting room." Such a house might require thirty iron sheets.
- Having an *imidugudu* to build a house on. One executive secretary stated that only one *umudugudu* existed in his entire sector.
- Acquiring land for an *imidugudu* plot. This was not easy to do. The executive secretary of one sector, for example, stated that everyone seeking a plot for a new house on an *imidugudu* would be required to exchange a piece of their land with the person who already owned the *imidugudu* plot. Such negotiations would involve two sets of family relatives and could be complex, difficult and protracted.

The result of these three challenges was that few youth in any of the sectors that the research team visited were even planning to build a house on an *imidugudu*. For most youth, doing so was well beyond their means. Local government officials knew this. The possibility that some youth might never be able to build their own houses was a prospect that government officials were well aware of, too. The limitations of government officials to deal with pressing realities surrounding the housing issue shed a harsh light on the narrow limits of Rwanda's decentralization reforms.

Despite the towering difficulties of implementing the rural housing policy, government officials had no choice but to enforce it. Some of the youth and adults who were interviewed were sympathetic, and not upset, with local officials about this issue. Indeed, their answers communicated the widely held view of Rwanda as a vertical society. One middle-aged woman, for example, explained that "the authorities here know [about the difficulty of building a house], but they can't do anything about it because their orders come from the higher authorities." Commenting about government regulations more broadly (which would include the requirement to build new houses on *imidugudu*), a twenty-four-year-old male youth expressed a similar view: "As far as regulations are concerned, when you tell the authorities that the regulations are hard for poor people, they tell you that the regulations come from higher authorities and it's the law. There's nothing you can add to a law: if it's there, you have to follow it. You can't modify it."

Such expressions of powerlessness before regulations that could not be altered—not only by youth and adults but by government officials as well—was a striking characteristic of responses of those interviewed on the subject of youth and housing. Respondents rarely questioned the rationale behind specific regulations. The difficulty lay in following them. Yet while the many regulations emerging from decentralization reforms were difficult, youth and adults mentioned most frequently the two that significantly complicated the male youth housing requirement: restrictions on tree cutting and the requirement that all new houses must be built on *imidugudu*. As one female youth put it,

> these two restrictions are the most difficult because the youth are staying at their parents' houses. It's like we're prisoners of the law. This is one of the reasons why the youth here are so poor. Now we have to build a house on an *imidugudu*. To do that, you need 100,000 francs [$185.20]. Without that money, you can't do it. But it's almost impossible to get that money. You have to buy roof tiles and wood. Just to buy a door for your house, you need 30,000 francs [$55.55]. Even if you work a whole year, you can't get that much money.

Consequences of the Youth Housing Challenge

The situation facing many male youth in rural Rwanda might be boiled down to the following. Every male youth is obliged to build a house in order to marry and become a man. Most are having tremendous problems in meeting this strict societal obligation, and will probably fail to build a house—and thus gain recognition as a man. Government regulations impede male youth efforts to build a house. This situation has created a crisis for youth with four serious consequences.

First, the housing expectation was so great, and the difficulty of building a house on an *umudugudu* was so difficult, that youth sought illegal remedies. A government official at the cell level explained the most dangerous of these: roof tiles were made at night, secretly, and in people's houses. Huge pits are dug in the center of houses, and firewood is brought in to create an oven for making tiles. The size of the fire can be so great, the official explained, that it can burn the entire house down. Youth are involved as workers in these schemes. They are not ringleaders. Many people, including their parents, might be directly involved. As the official explained, "If an adult wants to make roof tiles, they hire youth to make tiles at night. Since the youth is making money for the family, the parents will spy on the authorities to protect the youth, so the youth can bring money home."

The official also described two other illegal ways that parents may help their sons gain a house: "Some youth find ways to build houses on their land, even though it's illegal. For example, the parents ask the authorities for permission to fix their kitchen. But instead of fixing their kitchen, they build a house near the barn and connect it to the barn. It becomes a new house on their compound. They might also ask to build a new barn for their cows nearby. But they make a house for one son instead, and then put the cows in the older structure." When such arrangements are completed, they are considered awkward, unusual, and untraditional. Young men are supposed to build their own houses on their own land. The options described here are a kind of last resort. It was not clear what parents might do when they have several sons.

The responses by authorities to this desperate lawbreaking could be compassionate. Many understood that building a house on an *umudugudu* was difficult (and, according to some officials, unpopular with locals). Yet there were also reports during interviews of officials who responded forcefully to such illegal practices. An interview with a group of adult women and female youth revealed the following example, here explained by one of the women: "A son got married and brought his new wife into his parents' house. A government authority came and ordered the new wife back to her parents. Then he told the male youth to build his own house on an *umudugudu* before getting married." This example is illuminating in two ways. First, the idea of having two married couples living in the same house was thought by some to directly contradict Rwandan tradition. In subsequent discussions with Rwandan officials and adults, everyone contended that this solution to the housing crisis was unusual and an act of extreme desperation. The story also illustrates the degree to which government officials may involve themselves in personal affairs. In addition to requiring farmers to obtain permission before they repair their kitchen or build a new barn, as just described, they also have the power to separate spouses if a law (or, in this case, a tradition) is violated.

A *second* consequence of housing challenges to male youth is it has led to the theft of roof tiles. Because tiles are simply laid over the roof frame, they are easier to remove than iron sheets, which must be nailed down. Houses that are incomplete and not lived in are reportedly easy targets. Reports of theft (food and livestock in addition to tiles and household goods) were common in descriptions of rural life from those who were interviewed. According to one cell-level official, youth are the culprits: "A lot of [male] youth steal. When there's a case of robbery, it's always [male] youth who did it. The things they steal requires strength to take. Like they break into a house, steal goats, kill the goats near the house, and transport the meat on their heads. We think they sell the meat." The research findings indicate that such reports of theft did not suggest that respondents thought their situation was insecure. Nearly half (45 percent) of seventy-eight rural respondents to the question, "Can you tell me about the security situation here?" (question 18 in box 2.3), for example, simply reported that the security situation in their communities was under control. Another 27 percent of respondents agreed that the situation was essentially fine, with the exception of crimes relating to poverty. Stealing roof tiles was one such example.

One must reflect on the Rwandan context to appreciate just how people could view their neighborhood as secure even while it is wracked by endemic conflicts and difficulties. Rural Rwandans appear to define insecurity broadly as a truly significant outbreak of violence, when everyday tensions and difficulties explode. That is not taking place. Stealing roof tiles or goats, on the other hand, regularly occur as matters of necessity. Similarly, bar fights, accusations of corruption and witchcraft, and domestic violence, conflicts between neighbors over land and poisoning, seem to be so much a part of the everyday landscape of rural Rwanda that they are not seen as particularly unusual. And so, despite regular difficulties and threats, many Rwandans nonetheless consider their locales to be essentially secure.

A *third* consequence of male youth difficulties in building a house is migration. Youth mentioned two destinations. The first was to commercial farms, where male youth would be paid 500 to 600 francs [$0.92–1.11] a day to dig (reportedly, female youth never went there). This was significantly more money than could be earned for digging for a landholder in a rural community.[3] The chief purpose of these migrations was to make money to help construct a house. While there were no reported examples of a youth who was able to complete his house after working on a commercial farm, it was an option that seemed to attract reasonable numbers of male youth (precision on the actual proportion was impossible to gauge).

The second migration destination was Kigali (this group included female youth). Less than a quarter of seventy-four rural respondents to the question about migration (question 9 in box 2.3) found it appealing in comparison to rural life. The majority of this group were male youth who had had some secondary or vocational school experience. For more than three-quarters of respondents, however, migrating to Kigali was a high risk option, even an act of desperation. Many made reference to the high probability, in their estimation, of failing to get a job and becoming a wanderer. There were reports of migrants returning with little or no savings from their urban adventure. Others never returned. Female youth who migrated faced the prospect of returning from Kigali pregnant and perhaps with AIDS, many said. While some mentioned migrating to Kigali as a means of getting money to build a house, it appeared to be a prime destination for those thinking of escaping the pressures of rural life, as illustrated by a twenty-six-year-old male youth: "There is no advantage to staying in a rural area while you're suffering. I'm at home and my parents still feed and care for me. But in a few years, if I still can't build a house, I might migrate."

A *fourth* consequence of pressures on male youth to build houses and become men is decreased interest in secondary education.[4] The lowered priority on the pursuit of secondary education was expressed in two main ways. The first concerned the challenges of gathering enough funds for roofing. The chief means of doing so, for the majority of poor male and female youth, was to dig on the land of the relatively few people who both owned land and were not poor. By far the most common personal items that female youth said they purchased with their money were soap and skin lotion. The reason for this was the social expectation of female youth to be feminine, womanly, and attractive. In some areas, female youth also wove mats to sell for a profit. Significantly, some female youth also saved money as a way to attract a potential husband. With so many unmarried female youth in rural areas, and so many male youth having trouble building a house in order to marry, having a store of funds to contribute to a male youth's quest for housing promised to increase the marriage prospects of female youth.

Male youth might be able to purchase four or five roof tiles with a day's wages from digging. There were many reported ways for male youth to make money, such as serving as a porter or by renting land. One porter, a male youth of eighteen, related his work to both roof tiles and educational opportunity:

> Male youth are doing everything possible to get money in order to build their own home. Some migrate to dig for money. Others go to work as a porter. You get 15 francs [$0.03] for transporting one kilo, so if you transport 30 kilos, you get 450 francs [$0.83] per day. You have to transport the goods for three

hours to get paid. When I do this, I take part of that money and buy roof tiles, slowly by slowly. I want to do this until I have enough to build my own house.

The ones who don't get a chance to continue their studies are the ones who do this.

This male youth's plan for building a house is established, as is his understanding that he must pursue such a plan because continuing his education is not possible. Renting land for farming to make money was not often mentioned by youth who were interviewed. The reason may have been that it required a considerable amount of capital to get started. A male youth of twenty-four noted just how much time and work it required to follow this path: "You can rent a plot of land, 10 meters by 20 meters, for 5,000 francs [$9.26] for a year. There are two harvests in one year. You get that 5,000 by going to dig [on a commercial farm] until you get it. Then you rent the land and harvest maybe 50 kilograms of beans in a year. You eat 25 kilos and sell 25 kilos. Today you can sell a kilogram of beans for 300 francs [$0.55]." The plan for getting money to buy roof tiles required migrating to dig on a commercial farm for a while to save 5,000 francs (it was uncertain how long it would take to do this), return home to rent a tiny plot of land, farm it for a year, reserve half of the harvested crops for household consumption, and then surface with a profit of 7,500 francs [$13.89] by selling the other half. If the youth sought to rent the land for another year, his profit would only amount to 2,500 francs ($4.63).

That profit, from more than a year of hard work, might be enough to buy perhaps fifty roof tiles. Two years at the same level of proceeds would enable the youth to buy a single iron sheet. Even if the youth could put all of his earnings into roofing and other housing costs, it would take well over a decade to acquire enough materials to build a house. Yet this scenario was unrealistic because of the numerous other demands on the money that male (and female) youth make, such as helping to pay for certain foodstuffs, household goods, school fees and materials for siblings, and a host of other possible expenses. Many reported that male youth must regularly contribute to their parents' financial needs until they leave home. Female youth, in general, are not expected to make such a contribution. This was seen by some youth as a means to spur male youth to leave their parents' house and make a start in their own house and household. It was also reported that for many male youth living at home, having to pay their parents on a regular basis was a source of pressure on them, particularly for those who had not set up a house, or an alternative living situation, to which they could move.

The difficulty and length of time it took to accumulate roof tiles or iron sheet roofing for most male youth created a considerable disincentive for the pursuit of education. Secondary education took six years to complete, and one might run out of money to pay school fees and thereby never finish. Meanwhile, in the estimation of some poor youth, those who pursued secondary education instead of working to purchase roofing would have lost precious time in the race to build a house. As a male youth of twenty-four remarked,

we've seen people who have finished their third year of secondary school. Then they have no job and no money to continue their studies. They come back home and are stuck.

So it's better to dig than to go to school. When the secondary student comes back, he doesn't have a job. As for the one who stayed home, without going to secondary school, he has been digging and saving for his house all those years. The secondary school student will then try to achieve what the uneducated person has already gotten, but he won't make it.

The second way that education became a low priority in the wake of house building pressures arose from the impact of secondary school drop-outs who returned to their rural homes. Such drop-outs helped cultivate the impression that attending secondary school was a high-risk strategy for poor youth and their families. A male youth of eighteen who had dropped out of primary school after his fourth year shared an example that illuminates the risk associated with secondary school:

If you have a big brother who's been to secondary school and has no job, and you're in the fourth year of primary school, your parents may ask you, "Why should we continue to pay for our child in primary school?" So you leave school.

Look, there was a student who dropped out of secondary school after his third year because his parents couldn't afford to pay any more school fees. So the student returned home and is unemployed. That student has to work and dig to repay his parents [for the secondary school fees that they had paid].

Working to repay their parents set secondary school drop-outs even further behind in their quest to build a house.

Youth who attend secondary school but cannot finish tend to be those from poor families. Their parents may make tremendous sacrifices to find sufficient money to put them through school. There were several references to such families selling their only cow to send their son or daughter to secondary school. This represented an enormous family sacrifice, and it put considerable pressure on students to finish school, get a job, and repay their parents for their investment. At the same time, the proceeds from selling a cow, or perhaps a small piece of land, were often not enough to pay for six years of secondary school education, particularly when paying for other household demands during that time might be drawn from money set aside for secondary education. Nonetheless, youth, especially male youth, were expected to provide a return on their parents' investment, which was to complete school, get a job, and give some of your salary to your parents.

Reaching this goal appeared extremely difficult for a youth to do, particularly if he or she came from a poor family. Youth who failed, and male youth in particular, were frequently brought up during interviews with youth and adults as high profile disappointments, or worse. Given the prospects of failure facing poor youth who attended secondary school, and what would seem to be highly unrealistic expectations of success placed on their young shoulders, male youth faced unrelieved pressure, public embarrassment, and humiliation. The situation they may face is here described by the following comments from two poor male youth, aged twenty-one and twenty-two. The younger youth first shed light on the difficulties that youth can avoid by never attending secondary school: "Imagine a person who finished secondary school but can't get a job. It's worse for him than for us [who didn't go to secondary school] because we don't have high expectations in life. But educated people expect many things after they finish school, so when they don't get a job, they become wanderers. It's because of the frustration." The elder youth then raised the issue of parental pressure: "The reason they become wanderers is because of their parents. They feel guilty. The parents abuse their children who go to secondary school because of the sacrifices they made to pay the school fees. The parents make the students feel like failures and losers." Two comments about these descriptions are useful. First, while the percentage of rural unemployed secondary school students migrating to Kigali was difficult to assess, there were several references to the phenomenon of migrating to avoid humiliation. Second, given such high-profile difficulties, it is not surprising that evidence surfaced in the interview data of poor male youth that downgraded the potential benefits of attending secondary school and highlighted the difficulties that attendance invited. A secondary education, from this perspective, was risky. For some poor male youth, a safer course of action was to leave primary school and then start working and saving for a house.

Yet while the interview data provided potent examples of the symbolic power of secondary school students who failed to complete their studies and get a job, this did not mean that most youth viewed education as worthless. On the contrary: only 12 percent of youth respondents to a question comparing youth who went and did not go to secondary or vocational school viewed such education as not providing positive potential benefits.[5] But what also resonated strongly in their responses was the gulf between youth with and youth without education. Overwhelmingly, youth described "educated" youth as living in a separate social world. Educated people joined different associations, might not be willing to dig for a living, commanded a far greater level of social respect, had access to many more opportunities, and were more resourceful. Receiving education after primary school was "special," a poor male youth of twenty-five remarked. Youth with education "have a step ahead" of the rest, a male youth of twenty-seven asserted. A poor female youth of twenty-three contended that "educated" youth had a chance of becoming district mayors or even national government ministers. They also knew how to plan and save money. Such youth essentially described people belonging to the educated class, to which they did not belong.

Postprimary education, in short, was valuable. But the responses of poor youth strongly indicated an awareness of a situation in which very few Rwandan youth had a chance of attending secondary school. Illustrative of this is the fact that only a third of youth responding to a question on parent expectations listed the attainment of education, or a job requiring education, in their answer.[6] For youth who had never achieved a secondary school education themselves, the proportion fell to a fourth. Secondary education, in other words, was widely seen as possible for very few youth, and the examples of poor youth who had reached for secondary education (and, evidently, a jump in social class) and then failed had clearly left powerful impressions with other poor youth.

Here again one sees evidence of poor youth applying practical and risk averse strategies toward their situation. Better not to strive for things that are difficult if not impossible to achieve, the thinking went, particularly if such efforts invite frustration, embarrassment, humiliation, and failure.

Danger in Waiting: AIDS and Unwed Mothers

The girls in that family are getting older and there's no one to marry. At some point, boys will get them pregnant.

Male youth, age twenty-two

Because of the problem of not getting married, female youth are in danger of being infected by HIV/AIDS. When they produce three or four children while living at their parents' house, they won't be able to take care of their children. There is no chance for such a woman to get married.

Male youth, age twenty-six

These "old ladies" [i.e., unmarried female youth over age twenty-five], they are desperate. If you meet her in a bar and give her a beer, you can have sex with her and she gets pregnant. This leads to AIDS.

Male youth, age twenty-four

Some youth decide to go to Kigali to look for money. But even if they get money, it's usually because they end up as wanderers. Male youth in town can end up as thieves and the female youth end up as prostitutes. They can get HIV/AIDS or become pregnant. The youth are going to be exterminated by AIDS.

Female youth, NYC official, age twenty-three

Housing delays cause marriage delays. The collective view of youth and adults interviewed in rural Rwanda might be summed up as: when youth can't marry, bad things happen. Youth and adults reported that society viewed the unmarried as failures and so were subject to ridicule. Some turned to drinking beer and smoking marijuana. Others turned to theft, including of roof tiles. Still others ventured to dig in other areas in their quest to find funds to build a house. And increasingly, male youth migrate to Kigali. Many of those who ventured to Kigali were believed to become the homeless wanderer (*inzer-erezi*), in what appears to be the worst fate a person—male or female—can assume. In such a state, one may face *igisekuru* (social extinction), which an NYC official defined as follows: "When you don't supply a descendant, your family can be forgotten."

The dangers in waiting for marriage were just as serious, if not more so, for female youth. Many respondents contended that bad things do not happen nearly as often to married female youth as their unmarried counterparts (which included female youth who lived in informal marriages with male youth).

Female youth in recognized marriages each have a house, it is assumed they will have children, and so they are on the road to becoming socially accepted women. As a result, they do not become urban migrants, old ladies, wanderers, or prostitutes, or some combination of these, all of which surfaced as indicators of social destitution. It was also widely believed that young married women were not carriers of AIDS. Instead, it was poor, unmarried female youth who were viewed, more than any other group, as the incubators of AIDS.

Rural youth and adults mentioned AIDS so rarely during initial interviews that I added questions about the disease to the field questionnaire. When the subject was directly addressed with youth, some explained that it was, as characterized by a twenty-one-year-old male youth, "taboo." As a result, he continued, "people don't get tested." Others shared this belief. No one we interviewed said that many people in rural areas were getting tested. The test was expensive (reportedly 100–200 francs, or $0.18–0.37), and it may require a long walk to obtain one. Government officials confirmed this contention. "Youth don't want to get tested," one explained, "especially uneducated youth." Another official noted that he "understood" the disinterest in getting tested, since the cost—200 francs—"is a person's daily salary." Moreover, the disincentives against getting tested, in social terms, far outweighed the incentives. Respondents contended that treatment was hard to come by. The social stigma attached to being known to have AIDS was reported to be considerable. People who become sick claim to be cursed by witchcraft instead of telling others that they have AIDS, a male youth of twenty reported. They can also become pariahs. "Nobody shares a drink with an HIV-infected person," a male youth stated, "even though they know that there is no risk. People just avoid infected people."

The stories of female youth and AIDS that a multitude of respondents shared might be boiled down to this: poor, unmarried female youth grow discouraged while waiting to get married. Some never marry. They become "old ladies" instead of socially accepted women. Many find short-term sexual partners. They get drawn into sexual relations in exchange for money, a beer, or particular goods that help them appear ladylike and attractive (soap and skin lotion were the most frequently mentioned). These female youth were often referred to as "prostitutes," although there was little evidence of them entering into prostitution as a regular means of acquiring income. Instead, it appeared that they periodically exchanged sex for money or a tangible good. Unmarried male youth sought out such female youth, in part, because of their own inability to marry. Mention of condoms and protected sex was rare. Mention of pregnant unmarried female youth was common.

While male youth and men generally viewed poor, unmarried female youth as the primary AIDS carriers in rural society (and not their partners), it appeared that any female youth who left home faced the real possibility of a collapse in their social standing. Once away from their family homes, they may immediately be seen as prostitutes and wanderers who were almost certainly infected with AIDS. Lacking the ability to move about freely without the risk of social condemnation, and with far fewer economic options at their disposal than male youth, poor, unmarried female youth existed in a kind of sheltered trap. They lived in their family home, were unable to venture far from domestic routines without the threat of social ruin—and waited for a marriage that might never arrive.

PART THREE

Quest for Cash

URBAN YOUTH LIVES

Nothing moves forward. Parents are crying here. They have lost.

Female youth, age seventeen

It's terrible. The urban youth are very poor. Nobody cares about them. I wonder what their future will be. It's like they've been abandoned.

Adult man, age forty-four

There are some who say that prison is better than this life.

Male youth, age twenty-eight

Instead of dying of hunger, I'll steal. We are sad. It makes me sad to see my sister prostitute herself around because I cannot do anything for her. So I'll steal, and let them kill me. Death is death.

Male youth, age twenty-nine

CHAPTER SIX

Desperation on the New Frontier

URBAN YOUTH AND THE GOVERNMENT

Kigali is Rwanda's new frontier. While the literature on rural Rwanda is deep and diverse, there is precious little documentation about urban Rwanda. This state of affairs persists despite the fact that the roof of restrictions on urban migration has receded and Kigali's population is rapidly advancing. The urban youth situation is so dire as to be no longer ignorable, and the urban outlet for frustrated or adventuresome rural youth has become well established. Informal housing booms while government restrictions, policies and plans are unrolled. Formal employment is limited, unemployment and crime are rampant—yet ever more rural youth enter the city.

The three chapters in this part of the book mainly draw from interviews with one hundred male youth, thirty-nine female youth and twenty-six adults in two urban sectors (one densely urban, the other peri-urban), as well as government officials from all levels of Kigali's government structure: *umu-duguda*, cell, sector, and the city council. The sample of Kigali's urban youth described here cannot reflect the entire state of the urban youth population.

That is not the intention. Instead, it provides a window into Kigali life for the urban youth majority there. What follows in this part is a description of the pressing concerns, conditions, and context of Kigali's burgeoning majority of poor, undereducated youth.

Before turning to their story, however, a word is necessary about the minority of urban youth whose education and economic status tower above the desperate majority. As the nation's capital and primary urban center, Kigali is, of course, also home to many members of the small demographic of Rwandan youth with secondary or university education. Yet a good number of them, reportedly, are similarly unemployed: comments during interviews about severe competition for jobs that they may qualify for were common. In this regard, it certainly appears that unemployment, stress, and difficulty in urban life applies to urban youth in nearly all walks of life.

If life is reportedly hard for educated and unemployed urban youth, the blanket of difficulty spreads much more heavily and completely over members of their poorer, lesser educated brethren. As the epigraphs beginning this chapter illustrate, not one of the 335 youth interviewed for this book described the youth situation in Kigali as anything but desperate. This included youth who graduated from secondary school. Adult or government and nongovernment officials similarly described the situation as difficult for some youth and overwhelming for others. Moreover, the government's task, as virtually all of part 3 suggests, is a long way from easy.

Much of what is described here is not specific to Kigali's poor youth. Urban youth situations in other developing countries are also dire.[1] Yet the Kigali youth story is only just coming to light. Thus part 3 should be seen as a contribution toward understanding the particular plight of Rwanda's desperately poor and undereducated urban youth majority.

Governance amid Rapid Expansion

The current regime is Rwanda's first ever to loosen constraints on the movement of Rwandans. The urban outlet has opened an escape hatch from a pregenocide rural life so constrained that Uvin called it a "prison without escape in which poverty, infantilization, social inferiority, and powerlessness

In international circles, Kigali is increasingly renowned for its security, order, cleanliness, and quiet. This visual slice of commercial Kigali sheds light on several features of the capital city that the Rwandan government promotes. Unlike many other African urban scenes, there are neither beggars nor street vendors. The streets and sidewalks are devoid of garbage. Careful building upkeep is apparent: all appear to be recently painted. The motorcycle taxi drivers in the foreground wear helmets, as per a government regulation (they also must carry an extra helmet for customers). No one is barefoot. The dodgy housing and treacherous marketplaces that are commonplace in other parts of Kigali are entirely out of sight here. In its place is the familiar and compelling Rwandan vista of tall, overlapping hills on the horizon.

combined to create a sense of personal failure" (1998: 117). The new urban passageway has created an important new option (Sommers 2006b: 156). The government's decision may be seen as demonstrating acceptance of the reality that so many young people cramped on so little farmland could not possibly continue (even if, as I mention in the section on insecurity, there were reports of irregular forced returns of urban youth to the countryside by policemen). At the same time, the government's currently unfolding decentralization policies are partly intended to stem the tide of youth migration to cities. As a Kigali City Council official related, "The government strategy for decentralization is a solution for high youth migration. Decentralization will bring services closer to rural people, so youth will not need to migrate to urban areas." While the impact of this policy intention has yet to be evaluated, Rwanda continues to have one of the world's highest urban growth rates. And Kigali's current realities have created considerable challenges for urban governance.

This chapter examines many of the ways that the Rwandan government has responded to challenges arising from Kigali's rapid urbanization. Most of what I describe is drawn directly from interviews with government officials.

Contours of the Urban Youth Challenge

Addressing the challenges that Kigali's youth present is unusually difficult. The urban officials who made time to discuss their views with researchers revealed a government apparatus that viewed itself in distinctly different ways than its rural counterparts. While government officials in rural areas regularly communicated confidence in the implementation of government policies and programs, urban officials often admitted an awareness that, in many respects, they are overwhelmed. As a Kigali government official explained, "all of the issues" arising in interviews with the research team "are not new for us. The problem is we don't have enough means to fight all these problems." Alluding to the insecurity and unemployment in his area, the official added that donors should build a vocational training center there. This, he explained, would help youth "survive honestly." Implied here is a simple goal for the multitude of struggling urban youth: "honest survival." It also implies that some urban youth without options are forced to resort to some means of "dishonest survival," with prostitution and theft being the most frequently mentioned means.

While rural and urban government officials' views of their challenges differed, rural and urban youth views of government officials did not differ significantly. Urban youth regularly highlighted their difficulties with lower-level security personnel (the LDF, in particular). To be sure, Kigali can be dangerous. Robberies of all sorts were consistently mentioned by youth we interviewed. Security matters, in fact, routinely surfaced in interviews with urban officials and youth alike, and the LDF are the most prominent security corps on the Kigali streets. Given everyday security concerns that many youth face in Kigali, it was not surprising that issues relating to security arose far more often among urban youth than with their rural counterparts.

As did their rural counterparts, many youth in town stated that they wanted the government to have a larger presence in their lives. They also sought support and opportunities that might stabilize and improve their situations. Urban youth expressions of sympathy for government officials proved common. At the same time, and similar to strategies enacted by many rural youth we interviewed, many urban youth maintained a studied distance from government personnel.

The distance was reciprocal. An official working at the city council level argued that "the city is growing so fast, but people at the city council don't know the real situation." The reason supplied had to do with how officials performed their work: "They don't go out, they don't talk to people. The little information they get is from association leaders and others in the government." This view requires context. Kigali is huge and government officials are few. The problems are enormous. Yet the government is implementing plans, with striking confidence, to address significant urban concerns (e.g., a city council official explained that "there are measures in place to solve" the problems that plague youth, such as poverty, disease, and HIV/AIDS). Some of these measures and plans (including the unusually ambitious Master Plan) are detailed in this section. Nonetheless, social distance between government officials and youth—rural and most urban youth—was a persistent finding of this research. It was a pronounced characteristic of the youth viewpoint, and it is among the issues I address in chapter 9.

The statistics for Kigali are, as in most booming developing-country cities, difficult to quantify accurately. While published estimates state that Kigali's urban area contains 682,616 inhabitants (and a total of 1,027,993 in Kigali Province) (OZ Architecture et al. 2006: 38), a Kigali City Council official stated that these estimates were outdated. The working estimates that the council uses, he said, are "about a million people during the day and eight hundred thousand at night" (i.e., 800,000 residents and 200,000 daily commuters).

These are current estimates, he emphasized (as of 2007). He also shared the accepted estimate that "65 percent of the population in the city is between the ages of fourteen and thirty-five."

Down at the cell level, an official's difficulties in estimating the number of people living in his cell further illustrate the challenges of figuring out how many people reside in Kigali. Early in 2007, the official stated that the official population was just over four thousand. However, this figure was drawn from the 2003 census, which was based on data gathered in 2000—seven years earlier. "So the figure has no precision," he explained. The official estimated that, in his cell, "not even 15 percent of all youth" have jobs with monthly salaries, few had completed primary school, and—similar to our research findings in the rural areas—of the few youth who had attended secondary school, "most [had] dropped out after two or three years."

The description that the cell-level official related reasonably reflected the urban youth research sample. Of the hundred male youth and thirty-nine female youth in the urban research sample, nearly half of all male youth (48 percent) never completed primary school. Another 40 percent completed primary school but never attended a postprimary school. Only 9 percent attended secondary school, and none had a vocational education. Nearly the same proportion of female youth (46.1 percent) never finished primary school, while a larger proportion had attended secondary school than their male youth counterparts (25.7 percent). Just over 28 percent of female youth (28.2) had completed primary school. There were no vocational school graduates in the urban youth sample.

The economic standing of urban youth in the sample was low (see the Sample Selection Results section in chapter 2 for the wealth category definitions). Almost three in four male youth (73 percent) were destitute, while less than a quarter (21 percent) were characterized as poor. The remaining 6 percent were nonpoor. There were no wealthy male youth in the sample and only one wealthy female youth. But as with the male youth, nearly all of the female youth were either destitute (56 percent) or poor (33 percent). The youth sample was predominantly those between the ages of eighteen and twenty-four (66 percent), while nearly all of the remainder were between ages twenty-five and thirty-five (33 percent).

As with the rural youth, it is highly probable that most, if not nearly all, urban youth who said they were married were referring to informal marriages. Beyond this similarity, however, the urban youth statistics on marriage contrasted significantly with those of their rural counterparts. In the countryside, the proportion of married youth in our sample scarcely differed by gender (just less than a third of male youth compared to just over a third of female youth). But in Kigali, only 16 percent of male youth said they were married while nearly two in five (38.5 percent) female youth stated the same. Although the interview data for this book cannot conclusively explain this difference, informed speculation is possible. Recurrent references in part 2 to urban migration were frequently connected to male youth seeking to escape public humiliation. As I discuss in chapter 8, most urban youth were single and never expected to marry. With this evidence in mind, it appears that many more female youth arrived with spouses than their male counterparts did. Some husbands abandoned their young wives once entering Kigali, as mentioned in chapter 7. But clearly, some did not.

Trade Associations

The government's heavy emphasis on social organization for Kigali's youth-dominated population is unmistakable. "When we talk about youth," a Kigali City Council official explained, "we talk about youth in organized structures." The official then listed two kinds: youth in the NYC, and youth in associations. The official explained that all youth are "automatically members the National Youth Council: every youth at the cell level constitutes a general assembly of the National Youth Council." The other way that youth are organized in structures is in what the official called youth associations, although "trade associations" describes them more accurately. There are associations for youth in particular urban occupations, such as taxi operators, shoe shiners, and car washers. Given the ever-growing throng of young urbanites in Kigali, this description illustrates the limits of what government officials can do for and with youth, and how few youth they interact with.

From the government's perspective, the undereducated majority of youth in Kigali divides into two types: those who join trade associations and those who don't. Although government officials made it clear to us that they wanted all youth to join trade associations, they also admitted that most were either unable to pay association dues or simply refused to join one. Few youth interviewed for this book stated that they were trade association members.

Officials related many purposes and benefits of trade associations. "We organize youth into [trade] associations to teach them how to save the little earnings they get and how to develop income generating projects," a city council official explained (on the difficulties urban youth have in saving money, see the Money, Hunger, and Instability section in chapter 7). Officials encourage youth in associations to save their money in banks. They also promote the possibility of accessing "soft credit." The city council official described how he helped "shoe shiners" get better equipment so they could conduct their work "in a modern style." A crucial benefit of associations is that government officials can use them to relocate tradesmen. "When the Kigali City Council wants [shoe shiners] not to work just anywhere, we encourage them [through their trade association] to work in certain places." This promised to help workers provide better service and make it easier for customers to find them, he said.

Trade associations, the city council official continued, also "encourage unity." The *ingando* solidarity camps taught youth that "it was not part of the Rwandan culture to kill each other." The purpose of such activities was "to unite the Rwandan youth." Government officials regularly promoted the cause of unity with urban youth, and it is not difficult to see why. Rural youth continue to pour into poor Kigali neighborhoods, where most live desperate lives in social isolation. Their contact with the government is sporadic at best. Government officials regularly stated that they rely on associations to reach urban youth. As one explained, "the secret of Rwanda is that, from an early age, we are taught to be patriotic and love our country through the government structures that are being set up." Officials also use associations to try to keep a lid on conflicts. A sector-level official provided an example of an effort to resolve disputes between business owners and *chercheurs*, or male youth who search for spare car parts for customers:

> We tried to put the *chercheurs* along the road into an association. This was because spare car part shop owners were complaining about them. One boss could use *chercheurs* to send clients to his own shop [and keep customers away from other car parts shops]. Also, some *chercheurs* were stealing and being undisciplined. When car parts shop owners complained, we asked them whether they wanted the government to chase the *chercheurs* away. They said no. Instead, they asked to have them organized so that they know who is a *chercheur* and who is not. So we chose the ones who were known by the owners of spare shops and asked them to join a [new trade] association from then on. Now the owners are not complaining about stealing or indiscipline.

While it was unclear whether government officials asked or coerced the *chercheurs* to create an association, the membership fees required to join any trade association were, in the view of most urban youth who were interviewed, high. They reported that, in addition to the membership fee, association members also had to pay daily fees. These daily fees were particularly problematic, and youth reported that many youth who sought to join associations could not keep up the required costs.

Government officials in Kigali also rely on associations to communicate public health concerns. Yet the following comment from a cell-level official illustrates the heavy limitations of this approach:

> There is AIDS. There are many people who live with AIDS in this cell. We have two associations of people living with AIDS here. But the majority [of people with AIDS] are not joining these associations. We know them when they come for papers. When they want to go to hospitals to get the ARV [antiretroviral medicine], they have to bring [signed] papers from officials. So when they come, I talk with them. They are ashamed and feel uncomfortable talking about their "zero positivity" [seropositivity, or positive AIDS test]. When I ask them why they don't join associations, they say it is not good for one's reputation. So there are more infected youth than we know, and they are the most dangerous.

AIDS associations may be useful to attract assistance to those who are infected. But they also call unwanted attention to the fact that a person is infected. The stigma of HIV/AIDS infection can have disastrous consequences for youth. Some youth reported that people who are known to have HIV/AIDS lose their jobs. Lacking alternatives, female youth with HIV/AIDS may fall into prostitution as a means of survival (see chapter 8).

Kigali government officials admitted that their heavy reliance on associations to reach and communicate with urban youth yielded limited benefits. The main reason for this, in their view, was that so few youth were association members. One sector official in Kigali described how every *umudugudu*, cell, and sector office had limited staff and support to deal with the needs of prodigious numbers of youth in their respective areas. He initially stated that there were six thousand youth in his sector. Then he clarified what he meant: "These are the ones we have registered [in trade associations], the ones we have been talking to." They are also the ones who participate in *umuganda* (community labor) work in his sector. The official explained that "from time to time, we organize *umuganda* for all youth who are organized to clean the roads, plant trees, and so on." The official later speculated that "there may be another six thousand youth without jobs who we don't know [about]. There may be more than six thousand youth like that." In other words, government officials probably have no contact with most youth in their sectors.

The proportion of female youth who come into contact with government officials, the same official explained, is smaller still. "Not many female youth come to meetings" with sector officials, he said. In fact, "The six thousand youth whom we know are mainly male." Subsequent interviews with other city officials supported this assessment. The primary reason they supplied is that few female youth are association members. One official explained that male youth are "more active" while, according to Rwandan culture, "girls are always home, with their families." The few who "deviate" from this pattern, he continued, are prostitutes, house girls, or those who "look for small jobs in hair salons." One sector official explained that "the only female youth association" in his sector "is the one for prostitutes."

Interviews with government officials in Kigali collectively suggest that they mainly interact with a tiny proportion of urban youth: youth association leaders. A Kigali City Council official said that the leaders are mostly well-educated male youth. A sector official explained that "uneducated youth don't come to me because they aren't heads of associations. Only educated association leaders come to me." In general, government officials in Kigali rarely interact with any female youth and with very few male youth. Underscoring the distance between government and urban youth was the following description from a cell leader in the capital. He summed up his interactions with youth, who constituted the strong majority of residents in his area, in the following way. "I only speak to the association leaders," he said. I asked him whether he interacted with any other youth in his cell. "Never," he replied. Then he corrected himself: "Actually, I do speak to other youth. I tell the police that when they arrest prostitutes and thieves, they should bring them to me." Before they are carted off to jail, "I encourage them to change their behaviors."

Insecurity

Not one official, youth, or adult mentioned the presence of gangs in Kigali. They did not seem to exist. Yet far more youth appeared to be engaged in lawbreaking in Kigali than in rural areas. Youth and adults alike reported that the security situation in their Kigali communities was poor. Talk of "ambushes" by thieves, or of being forced to hand over money to night patrol members, was common. Violent fights involving drunken men at bars at night surfaced in many accounts of the security situation. Just as notably, there were few reports of house robberies: thefts and assaults mainly took place when people went out at night (staying home was a protection measure). Most viewed petty thefts as driven by hunger and desperation: it was what *inzererezi* and *maibobo* (street boys and girls) performed. Such theft was both commonplace and high risk, the latter because if neighborhood residents caught the thief, they would probably beat and perhaps kill the person.

In response to the pervasive insecurity in Kigali, an NYC official explained that the government had "Four different ways to take care of security [in Kigali]: national police, military police, LDF, and people's night patrols." The LDF are low-level security officials who wear pink suits and serve as volunteers. The people's night patrols consist of male youth who protect their neighborhoods at night (all households make mandatory contributions to compensate them nominally).

As I detail in chapters 7 and 8, many urban youth and adults reported routine abuse and harassment against them by all of these security groups. They said that the LDF and policemen regularly harassed and fined them for selling goods without permits—and then confiscated the goods. They also destroyed housing that was not up to code. Another duty that policemen perform in Kigali, a government official in Kigali explained, is to "pack youth into police cars and take them to their rural homes." The official said that such efforts are unsuccessful because "in less than a week, those youth are right back in Kigali."[2] Not surprisingly, Kigali youth call all policemen *panda gari* (police car).

Housing

The Rwandan government has ambitious plans to transform Kigali. The starting point for most of its poor residents is low. A handful of facts are useful in illustrating this. According to a survey of water use in four sampled sectors in Kigali, an international official involved in the Kigali Master Plan said that the average water use is 15 liters of water per person per day. In contrast, they continued, "a typical American uses 700 liters of treated water per day". The city is densely populated. The Kigali Master Plan document stated that "the vast majority of Kigali's population" lives on only 10 percent of the land. Approximately 83 percent of Kigali's population live in informal settlements (OZ Architecture et al. 2006: 52). The international official added that all houses and building materials are considered illegal in such areas and that Rwanda has no building code.[3]

According to two sector government officials, rural youth were attracted to newly expanding areas where irregular, unplanned, and informal housing was expanding. Gatsata sector, for example, rests on the edge of an important market area. Yet a sector official explained that it was considered a rural area before 2000, when it was incorporated into the city of Kigali. As a result, "youth like to come there because of the lack of housing regulations and the job opportunities nearby." The Master Plan is reportedly coming to Gatsata. "There was a consultant from the Kigali City Council who came and explained how the council wants Gatsata to be," the official recalled. The consultant met with Gatsata leaders, businessmen, opinion leaders, and "normal citizens." While planning continues, uncertainty and rumors about how the Master Plan will be implemented remain. It is a matter of some concern, as illuminated by one government official in Kigali: "What's obvious about the Master Plan is that they don't talk about places where they'll relocate people. They only talk about putting in infrastructure. The authorities only say that they'll build new roads and water points. But they don't talk about relocating people." The official added that "there are wealthy people who want to invest but will wait for the Master Plan to come first, to ensure that their investment won't be destroyed."

Urban Youth and the National Youth Council

In response to the question, "Are there organizations who support young men/women like you?" (question 4 in box 2.3), not one youth we interviewed stated that there were such organizations in their areas. There were slight qualifications to this finding, such as one male youth who stated that "there are only organizations helping educated youth," adding despondently that "it seems there's no place in Kigali for uneducated people." Some also stated that youth infected with HIV/AIDS qualified for assistance.

The government office tasked to support Rwanda's youth is the NYC, an elective but, for all NYC officials except those at the level of the executive secretariat, a volunteer position. Their task in many Kigali neighborhoods is, without question, unusually difficult. As a sector-level government official explained, "the National Youth Council in Kigali has a big job to do because there are too many youth." The NYC officials, the official continued, have three main responsibilities: "to sensitize the youth to join associations, be patriotic, and fight against AIDS."

In addition, the means that NYC officials have at their disposal, cell-level officials related, were so meager that there was little that they could do to support masses of needy youth. They are, in other words, besieged, and those who were interviewed for this report openly stated as much.[4] As one NYC official explained, "when one analyzes what we do for youth, it is next to nothing.

The youth here are accusing us, and they are right." Conveying the frustration arising from their position as elected youth officials, one then described their situation as follows: "The only thing we can do is advocacy, but to whom? We just collect the information and bring it to the cell office. The cell officials themselves don't have enough means to handle the youth's problems. So we tell the youth to be patient, that their problem will be solved soon." The pressure on elected NYC officials to deliver some sort of support, relief, or advice to poor youth was considerable. At the same time, promising things to young people in need and then not being able to deliver on the promises only aggravates their relations with youth, invites still more criticism of their work, and further frustrates their desperate constituency.

Powerlessness, indeed, was a persistent theme in interviews with urban NYC officials. The officials displayed a fairly sound knowledge of urban youth issues but an inability to address them. If they want to survey the youth situation in their cells, for example, NYC officials must contribute their own personal money. They have no funds in their budget, NYC officials reported. Groups of youth come to them for assistance to form volunteer groups (such as karate and soccer teams). But an NYC official said that "nothing is done" when NYC officials submit requests to support such activities. Sports activities only take place in their area when secondary or university students are on school vacation, the official continued. "When it is school holiday vacation and students are around," he said, "there are good activities. But when students go back to school, these activities are kind of stopped." Budget funds earmarked for NYC activities never seem to arrive. One NYC official noted that "money comes to the sector office, but people up there don't give the money to the cell level."

The main activity that NYC officials at the urban cell level perform does not require funding. Officials called it "sensitization." This consists of summoning youth to meet with them. However, because youth lack free time, "we meet very few," another official explained. Another reported problem is the fact that "there are no meeting places" for NYC activities, an NYC official said. When NYC officials in Kigali do actually meet with youth, "the first thing we tell them is to go for a HIV/AIDS test" to see if they are carrying the virus, one explained. Such advice does not appeal to many youth because youth often ask them, "Why humiliate myself and say that I'm HIV positive and then not get anything?" NYC officials are well aware of the severe stigma attached to having the HIV/AIDS virus. Yet the government nonetheless tasks them to encourage youth to take the test. Such efforts appear to further undermine the already low credibility of the NYC among urban youth.

Kigali irinjirwa ntisohokura.
(Once one enters Kigali, he/she can't escape.)
Popular Rwandan proverb

The rural youth are coming to look for life in Kigali.
Either they don't know how to read or write or their
education level is not beyond primary school. They
don't have formal jobs. They have a bad situation.
Government official in Kigali

CHAPTER SEVEN

An Inconstant Existence

Coming to Town

In prior field research, rural Rwandan youth that I interviewed referred to the prospect of migrating to Kigali as an impossibility. A youth leader explained that "youth don't have the heart to go to Kigali because they don't know Kigali." Another male youth asserted that "youth can't go to Kigali because they don't know anything and they can't go just to wait around" for a job (Sommers 2006a: 92). Female youth I interviewed viewed urban migration as similarly out of the question.

Those interviews in 2000–2002 in northern Rwanda did not reflect the ideas and actions of all young Rwandans at that time, since Kigali was already in the midst of stunning population growth spearheaded by incoming rural youth (and, following the 1994 genocide, refugee returnees). But they do underscore one finding arising from research for this book: that nearly all Rwandan youth migrating to Kigali arrived with little more than hope. Just about every urban migrant youth who was interviewed stated that they arrived without prior knowledge of the city and with severely limited connections or networks—if they had any at all. They arrived to build a better life in town. Some male youth, having found adulthood difficult to achieve, were seeking relief from the pressures of becoming men. The generally harsh indoctrination into urban life is illustrated in the following comment from a destitute twenty-year-old male youth: "I came to Kigali alone. People used to tell me that there is cash in Kigali. But I was disappointed. They lied to me."

Of the seventy-six urban youth who responded to the questions, "Where did you come from, how did you get to Kigali, and did anyone help you get here?"[1] only 12 percent stated that they were from Kigali. Of those who had migrated to Kigali (sixty-seven respondents), approximately three-quarters of both male (72.5 percent) and female (75 percent) youth said that they either followed or arrived with someone to Kigali (usually a peer, sibling, or spouse) or followed a job offer in the capital. Many of those who came alone were either orphans or had experienced some sort of family abuse at home.

In sharp contrast to findings with rural youth, the themes of roofing and house building rarely arose among urban youth. Migrating to Kigali appears to significantly shift the context of male youth thinking away from working toward manhood to other, more immediate concerns such as finding money (and not always through work) for food, cigarettes, beer, and other things (such as a session with a prostitute), and help pay for house rent. While these issues are addressed in the Money, Hunger, and Instability section of this chapter, it is useful to note here how a young man's passage from rural beginnings to urban life in Rwanda may not remove expectations of manhood. They only seem to set them aside; perhaps temporarily, but perhaps permanently. As an educated female youth of twenty-two explained,

> The situation of the youth is really bad. There was this guy who left Butare to come here to Kigali because life was difficult for him and his family there. His house roof was leaking. He couldn't afford to build a proper house with all the roof tiles it required, so he came here. Many other people do the same: they come here, but once they arrive, they realize that life is not as easy as they thought it would be. And instead of the issue of building a house, which they had in their village, in Kigali they face another issue—paying the house rent.

Shame played a part for a significant minority of those who were interviewed. For example, 9 percent of eighty-six respondents (eight people) to the question, "Why did you come to Kigali?" either highlighted in their explanations that they moved to Kigali because of their inability to become adults in their rural communities or their inability to return home, or both.[2] All but one of the eighty-six were male, and two were adult men. The responses reflect the sorts of pressures that created so much difficulty for rural youth.

A man of thirty-six left rural Cyangugu for Kigali at age thirty-two because, as he put it, "people in my village were making fun of me because I couldn't afford a wife. That's why I decided to migrate here; to a new place where nobody cares about me. They are all poor around here, and they only care about how to make money and survive." A powerful characteristic of urban life that emerged from the interviews was shared desperation. Shame caused by an inability to become adult men and women might haunt a youth in rural areas, but it was irrelevant in an urban environment where survival was the dominant priority. In that sense, the anonymity of urban life created a luxury of sorts, as young people could unburden themselves from the humiliation and adulthood expectations that infused rural living for most youth.

The move into town also changed the nature of parental expectations on youth. Responding to the same question ("What do/did your parents expect you to be?" question 10 in box 2.3), nearly two in three urban youth (thirty-three of fifty-one, or 65 percent) supplied vague answers, stating merely that their parents wanted them to have a good life, or a better life than they had. This contrasted sharply to answers from their rural youth counterparts, most of whom stated specifics, such as education, an occupation requiring educational achievement, or becoming recognized as an adult man or woman.[3] The difference suggests that urban migration redefined what a young person might achieve in life. Expectations that a youth would obtain the traditional trappings of success appeared to more or less evaporate (or at least decline). At the same time, migrating to Kigali did not remove parental (and societal) expectations entirely: it was apparent that most youth still needed to demonstrate success. Indeed, it was difficult to ever return to one's rural home without some indication of urban achievement. As a female youth of twenty-one noted, "once you're here in Kigali, it's difficult to go back to your village because people expect us to succeed here." As is revealed in chapter 8, most migrant youth don't. As a result, they may rarely, if ever, return to their former rural homes.

Notably, there was a virtual absence in interviews of links to networks of reasonably successful relatives recruiting nephews or cousins to work in their urban enterprises, or religious networks—so common elsewhere—facilitating the migration of young people into cities.[4] While such things very likely took place in Kigali (more likely with more economically stable migrants, perhaps), no evidence of either kind of recruitment surfaced in any of the youth research data. In many other countries, urban migration is frequently a low-risk strategy because family or other networks (such as religious group affiliation) facilitate youth movements from villages to cities. An uncle may recruit young nephews (and perhaps nieces) to work in his urban enterprise as trusted junior employees. Pentecostal entrepreneurs may use church networks to recruit "saved" rural youth to work in their businesses. Regardless of the connection, bonds of trust secure arrangements for youth to migrate to cities.

This did not appear to be the case, in general, for Kigali migrants. There seemed to be no widespread tradition of trust-based networks that essentially recruited young people from villages to urban areas. Whereas a common low-risk strategy for a youth elsewhere was to access family or group networks and migrate to urban areas, a central low-risk strategy for many rural Rwandan youth was *not* to migrate. This characteristic was in vivid display in my interviews with rural Rwandan youth for earlier research (2000–2002). During that time, the interview data suggested that many rural male youth were reluctant to migrate to Kigali because "the fear of moving to a new place without assistance or a base of support made urban migration unlikely." The idea of venturing to Kigali to stay with relatives based there struck many male youth interviewed during that period as preposterous. For them, "migration lacked precedence, and potential migrants lacked networks" (Sommers 2006a: 92).

As a result, youth migration to Kigali in general carried with it a different—and fairly unusual—kind of profile than is common elsewhere. Many urban youth in Kigali were migrants, and while many in the research sample arrived with assistance, that assistance either proved tenuous or promised limited or no stability. Indeed, some rural youth and adults we interviewed equated urban migration with an escape from unduly humiliating or difficult circumstances, as with secondary school dropouts enduring lives of public failure upon their return home or older youth remaining unable to marry. Evidently, some rural youth grabbed at just about any opportunity they could get, however tenuous, to leave for the capital. Others migrated because they lacked alternatives, as illustrated by a twenty-four-year-old, destitute male youth:

> Life was very difficult in the countryside. When I came back from Congo, I found out that my parents were dead. I decided to migrate to Kigali. I was fourteen years old. I came by foot because I didn't have money to pay the bus ticket. It took me two days. When I got here, I got sick. I was staying in a house with two hundred other people (199 plus me). We were paying 80 francs a day [$0.15] to stay there. The conditions were horrible. Can you imagine living in a house, two hundred people in one house? No air to breathe inside the house. I learned to appreciate the morning. Every morning was a blessing for me.

I got a job in a restaurant run by Ugandans. I was getting paid 300 francs [$0.55] a day, so I decided to move to another house with a friend of mine. We were paying the rent of 1,500 francs [$2.78] a month each. My friend was smoking weed [marijuana], but since I wasn't smoking, I decided to move to another place. I found a lady and decided to live with her. We had one child, another one died recently. I can't even bury my own child.

Despite many rural Rwandan youth having grown up in a risk-averse culture, desperation and the need to escape difficult social and economic conditions in the countryside pushed them to become risk-taking urban migrants. The pull of urban life, so common among urban migrant youth in other parts of Africa (Sommers 2009: 21–22), was far less pronounced in Rwanda.

Once in Kigali, many migrant youth we interviewed reported that the friends or spouses who had brought them to town abandoned them soon afterward. Others who had been promised jobs found that they didn't exist or didn't last long. One of many accounts of these kinds of travails sheds light on the difficulties that so many encountered. A male youth of twenty-four recalled his entrance into the Rwandan capital: "I came one year ago from Ruhango [located 27 miles southwest of Kigali]. I followed a friend of mine, but he wasn't nice to me when we got here. He left me after a week. I had to find a way to survive, and it was hard. I don't want to talk about it. Here I am now, still in Kigali." And so, for many urban youth, it began. Some incoming female youth were abandoned immediately by boyfriends or spouses. Such stories might inspire condemnation of others for tricking the newcomers to Kigali. Yet one also must account for the general irregularity and instability of nearly all urban youth lives reported in the research. The data largely describe life of the desperately poor. Constancy and stability were not often features of lives driven by survival.

Urban Landscapes

In 2002, houses along the main road heading out of Kigali and toward Byumba did not reach very high up the hillside. Above the small car parts shops, garages, restaurants, and stalls that clung to the roadside, there were perhaps two or three lines of small houses. Above those residences, rural Rwanda began: all that could be seen from below were woods and pathways leading up the hill and into other valleys.

A view from the unregulated urban "countryside," where children and youth abound and most people live in rented rooms or houses, such as the one behind the children.

No longer. The treeline is now near the top of the high hill, and a tumult of mostly makeshift mud houses clots the view beneath. Rising from the roadway, one left the thicket of enterprises and the dense traffic of cars, trucks and young people, most of whom amble along the road searching for work or some glimpse of economic opportunity. Members of the LDF can also be observed dotting the throng, due to their worn but still light red (or pink) uniforms. The roadside is the most highly regulated area of Nyamabuye Cell, in Gatsata Sector, youth and adult residents report, and it is here, they say, where the LDF rule the roost. Just above this tarmac highway, one walks up steep, narrow footpaths that residents also call roads. These "roads" are rutted by rain gulleys and are strewn with garbage. As the din of the traffic below becomes fainter, it is clear that one is entering a new area. Residents call it "the countryside," which one youth living there defined as "upon the hill." Just below, along the tarmac roadway, he explained, is "town."

Up in this urban "countryside," mud house and apartment dwellings stand alongside shops and homemade banana beer bars. The area is crowded, although the pace is much slower than down on the tarmac road. With remarkable regularity one sees small children and youth: there seem to be few adults anywhere. Schools and churches, for that matter, are few and far between, too. Some youth hawk various wares displayed on cardboard or cloth, selling sandals, soap, toothpaste, salt, batteries, and other household goods. One who camped out just above "town" set up a makeshift shoe repair shop on a cloth. Why did he locate his enterprise in the "countryside?" "If I tried to fix shoes in town," he explains, "I'd be forced to join a [trade] association with four or five other shoe repairers, so I could work there." That option, he continued, was impossible. "I can't join a [trade] association due to poverty. It's too expensive: maybe you have to pay 10,000 francs [$18.52] a year." A woman customer disagrees: "It's 10,000 francs *a month*," she insists.

Here, in the space of a few hundred meters, is the invisible dividing line between business areas and the poor neighborhoods where most Kigali residents reside. Just as commerce dominates in "town" areas, so does government regulation. It is an area where economic risks and potential gains thrive. Jobs are possible there, but unregulated economic efforts may be stopped in their tracks: if an LDF discovers someone with goods to sell without a permit, youth and adults explain, the goods can be confiscated and the person can be fined or even arrested. Up on the hillside—or, in the peri-urban area of Nyabisindu Cell, Remera Sector, where the team also conducted research, down in the valley—another reality exists. In such places, the government's presence is

A shoe repairman sets up temporary shop in one of the many
unregulated areas of Kigali.

thinner and more sporadic. This may have its good side—the "countryside" cobbler doesn't have to join a government-regulated trade association, and the LDF's shadow isn't as far-reaching. Yet such urban "countrysides" have distinct downsides, too. A resident can be forced from housing deemed illegal, and many report that violence and robbery are commonplace. The research team was warned by many youth that they should exit the countrysides before six in the evening, as the approaching darkness, many warned, was when thieves thrived ("countryside" areas generally lack electricity). The community night patrols are among those who rob people, some also reported.

This is the world that youth and adults described during interviews, and it is the stage for the discussion that follows.

Money, Hunger, and Instability

Look at me! I worked hard yesterday and now I have nothing left.
> Male youth, age twenty-five

Because I prefer avoiding trouble, who am I?
> Male youth, age twenty-six

I'm still alive: that's all that matters.
> Male youth, age twenty-seven

An irony surfacing from the field research for this book is that many youth migrated to Kigali because of the promise of making money and, at the very least, of stabilizing their lives and providing some chance for a bit of success. Yet the more typical result was just the opposite: a life of chronic instability in which income, and food, arrived only with irregularity. The irony was not lost on a twenty-seven-year-old male youth who observed that, in his words, "I'm struggling to survive in Kigali. But in fact if I could go back [home] to Butare, I would. I want to go back. At least in Butare I can get food every day; not like here. In Butare, I couldn't spend a day without getting a job digging for other people and making 500 [francs, or $0.92] a day. In Kigali, I never know if I'll work or not." And without working, many youth stated, there might be no way to get food to eat.

Money in some way or another surfaced constantly in conversations with urban youth and adults. There were concerns about how and whether one might find some, how much things cost, how much one might make in a certain activity, and how money could be lost. There was hardly ever enough money on hand, and when it was, it was difficult to find a safe place to keep it. Money could come and go in a matter of hours, spent on rent, beer, cigarettes, a prostitute, occasionally some money to send home—and food. Many if not most urban youth we interviewed were either hungry when they were interviewed or were concerned that hunger would visit them again soon. Most appeared to eat, at most, one plate of food per day. Few cooked. The irregularity of income meant that urban youth lived day to day. Uncertainty reigned. One might lose their job or accommodation, or even a friend, any day. Indeed, there seemed to be little to depend on in city life except the difficulty of making ends meet—and getting enough to eat.

There were regular indications of this constant inconstancy in the research findings. The unceasing thinking about money, and the prominence of food in this thinking, is apparent in the following quotations. A single thirty-year-old male youth described how he spent 1,000 francs ($1.85) when he managed to earn that much: "I use 200 [$0.37] francs for food, and the rest is for the rent and other needs like buying water, cigarettes, or banana beer. It doesn't happen every day, and because I don't know if I'll get a job tomorrow, I try to save sometimes." A single twenty-three-year-old male youth who peddles goods on the street described how he managed his money in the following way: "I sell my stuff in this box every day. I first think about what I'll buy for the day after [selling goods]. Mostly, it's cigarettes. Then I think about food, but that comes after I've made sure that I've got enough money to buy what is missing in my box. Some days when I don't sell much, when I have a bad day, then I don't have a lot of money and I just eat instead of thinking about what I'll buy for tomorrow." The difficulties of getting enough money, and food, do not only affect urban youth. Here, a single thirty-nine-year-old man describes his current state:

> The first thing I think about when I get money is food. Life is becoming more and more difficult in Kigali, and food is very expensive. In 2000, a kilo of potatoes was 25 francs/kilo [$0.05]. Now it's 130 francs [$0.24].
>
> But I can't afford to cook at home. I eat cooked food in restaurants. I use the rest of the money for rent and drink and smoking. It's not easy for me to get a job [in construction]. We are so many here.

Even those with comparatively stable lives faced regular difficulty, as illuminated by the following description of daily economic challenges from a married female youth of twenty-five who ran a small shop: "At the end of the day, the average profit is 500 [francs]. We save 200 for the rent and use 300 [$0.55] for household needs. There are times when we're lucky and have more than 500. It is then when we eat good meals. Otherwise, we eat to survive."

Since urban youth and adults regularly mentioned the cost of things which they bought or paid during interviews, some context is useful. Table 7.1 lists the cost of things according to those whom we interviewed in Kigali.

The prominence of food in people's thoughts was conspicuous and widespread. An indication of its importance arose in responses to question 20 (in box 2.3), "When someone talks to you about 'peace,' what does it mean to you?" The responses were more often connected to biological survival than either economic stability or physical security. More than half (54 percent) of the ninety-five respondents connected peace to food or to eating food. The rationales were consistent as well, illustrated by the idea of a male youth that "you can't talk about peace when you are hungry." Another believed that "hunger is the biggest threat to peace. All these robbers steal because they're hungry." In contrast, only 35 percent of respondents connected peace to work or a job. Of these, some contended that, as one respondent argued, "jobless people are a threat to peace." A similar proportion of respondents—37 percent—raised the issue of security, or related issues such as robbery or violence as connected to peace. While this was a fairly surprising result because many youth listed theft and assault as commonplace in their areas, it further highlights how addressing immediate hunger needs was more pressing than protection. Most of Kigali's urban youth are in dire straits, and no one who was interviewed, from youth to adults to government officials, contradicted this view.

This finding was underscored by results from the question, "Do you have a plan for improving your situation?" (question 6 in box 2.3). Approximately a third of all youth, and 44 percent of all adults, had no plan whatsoever, and many of the 107 respondents found the question strange. A destitute, twenty-three-year-old female youth, for example, asked "what do you want us to plan?" Her plan, she stated, was "just to survive day after day." The remaining youth and adults stated that they had plans of some sort, although most were much more like hopes or dreams than actual, realistic plans. Some expressed a "plan" of somehow getting enough money to join a trade association (which would, of course, first require the person to get a job in that trade). Nearly half of the respondents (46 percent) had plans of some sort relating to a business activity. A mere 5.5 percent had plans connected to more education or training (such as driver's education). Most responses were short on specifics, but there were exceptions. One male youth was purchasing land and animals in his rural home area, for example. Another provided a detailed plan (in response to

TABLE 7.1

How Much Things Cost in Kigali

Item	Cost in Rwandan Francs	U.S. Dollar Equivalent*
Food, per meal		
Low	150	0.28
High	500	0.92
Average	200	0.37
Rent, per month		
Low, per person	500	0.92
High, per person	10,000	18.52
Average, per person	2,300	4.26
Average, per unit	5,500	10.18
Trousers		
To buy used	1,500	2.78
To have mended	200	0.37
Washing clothes, per load	300	0.55
Banana beer, per bottle	50	0.09
Haircut		
Man	100	0.18
Woman	200	0.37
Night patrol contribution, per month for each household or business	500	0.92
Cigarettes		
Single	20	0.04
Average cost per night	100	0.18
Visiting a prostitute		
Per session, low	100	0.18
Per session, high	1,000	1.85
Per night, low	1,500	2.78
Per night, high	2,000	3.70
Condom	50	0.09
Trade Association Entry Fee		
Low	2,000	3.70
High	30,000	55.55
Trade Association Daily Fee		
Low	50	0.09
High	500	0.92

* During the period of field research in rural Rwanda and Kigali (November 2006–March 2007), approximately 540 Rwandan francs had the equivalent value of one U.S. dollar (540 francs = US$1).

Notes
- Most youth reported that they ate one meal per day. Most eat out because they lack the facilities to cook and eat at home.
- Respondents reported that as many as eight people shared each housing unit (usually two rooms), with up to four people sleeping in each room.
- One female youth mentioned occasional costs to help care for the ill, the needy, and for those who died. She had contributed 200 francs ($0.37) for the coffin and cemetery fees for someone who died and did not have relatives.
- Few youth said that they were paying premiums to the government's community-based health insurance program, Mutuelles de Santé. While some reported that they did pay, most said that they could not afford to pay the premiums.
- The reported estimated entry fees for trade associations were 2,000 francs ($3.70) to join a wheelbarrow association (to carry water); 3,000 ($5.55) to join a street-cleaning association; 10,000 ($18.52) or more to join a porter association; 20,000 to join a mechanic association; 5,000 ($9.26) to join a taxi association; and 30,000 ($55.55) to join a car-washer association.
- Reported estimates of how much it would cost to start up a business include: 10,000 francs ($18.52) to sell out of a box (or on a piece of cardboard or cloth); 50,000 ($92.60) to start a hair "saloon" (salon); 70,000 ($129.63) to open a tailoring business; and 150,000–200,000 ($370.37) to set up a garage.
- Other costs mentioned by respondents include purchasing other clothes, hospital fees/government health care, taxes, roof tiles and transportation fees (if building a house), school/vocational school fees and uniforms, fines levied by LDF (500–5,000 francs [$0.93–$9.26]), and purchasing marijuana.

another interview question) for acquiring vocational training—by becoming a prisoner. The destitute twenty-two-year-old explained that

> if someone told me to go into a prison and promised that I'd be released after one year, I'd accept. Do you know why? Don't you see prisoners every day coming out, constructing houses, and building bridges? This is a training experience. They even have music bands inside prisons, as well as workshops where they make chairs and repair electronic items like irons, radios, and TV sets. If I went there for a year, I could get training for more than three jobs at the same time. And after I got out, I wouldn't be jobless. But without prison, well, come back in year and see how I'll be. There will be no improvement in my situation.

The responses further illustrate how few urban youth seemed to have viable support networks or job-related opportunities in Kigali. Very few youth believed they could improve their social and economic situation on their own.

Responses to the question, "Who might help you with your plan, so that you might find success?" (question 7 in box 2.3), highlight the high degree of social and economic isolation that characterize many if not most urban youth lives. Indeed, the contrast with the findings with rural youth is startling. More than half (55 percent) of the forty-nine urban youth respondents said that they didn't know anyone who could help them, that "no one can help me," or that "only God can help me." The proportion of urban youth respondents expressing these sentiments was significantly higher than that of rural youth (33 percent). It was not only youth with lower education levels who expressed these views, as more than half of urban youth in the sample (53 percent) who had achieved a significant degree of educational accomplishment (completing primary school) were part of this group. In addition, almost twice as many rural-dwelling youth responded to this question with the expectation that either the government or associations might assist them with their plans (42.5 percent of rural youth compared with 22 percent of urban youth). Taken together, the findings suggest that urban youth were much more likely to feel isolation, and perhaps despair, than rural youth. It also suggests that urban youth generally had much more distant relations with government officials than their rural counterparts.

A substantial distance between urban youth and urban government officials, of course, is much more the norm than the exception in large cities. In developing countries in particular, prodigious numbers of urban youth tend to stress urban infrastructure, resources, and services. Nonetheless, the

Rwandan context for relations between urban youth and government requires some description. First, far more youth in Kigali seemed to be engaged in outright lawbreaking than in rural areas. However, much of this lawbreaking, a great many urban youth and adults explained, was motivated by sheer desperation. Many urban youth described some of their male counterparts as being driven to theft by desperation, as mentioned in the Insecurity section in chapter 6. The level of youth and adult compassion and understanding for such thieves in their midst, even if they had been victims of theft, was striking. Significantly, and quite unlike what would be seen in a great many other African cities, our research uncovered no reports of organized crime outfits or even large gangs: the reported crimes were mainly carried out by desperate young people.

A second form of urban lawbreaking was similar to what respondents in rural Rwanda reported to us. These were activities that broke government regulations. As in rural areas, some of this illegality concerned housing, and exposed lawbreakers to considerable consequences: for example, houses that did not meet government regulations (such as those made with mud walls instead of concrete) could be torn down. This appeared to occur fairly regularly. But the most consistent form of regulation-breaking lay in selling goods without a permit. Youth and adults alike explained that obtaining government permits to sell goods in a particular place (in a market or along a street) was, from their perspective, difficult or impossible. The reason given was that it took funds, and perhaps connections, to obtain such a space. Most had neither. As a result, many youth and adults tried to make money by hawking their goods on foot and without a permit. They knew that this "unorganized commerce" was illegal and it invited intercession by the LDF or the *panda gari*. What has ensued is a kind of economic cat and mouse involving people trying to hawk goods without getting caught and government officials on the lookout for precisely this sort of economic behavior. A government official in the midst of such activities accepted that the situation was difficult for people living in his area. But the activities were also illegal, and he had to do his job. As he explained,

> This unorganized commerce—people wandering around with fruits, vegetables, mosquito nets, and other things—is now prohibited. We were asked by the Kigali City Council to find a place in each sector to set up a small market for these people. Here in this sector, we gave them a place.

But these sellers worked there not more than three days and left. When we asked them why they left, they said that people there are poor, they don't use vegetables or fruits. So since they weren't finding customers, they left.

Poor people from poor neighborhoods naturally want to sell things in areas of town where commerce thrives. As most poor youth and adults eat in restaurants, few people purchase fresh produce in poor neighborhoods.

The need for street peddlers to hawk their goods elsewhere invites regular interactions with government officials, particularly members of the LDF. The LDF held sway in descriptions of the challenges that urban youth faced while selling goods, or attempting to do so, on the streets. Typically, it appears, an LDF member would stop a street peddler to see if they were conducting illegal economic activity. What ensued next is a matter of conjecture, because officials, and an LDF member who agreed to be interviewed (only one consented), emphasized that most were carrying out their duties properly. As a government official explained, "When one is caught with goods, for example mosquito nets, all the goods are confiscated and taken to the nearest government office. So if one has, for example, goods worth 20,000 francs [$37.04, a sizable sum], he or she may give 1,000 [$1.85] to the local defense and remain with his or her goods. Some may even give 5,000 [$9.26] instead of losing the whole business. It is a kind of corruption, but it is very hard for us to fight it: you cannot be at all places at the same time." Selling goods on streets was one of the only types of potential work available to many youth, female youth in particular. The work was not impossible—one did not seem to get caught every day—but it made difficulty and risk a regular part of working life. The loss of capital if caught could also be considerable. For some, it was worth the risk. For others, there may not have been viable alternatives to street selling. And certainly not all LDF members responded in the same way when they encountered unlicensed street peddlers. Some would negotiate for a particular fee, as suggested by the government official. But others, reportedly, confiscated all of the goods. Many youth contended that this was sheer corruption, since the LDF officers kept the goods themselves and did not turn them over to government offices.

Whether or not the youth were right about what became of the confiscated goods, the situation itself was more complicated. From the perspective of the LDF, their lack of a salary might naturally set up a need or interest in gaining some profit from their work. In any case, the street peddlers were breaking the law. As a result, as an LDF member explained, "Those sellers are doing business in disorder. They are avoiding taxes by trying to sell things at a cheaper price.

So when they do this, the sellers who pay taxes [i.e., legal shopkeepers and market peddlers with permits] lose. This is because the legal sellers have to add the payment of government taxes to the prices for goods. So their prices are higher than for peddlers who don't pay taxes. So they keep complaining." From the perspective of youth engaged in this sort of work, interactions with LDF could be regular, and regularly unpleasant, affairs. Some LDF appeared to be much more vigorous with street peddlers than with other violators. Complaints about LDF members demanding goods or cash, or both, from peddlers were common in interviews with urban youth and adults. One particular story of an LDF shaking down a youth was humorous, and illuminates the degree of power that LDF members can exert. During an interview with some male youth and men, a poor man of thirty-nine asserted that the LDF members "confiscate stuff. They always ask for money. I'm telling you these LDF are even poorer than us. They are *abatindi* [low-status, destitute people]!" In response, a male youth of twenty-five told the following story: "The other day one asked me to follow him. He said, 'I've been told you sell weed.' Then he searched my pockets. He found a small piece of paper and asked me what it was for. I said, 'It's a piece of paper. You can write on it.' He asked, 'Why is it crumpled?' I answered that 'it's because I use it in the bathroom as toilet paper.' Then he released me." There was, in addition, regular mention of the *panda gari* and community night patrols variously arresting or intimidating youth, and in the case of night patrols, demanding money from youth at night.

Three useful points might be drawn from these comments about the LDF. First, it was widely believed among youth and adults that the security situation in their Kigali communities was poor. Dangers arise most particularly in the dark of night. Talk of "ambushes" by thieves, or of being forced to hand over money to night patrols, was common. Violent fights involving drunken men at bars at night surfaced in many accounts of the security situation. Just as notably, there were few reports of house robberies: the danger mainly seemed to lay when people went out at night (staying home was a protection measure). And, frequently, talk returned to alleged abuses by the LDF. As one twenty-year-old male youth asked, "How are we supposed to survive if the LDF confiscate our stuff? Stealing shouldn't be an option to get out of poverty." Again, one can see a kind of sympathy for what might be called "desperation theft."

Second, statements from poor urban youth during interviews broadly express a sense that they were outsiders—even though, in demographic terms, youth thoroughly dominate Kigali (an estimated 65 percent of the city's population). The best survival strategy seemed to be to avoid trouble somehow. Gauging from what government officials and youth themselves related, night patrols and LDF members reported robberies or assaults to police. Youth did not, or rarely did so. This is significant because officials and civilians alike reported that poor Kigali neighborhoods were dangerous and filled with criminal activities at night. Some youth noted that night patrols had somewhat improved the security situation, although others were skeptical because of reports that some night patrols robbed people, as well. Reporting sexual assault or rape to the police appears to have been particularly rare.

Underneath all of this was a persistent sense that most urban youth viewed their lives as unstable and insecure, and that there was little they could do to improve their situation. A life led among other young and poor people did not often lead to encounters with other kinds of city dwellers. Some youth stated that they could not trust educated people, as they contended that such people would trick or exploit them (this sentiment may have been one reason why some youth avoided joining trade associations, as educated male youth lead most associations). At the same time, some youth said that it was hard to trust anyone. "People here don't trust each other," a twenty-four-year-old male youth explained. "They are suspicious." Many other youth appeared to agree with him. Expressions of distance from others could take on fairly extreme forms, such as the following comment from a twenty-three-year-old female youth working as a prostitute about how officials viewed prostitutes: "The only threat to my peace is that I'm taken as an animal. The officials are always herding us as if we were animals. Whenever they come to this cell, the first place they go is this area, to hunt for us." In fact, that did not appear to be the only threat to the peace of female youth in her profession. As chapter 8 details, descriptions from female youth working as prostitutes indicated that sexual assault and rape occurred regularly and that night patrols were among the culprits. It seemed highly unlikely that prostitutes themselves would ever report such crimes, given the way that police routinely treated them. It also seemed likely that molesting and raping prostitutes was common, since one could do so, evidently, with impunity.

A third point we can draw from urban youth's attitudes toward the LDF is that figuring out how and where to save money is a persistent urban youth problem. Young people unaccustomed to having even small amounts of cash were clearly challenged when any sort of financial windfall, however small, came their way. Some fretted that money in their keep didn't stay there long: they would end up spending it on food, beer, cigarettes, and other items. Government officials explained that joining an association could help youth

TABLE 7.2

Reported Youth Incomes in Kigali

Profession	Income in Rwandan Francs	U.S. Dollar Equivalent*	Profession	Income in Rwandan Francs	U.S. Dollar Equivalent*
Chercheur ("searcher"/middleman), per day			Selling water		
Low	1,000	1.85	Per day, low	400	0.74
High	5,000	9.26	Per day, high	1,000	1.85
Lucky day	20,000	37.04	Per jerrican	100	0.18
Mechanic, per day			Selling clothes, per day		
Average	3,000	5.55	Low	500	0.92
Lucky day	20,000	37.04	High	1,000	1.85
Guard, per month			Bricklayer		
Low	10,000	18.52	Per day, low	600	1.11
High	30,000	55.55	Per day, high	700	1.30
Porter, per day			Per brick	10	0.02
Low	200	0.37	Working in a restaurant, per day		
High	1,500	2.78	Low	300	0.55
Lucky day	3,000	5.55	High	500	0.92
Prostitute, per session			Barber, per day		
Low	100	0.18	Low	500	0.92
High	1,000	1.85	High	1,500	2.78
Lucky day	4,000	7.41	House girl/houseboy, per month, room and board included		
Selling produce / small commerce, per day					
Low	500	0.92	Low	1,000	1.85
High	800	1.48	High	3,000	5.55
Odd jobs			Construction site assistant, per day		
Per day, low	200	0.37	Low	700	1.30
Per day, high	600	1.11	High	1,000	1.85
Per job, low	100	0.18	Builder	2,000	3.70
Per job, high	200	0.37			

* During the period of field research in rural Rwanda and Kigali (November 2006–March 2007), approximately 540 Rwandan francs had the equivalent value of one U.S. dollar (540 francs = US$1).

Notes
- Less common jobs include selling posters on the street (up to 2,000–3,000 francs [$5.55] on a lucky day); being a street singer (up to 1,500 [$2.78] on a lucky day); being a trainer at a garage (up to 5,000 [$9.26] per day); and serving as an investor (investing money to purchase and resell goods; up to 5,000 per day).
- One demobilized soldier noted that he received 20,000 francs ($37.04) for reintegrating as a civilian. Another said that he received 30,000 ($55.55).

open bank accounts and invest their savings together. But since most of the male youth interviewed were not association members (and none in the female youth sample), the difficulties of saving money remained. A twenty-four-year-old male youth explained his solution to this problem, which was tied to the significant threat of night crimes on the streets (but not in homes): "I can't walk in the evening with a lot of money on me. I always bring less than a thousand when I go to a bar. I leave the rest of my money at home under my bed, even when I'm sleeping. My money is always under my bed." A remarkable research finding in rural and urban Rwanda was that house burglary is rare. Urban youth and adults reported that thieves rob outdoor kitchens, sheds, animal stalls, and people outside at night. But they rarely broke into people's homes. In other African cities where I have carried out research (such as Dar es Salaam, Tanzania, and Freetown, Sierra Leone), hiding money under your mattress would be unthinkable.

A few youth respondents mentioned one financial institution that they trusted and took part in: *ibimina* (informal savings associations, first mentioned in chapter 3). A difference from the rural version was that urban members typically contributed money every day (around 200 francs [$0.37]), while rural members contributed once a week. Payouts also seemed to occur much faster: members of a fifteen-member *ibimina* would have to wait no longer than 15 days to receive their payment. *Ibimina* membership, of course, may help some youth acquire capital. But it did not ultimately resolve the challenge of saving or investing capital.

Some youth mentioned their sudden surges in income as signs of good fortune in their work. Table 7.2 lists occupations mentioned by youth and their range of reported income.

Not listed are other sorts of occupations that urban youth and adults reported. These were being a "wanderer," who is much worse off than a "searcher." While a *chercheur* waited by roadsides to buy and sell goods, such as car parts, as a service to customers, *inzererezi* appeared to be without an occupation or a residence. They reportedly slept in different places at night and wandered the streets during the day, looking for money or food, sometimes through petty theft. In truth, an *inzererezi* is less an occupation than a position of itinerant poverty, a description that also applies to *maibobo*, or street boys and street girls.

The third occupation on the lowest social status rung is prostitution, the most common female youth occupation in the sample. Nearly one in three female youth in the urban research sample (31 percent) said that they were prostitutes, while one in five (20 percent) worked in "small business" (selling goods without a permit). Other jobs included student, restaurant worker, tailor, and house girl. Jobs for female youth constituted a much shorter list than that reported by male youth, which included all of the occupations listed in table 7.2 except prostitute. The primary reported reason for this greater range of occupations for males was physical strength: youth explained that male youth are able to carry out certain jobs, such as working as porters, for which female youth were never hired.

As a result, male youth generally had significantly more options in town than female youth. It was also much more likely that female youth would be stuck in appalling situations without viable alternatives. In the next chapter we turn to the disturbing situation of poor female youth in Kigali, and gender relations involving male and female youth in town.

I'm a prostitute. That doesn't mean I like it, but I had no choice after my husband left me. He was beating me. Can you imagine being beaten when you're pregnant? Once he beat me so badly that I couldn't leave the house for five days.

Now I've got a child to raise on my own. We haven't eaten since yesterday. I haven't gotten any money for today, so if somebody comes and gives me 500 francs [$0.92], how could I say no to him?

Female youth, eighteen years old

There is a lot of poverty here. Girls are selling their bodies because of that. A girl can sleep with a man for 100 francs [$0.18].

Male youth, age twenty-three

People here are not afraid of HIV/AIDS. They think about how to get a job and make some money for food and after that, there is tomorrow. It's another struggle for another day.

Male youth, age twenty-four

What prevention?

Female youth, twenty-three years old and working as a prostitute, when invited to comment on HIV/AIDS prevention efforts

CHAPTER EIGHT

Prostitution, AIDS, and Fatalism

Desirable Pariahs

The situation facing many urban female youth is desperate. No group of Rwandan youth faces circumstances so grave. Their desperation is tied to limited options and the horrors of life as a prostitute. Many female youth descend into prostitution because they lack alternatives. Many female youth who are not prostitutes appear to be one misfortune away from the descent. While the sample is small, the findings nonetheless spotlight a potentially serious emergency with profound social and public health implications. Due to AIDS, the threat of disaster appears to be affecting a large proportion of male and female youth in Kigali.

Prostitution was the most common female youth occupation in the research sample. Although nearly one in three female youth in the research sample were prostitutes, it is entirely possible that the proportion was even higher, since some prostitutes may have concealed their involvement in prostitution because it is illegal and carries the status of social pariah. The average age of female youth respondents working as prostitutes was twenty-one. All were destitute (per the definition in chapter 2). Only one of the twelve had attended secondary school, and 17 percent had never attended any school. Three-quarters were single. The research did not record how many had children, although there were strong indications that most were mothers. Some information was hard to extract: only six female youth who stated their job as "prostitute" would explain how they got to Kigali. Four of those six had followed their husband or boyfriend to the capital and then had been abandoned by those males. Urban support networks beyond their exiting male partners did not seem to exist. At least some prostitutes were victims of regular violence: references to being beaten by customers were common during interviews. Many female youth who worked as prostitutes had visible bruises or scars.

Urban youth and adults considered prostitution as a last-chance, no-alternative net that young women fall into and then, in nearly all cases, cannot escape. The entrapment surfaced in responses by prostitutes to the question, "Do you have a plan for improving your situation?" (question 6 in box 2.3). The responses fell into three categories: those without any plans whatsoever (42 percent), those with particularly unrealistic plans (such as getting a rich man to rescue them, which one considered "a dream") (33 percent), and those with plans for developing a business or returning to school (25 percent)—the last was possible only provided they somehow receive assistance. Those without any plans illustrated the difficulty of finding a getaway. One respondent, for example, stated that "my plan is just to survive from day to day." Another said that imagining a plan for herself was like a convict serving a life sentence. "Right now, I'm like that prisoner," she explained. "My life is not going to improve, so why should I waste time thinking about a plan?"

While some youth prostitutes described theirs as a chosen occupation, others viewed prostitution as an act of survival. Female youth had considerably fewer economic options than male youth. As many were virtually alone in town, one mishap was all that it may have taken to push a female youth toward that profession. As one female youth remarked, "Most female youth are prostitutes. There are not many jobs for girls here. They can't sell things around anymore due to the *panda gari* and Local Defense Forces. There are some who work in restaurants or shops, but they are few compared to those who are prostitutes." Some female youth explained that it was not unusual for house girls—a much-desired female youth occupation—to get pregnant. Once that happened, they usually lost their jobs and had no alternative except prostitution. As a twenty-six-year-old female youth explained: "When girls work as house girls, they sometimes get pregnant and go back to their village, give birth there and come back to Kigali to become prostitutes." Pregnancy for single female youth living in town shamed their families and forced the youth's return to the city. And once they became prostitutes, it seemed almost impossible to regain acceptance by their families.

The prostitutes' state of severe social and economic weakness is illustrated by descriptions of female youth exchanging sex for a place to sleep, or a meal, for as little as 100 francs ($0.18). They routinely charged an additional $0.37 to put their lives at grave risk. Two hundred francs was a common additional charge for customers who wouldn't wear condoms. The extra money may have been appealing because 200 francs bought a plate of food. Some female youth became prostitutes because they *have* AIDS, not the reverse. As one female youth observed, "anyone who is infected with AIDS loses his or her job. When girls lose their jobs due to this weakness, they become prostitutes. And then their problem is that there are different prices. There are mean people who say that if the girl wants him to use a condom, he will give her like 300 [francs], and if he doesn't use it, it is 500. So the girls prefer not to use a condom." This comment exposes the dynamics of desperation in a particularly chilling and alarming way. Prostitution is a death sentence for prostitutes and their customers (most of whom are male youth) because the likelihood of contracting HIV/AIDS is exceptionally high.

Many prostitutes did not have condoms available. As a nineteen-year-old prostitute explained, "maybe I'm infected with AIDS. I've never been tested, and I have to admit that I don't always use condoms. At the beginning, I was using them, but not anymore. You can't afford to buy them every day and most of the time I'm drunk before I sleep with a man so I don't think about giving condoms to my clients." At the same time, male youth may not bother to purchase one. One youth provided one reason: "Condoms are expensive. Fifty francs [$0.09] is too much for youth here." Beyond expense, a destitute twenty-three-year-old male youth remarked, "I haven't seen any condoms since I came to Kigali. Nobody uses them. When somebody eats once a day or once in two days, don't ask him to buy a condom to have safe sex." Government officials spoke with youth about the dangers of AIDS and the importance of protection, but their urgings evidently had little positive impact. The same young man explained that "when your stomach is empty, you can't think about anything else. Sometimes the authorities come and talk to us about AIDS, but we don't really listen. They think we do, but we can't because of hunger." Given the collective behavior and general desperation of male and female youth, it appears virtually certain that the AIDS epidemic was spreading rapidly through Kigali's population.

The connection between food and AIDS was frequently explicit during interviews. Many youth seemed much too desperate and preoccupied with immediate needs to think deeply about the prospect of contracting AIDS and a possible early death. Many male youth reported that once they get a bit of cash, they may get drunk and search for a prostitute. "If one day I get drunk," a male youth of twenty explained, "we are human beings and want sex. If unfortunately I go to the prostitute who is infected with AIDS and don't protect myself, I'm done." Another male youth remarked, "there are some prostitutes that we know are infected, yet men still go to them." Sessions with prostitutes often take place after men leave bars, and as one male youth observed, "one needs to be sober to wear condoms." Such statements suggest that while youth were aware that the possibility of contracting AIDS through unprotected sex with a prostitute may be high, many appeared to be resigned to their fate. As one female youth predicted, "AIDS will sweep us up. You can't go into prostitution and not expect to get AIDS."

This frightening cocktail of desperation and the apparent pervasiveness of fatalistic behavior regarding HIV/AIDS strongly suggests that the actual rate of HIV/AIDS infection among Kigali youth was far higher than the accepted estimate of 3.4 percent (Institut National de la Statistique and ORC Macro 2006: xxix). Indeed, one male youth directly challenged the publicly hailed 3 percent national infection rate: "You cannot tell what the AIDS situation is. This is because you cannot know the real figures. They keep mentioning that it's 3 percent, but I think it's more than that. If you see how prostitutes are around here, you can't say there's almost no AIDS." The research also illustrates just how difficult it can be to record accurate indications of the prevalence of HIV/AIDS in a population. The severe stigma and economic vulnerability attached to being publicly known to have HIV or AIDS means that "it's everyone's secret," as one male youth stated, and thus difficult to gain an accurate account of the prevalence level. Despite the personal secrecy surrounding who might be infected, urban youth displayed an ease in speaking about AIDS generally. This stood in striking contrast to rural youth, who were much more reticent to talk about it, perhaps because they were surrounded by families, friends, and the world of social expectation. Urban youth, in contrast, openly engaged in risky sexual behavior themselves or seemed to know many others who acted similarly. They did not consider such behavior shameful. Prostitution and drinking, of course, were present across rural Rwanda. But in Kigali they were accepted antidotes for urban living.

The strong and widespread awareness that the prevalence of AIDS infection in poor Kigali communities was probably high and expanding shocked our research team. The descriptions from respondents about AIDS—such as "We cried and tears dried," "We are worried," "Our lives are in danger," and "AIDS will kill us"—evoke a youthful population on the knowing edge of impending devastation. As one male youth noted, "AIDS will affect us all in one way or another. I can be infected due to many reasons. I may want sex and if I have 500 francs I go for one [prostitute]. If I don't have enough to buy a condom, or if I'm drunk and out of my mind, I don't use one. Then I'm finished." An awareness of doom among youth appeared to be near complete. All eighty respondents to questions about the AIDS situation in their area, for example, clearly recognized the gravity of the HIV/AIDS threat and expressed a strong sense that the situation was severe, threatening, and quite likely to leave ruinous results.[1] Not one respondent suggested that the AIDS situation facing urban youth was anything but serious. No one predicted that it might improve. There was also a considerable degree of compassion in this situation of shared decline. While some prostitutes complained bitterly about customers who refused to wear condoms (some are so mean, one related, that they deliberately break or "tear the condom" right in front of them, even when "they know they are infected"), people did not blame prostitutes for the spread of AIDS. Instead, many respondents simply stated that prostitutes, together with their customers, spread HIV/AIDS. Some youth were remarkably empathic about the lives of prostitutes. For example, a destitute male youth of twenty-eight said that "there's no good life in prostitution! Do you think they are happy? I'm sure they cry in secret when they're alone."

Back from the precipice are everyday problems, some of which are a consequence of the fact that, as one government official stated, "prostitution is an illegal profession." The vulnerability this creates can lead to arrest and temporary stays in jail. But living beyond the limits of the law also exposes prostitutes to exploitation and violence. As a twenty-two-year-old prostitute explained, "for us prostitutes, there is no security. We are very vulnerable. And the big problem is that we can't go to officials when we are violated [i.e., raped] because of what we do in Kigali." Another prostitute noted that "Sometimes those night patrol guys will ask me for 'something else' that's sweeter than money. They are bastards, those poor losers!" In addition to being vulnerable to rape and being unable or reluctant to report the crime, prostitutes also said that some customers refuse to pay the agreed fee following a session with a prostitute. Since so much of their living is hand to mouth, and since many have children, every such breach of contract is serious.

Government officials reported that they make efforts to address the problems that prostitutes faced. They had some successes. One government official in Kigali recalled one effort: "We asked some prostitutes to quit prostitution and join in an association so we could assist them. But they continued in their work. So in the last week, there was a curfew for them. We captured those who came to the meeting and other prostitutes. We gathered them together and talked with them about many issues, such as how they could quit prostitution, create new jobs and join associations. We even talked about AIDS." Another Kigali government official offered an example of his efforts to stem the prostitution tide: "Once we caught some girl prostitutes. We talked to them to sensitize them to change their behavior. We had around sixty girls. We know where they stay. When we call them, some come. We even have a project for them. They are to be trained in a vocational training center." What is illuminating about these government actions is how officials addressed the prostitution challenge. In both cases, prostitutes were first arrested, as their activities were illegal. Afterward, instead of taking them to jail, the officials provided counsel. It represented a sincere, if inadequate, endeavor in the face of a massive problem.

Gender Relations in an Urban Setting

Normally one is working for his own stomach. Working for two is hard.

Male youth, age nineteen

The pervasiveness of prostitution in Kigali provides an optic for gauging gender relations among poor urban youth. The research findings strongly suggest that most poor urban youth lived their lives only in the present. Planning for the future is difficult in any case because saving money is so hard, and obtaining money was their predominant preoccupation. Money provides access to food, paying rent, and engagement with the opposite sex. Prostitution was by far the most prevalent reported type of engagement between male and female youth.

Urban youth lives were frequently so unstable that planning for marriage was exceptionally difficult. Some of those who attempted to build a more stable urban life were stymied by government regulations, as in rural areas. Similar to their rural counterparts, an unusually enterprising urban male youth may be able to build only the sort of cheap housing in town that is impermanent, illegal, and vulnerable to destruction by inclement weather or government authorities. As one male youth explained, "we try to build houses [in the city] and the authorities destroy them. Then girls blame us because we don't marry them."

The overwhelming majority of urban male youth we interviewed never got that far. Some male youth defined manhood in town as obtaining "a good job" and getting married. Male youth in Kigali rarely mentioned the need to build a house before marrying, as renting living quarters was an acceptable marriage prerequisite in town. These expectations were virtually the same as those for male youth in rural areas who had at least some postprimary education. Very few single male youth in Kigali expected to marry. Many said that the marriage requirement for them was simple: to be the provider of a stable income. But not many in the research sample had achieved that. Lacking this prerequisite, urban male youth viewed marriage as out of the question or, even if it might occur, some expressed concern about being disrespected and abandoned by a wife when the husband's money runs out. A good wife was commonly defined as a woman "who can accept living with me even in poverty and not leave me when there's no food," as a destitute male youth of twenty-three stated. Yet few expressed any realistic expectation that such women were available in town, which is illustrated by the following comment from one male youth: "I don't think that any woman would marry a poor guy like me." Several male youth said that they would marry any woman who would accept them. The lack of a stable income in a prospective marriage might also yield a situation where male youth would be unable to exert the sort of masculine power that, in Rwandan culture, is a husband's right. As a nineteen-year-old destitute male youth commented, "I don't think I'm ever going to marry. Life is so hard for me, so why bring a wife home? She won't respect me when there is no food on her plate. And I won't even be able to beat her up because these days women have the power. You touch them and they go to the police. So, no thanks. I'm okay like this. I don't need more trouble."

Many urban female youth expressed a fear of domestic violence, although none reported to us that they had ever taken a complaint to the police. Most female youth in the research sample were single, and most who were single sought a husband who could provide either respect or financial stability (or both). As with their rural counterparts, most single urban female youth suggested that marriage was possible. In response to the question, "How do you choose whom to marry?" (question 12 in box 2.3) most female youth focused on the qualities they sought in a potential husband. Overall, less than half of all urban respondents to this question (twenty-five of fifty-three, or 47 percent) included mentioned love, God, beauty, shared values, and character as appropriate qualities in a potential spouse. Some of their statements were touching. "Of course, nobody wants an ugly wife," a destitute male youth of twenty-four declared, "but she has to be beautiful inside first. That's the most important thing." Nonetheless, nearly all of the responses citing such qualities also referred to the issue weighing on most urban youth lives: the struggle to find money and somehow press ahead. Slightly more than half of the respondents (twenty-eight of fifty-three, or 53 percent) emphasized the economic requirements of marriage in some way (getting enough money to marry; marrying anyone who would accept to marry them, given their bad economic situation; not thinking about marriage because no one would marry them). Many male youth in Kigali, like their rural counterparts, were concerned that they would never become eligible for marriage.

Yet urban life appeared to provide many male youth with at least one comparative advantage. The pressure to build a house and get married, which weighed so heavily on rural male youth, rarely surfaced during interviews with their urban counterparts. Young men in cities may face exceedingly limited marriage prospects. But at least the pressure to attain social definitions of success eased significantly. This was underscored by a comment from a destitute adult male of thirty-eight, who explained that he had migrated to the city because "it had become too embarrassing to still be single" in his rural home. The man explained that he "couldn't afford to get married" either in his village or in town. But at least in Kigali, he added, "I don't feel embarrassed."

For some male youth, failure to create a stable life in town may lead to a forced return to one's rural home. It was not clear how often this took place: some urban youth said that they never returned to rural areas—even for brief visits. Others might return, but it appeared to be as an admission of failure. As an eighteen-year-old male youth said: "You can't imagine how difficult it is for us here! Kigali is so tough. Only the strong people survive here. Those who aren't strong, they return to their villages." When the youth was asked what happened to male youth who have to return to their home village, he replied, "Villagers make fun of them. They ask them: where is your bicycle? You couldn't even buy a bicycle? Can you build a house now? So returning home is hard, too. One needs to be prepared before going back there. You need to have money." Comments such as this suggest that returning to rural communities also meant returning to the pressures of becoming men, a situation that male youth hoped to escape when they migrated to Kigali. Fear of being shamed or humiliated if a youth returned to his family home with little or no money regularly surfaced in interviews with male youth. The sense of entrapment in a hard city life was palpable in some male youth accounts, and if many could not see when return to rural life was possible, others seemed to accept their fate as urban residents. One male youth, who was single and destitute, acidly summed up his plight in the following way: "Look at me, I've got nothing. I was twenty-four years old when I left Byumba [32 miles north of Kigali]. It wasn't easy to live there as a single person, with no wife, so I came to Kigali and started working in construction. If I ever get children, I'll tell them never to leave the countryside. If they even mention Kigali, I'll beat them. My advice to people in the countryside is to stay and live there, even if I won't ever return." Summing up prospects for the future, he concluded, "Look, I'm thirty years old now. They say the best is yet to come, but prices are going up. I don't think things will get better."

Although migration to Kigali may have promised respite from social expectations that pervade rural Rwandan communities, it consistently failed to provide this. In town, most youth described lives as individuals, perhaps alongside a few peers, striving for stability. Within this milieu of everyday struggle, few youth we interviewed expressed realistic plans to marry. It was female youth who appeared to suffer disproportionately from this situation. While poor male youth in Kigali had largely shed social pressures to become men, and have a comparatively free, if highly unstable, life in town, the modicum of security that life in one's rural family home afforded single female youth did not exist in the big city. Male youth may have had no better chance of getting married and becoming men in Kigali than in rural areas (in fact, it appears to be worse). But the quest for cash was generally easier for male than female youth, who had few options beyond prostitution.

In this sense, many urban female youth were heavily dependent on male youth and men for survival (such as through prostitution), and to a degree extending far beyond their female youth counterparts in rural Rwanda. The

On a Kigali side street, a male youth insists on a portrait to demonstrate his urban cool. The youth on the far right wears the apron that allows him to sell mobile phone cards on the street without harassment from the authorities. Selling phone cards is one of a tiny handful of street-vending activities that the government permits.

In a peri-urban community of girls and female youth, and their young children, two female youth take time out from cooking and washing clothes to rest in the shade.

inability of many male youth to marry appeared to lead female youth directly toward prostitution and away from informal marriage, or mere cohabitation. Prostitution, evidently, was the primary, and perhaps the only, way in which a great many young men and women in town had sexual relations. Ultimately, as illuminated by the following comment from a destitute male youth, what most male and female youth mainly share in Kigali is fatalism: "When I want sex and you say it costs 500 [francs, or $0.92], I couldn't pass it by. So it's up to you to protect yourself. For me, I want what I need and I don't care about you being pregnant or not. I take the risk of you infecting me [with AIDS] and your risk is getting pregnant." Amid a shared sense of doom and finality, and the evaporation of marriage and adulthood as obtainable goals, the primacy of economic desperation surfaced again and again during interviews with Rwanda's urban youth. A young man with 500 francs will most probably visit a prostitute. The young woman will inevitably receive him. For many, the persistent need for cash and food transformed the AIDS threat into a mere dimension of Hobbesian living. Kigali contains a mammoth youth underclass.

In the end, AIDS is part of a landscape so daunting that many youth—rural as well as urban—assume a philosophy of profound resignation. The collective evidence from urban and rural youth delineates an approach to life that goes beyond the mere acceptance of one's fate and strategies for avoiding risk. Hope does not seem to be a part, or much of a part, of life's quotient for too many youth. Certainly the approach to AIDS as described in this chapter suggests this. But philosophical commentary from urban and rural youth underscore it. One after another, rural and urban youth shared an approach to life in which expectations for advancement had no place. "You may ask a girl why she's a prostitute," a young man in Kigali explained, "and her answer will be that she'd rather die from AIDS than hunger." Since hunger haunts so many urban youth lives (and, one might surmise, pleasures are so few), he asked, "where's the advantage of not being infected?"

Similar sentiments were found among many other urban youth in the sample, as well as among rural youth. Faced with the inability to marry, a male youth from rural Rwanda predicted his future with the following statement: "You stay at your parent's house until you get old and die." Without outside support, a female youth from the countryside commented that "moving up" in society isn't possible unless you get support. If you do not, "nothing will be done to improve your situation." The gathered view strongly connects to a finding that Uvin provided about pregenocide Rwanda: "long before the

1990s, life in Rwanda had become devoid of hope and dreams for a large majority of people: the future looked worse than the already bad present" (1998: 117). Despite Rwanda's renowned advances, the lack of hope among today's generation of Rwandan youth suggests that little seems to have changed. For most, the same bottom line persists: things are getting worse.

Perhaps the final sentiment emerging from such a longstanding approach to living is less about punishing everyday circumstances or diminished expectations. Another way to read the acceptance of life's considerable limitations is that most youth make do. They endure.

PART FOUR

Visions and Realities

RWANDA AND BEYOND

When you don't have a house, you become a problem
for your parents and for your community. People start
talking badly about you and you get frustrated, even
humiliated. When you don't build a house, you end up in
the city to escape this humiliation and frustration.

Male youth, age nineteen

CHAPTER NINE

Stuck Youth

Rwanda faces the imminent prospect of producing almost an entire generation
of failed adults. Many are stuck, struggling to become adults but unable to
gain acceptance as one. The potential outcomes of this situation are alarming.
There were strikingly high levels of frustration and anxiety affecting nearly
all of the male youth the research team interviewed in rural Rwanda. They
were unable to construct a house, a reality that no government official we interviewed in rural Rwanda denied. The fact was obvious to the officials. Their
challenge, it appeared, lay in attempting to report the dire housing situation
to their superiors at the district and national levels and then devise adequate
responses to it. *Imidugudu* villagization is the emphatic policy of the land,
however, and questioning it, or being seen to question it, did not seem to be a
viable option for low- and midlevel officials. Doing so runs the risk of being
seen as unpatriotic, which could invite disastrous personal consequences. In
this way, government officials are stuck, too.

Without a house of their own, male youth have no chance of obtaining
the other prerequisites of adulthood: securing a socially acceptable marriage,
having children in that marriage, and supporting their family. Male youth
unable to achieve manhood must endure the hardship of public humiliation,
of being seen as a "failed" man. One of the most tragic aspects of Rwanda's
youth situation is that so many male youth drop out of primary school and
work for others to create some savings with which to build a house. Yet many
reported that they follow this path while knowing they may never complete
their house. They continue because they "have no choice" but to keep trying.

The incapacity of so many male youth to marry crushes most female youth, too, since without a proper marriage, most have no chance of gaining social acceptance as adult women. The vicelike grip of time presses them more tightly then their male youth counterparts: as I've already noted, no one can legally marry in Rwanda before the age of twenty-one. The government has made sure that the controversial but timeworn outlet for unmarried women, polygamy, is not only outlawed but vigorously repressed.[1] By age twenty-four or twenty-five, an unmarried female youth may have to face the prospect of never getting married and consequently living life, essentially, as a social outlier, a family embarrassment, and a drain on her parents' resources.

The presence of a higher percentage of women in Rwanda's parliament than in any other nation, and the government's determined efforts to represent and respond to the concerns of women, has yet to alter these fundamental realities. One reason is that the government's primary gender focus is on more senior women. "'Gender' means women," a Kigali City Council official explained. Regarding the representation of female youth, he continued, "you find that women structures are for older women, while female youth are in youth structures." Yet in all of the rural and urban sectors that the research team visited, female youth were underrepresented in the primary government structure for youth (local-level NYCs) as well as in the main government-supported youth structure (youth associations). Educated male youth dominated both. Female youth appear to lack adequate representation in government and nongovernment organizations for both women and youth.[2]

The situation facing the poorest female youth constitutes a high-risk emergency. An illustration of the dire situation of poor urban female youth arose in the Kigali research sample. Though the sample was small, prostitution was the most common poor female youth occupation. Conditions facing many urban female youth were not only serious in terms of livelihoods and health, they also raised human rights issues. This was highlighted by comments from prostitutes that they refrained from reporting sexual abuse because prostitution is illegal and they could be arrested or have their allegations ignored. Among the results of the dire female youth situation are illegitimate children, urban migration, and an apparent spread of the HIV/AIDS virus.

A tumble of consequences that stem, in large part, from the inability of most male youth in rural Rwanda to build houses extends beyond the housing crisis in the countryside and emergency conditions afflicting poor female youth. They are summarized in this chapter. In addition, the section titled A Regulated Life: One Exception describes one exceptional case where the situation for rural youth was far less stressful. This is followed by an analysis of Rwanda's current situation in light of the book's findings, an examination of the contrast between the circumstances and outlooks of Burundian and Rwandan youth, and, finally, recommendations for Rwanda and for youth work in postconflict and development contexts generally.

Urban Destitution

Failed adulthood is fueling Rwanda's rapid urbanization. The research data yielded persuasive evidence that calamitous housing, social and economic conditions in rural locations, and an interest in avoiding being labeled a failure compel some rural youth to "escape" to Kigali, which is by far the main urban migration target. One especially troubling urban migrant profile was male youth who entered secondary school and failed either to finish or to find employment afterward. It was widely reported that such youth flee to the capital to leave behind especially humiliating social conditions in their rural communities. Yet Kigali provided most youth with unpalatable options, too.

The concept of fleeing or escaping to Kigali invites a sense of rural youth as refugees in their own country. The case of rural youth flight in Rwanda, in fact, creates an illuminating contrast to general rural–urban migration trends in Africa in at least two ways. In other countries, the "pull" of urban attractions helps motivate rural youth to shift to cities. Mats Utas dramatized this tendency in his depiction of modern and traditional worlds in Liberia:

> To most Liberians, modernity is what comes from overseas and predominantly takes the form of commodities (technology, clothes, etc.), communications, the western form of education, the world religions such as Christianity and to some extent Islam. Modernity comes in the guise of consumption. . . . Tradition on the other hand is what is locally produced, whether it comes in the form of commodities, or of ideas. Traditions also occupy a space largely dominated by elders, thus youth, contesting the powers of elders, are prone to seek status in the modernities. (2003: 44)

In Liberia and elsewhere in Africa, the traditional world mainly continues in rural areas while modernity thrives in cities. Cities are the location for all things modern: the Internet, traffic jams, big buildings, and the latest videos, music, slang, and fashions. Cities can be a proving ground for male youth, allowing the successful ones to demonstrate their manhood when they return to their rural homes with money in the pockets (Sommers 2001a, 2009). Suddenly, marriage and manhood are possibilities.

Not so in Rwanda, where our youth respondents rarely mentioned these options. For them, the push-pull dichotomy so common in urban migration studies is virtually bereft of any kind of "pull."[3] Rural and urban youth in Rwanda scarcely ever mentioned the wonders of city life and its various attractions. Instead, Kigali was risky and dangerous. Since Kigali was a place where people went and never came back from, it was mainly a destination for the desperate, not the curious. Moreover, this book's hypothesis that a youth's location in the countryside would influence urban migration trends was found to be false. For rural youth, the decision to migrate to the capital was not influenced by whether they lived in a remote rural area or one that was accessible to a main road (where logistically it would be easier to get to Kigali). Dropping out of secondary school and failing to achieve adulthood influenced youth decisions to migrate to Kigali. Their location in the countryside did not.

In a striking contrast to Utas's depiction of Liberian youth, there was no evidence in our research that Rwandan youth are contesting the power of elders, who help define what manhood and womanhood are. Youth resistance in the countryside was plainly evident and it ran counter to the controlling tendencies of the government: not attending an *umuganda* activity, a NYC meeting, or a *gacaca* session by claiming that they didn't hear about it, for example. Since this was so common, one can wonder whether a poor female or male youth living in the bottom of a valley was indeed missed if they didn't show up. Sidestepping housing regulations, such as seeking permission to expand the outdoor kitchen but actually creating a tiny living quarter for a son and his new wife, was not uncommon. Yet resistance against cultural mandates in rural Rwanda appeared to be rare. Youth are mainly pushed to the capital to escape culturally defined failure in their rural homes. They do not challenge it.

A second difference in urban migration patterns in Rwanda from broader African trends is that so few urban youth ever return to their rural homes, even for short visits. This appeared to be particularly the case for those who had nothing to show for their urban exodus—no regular job, no bicycle, no savings. There was a strong sense that the rural-based families of single female youth with children may not welcome them back home. Male youth with no evidence of success or progress as urban youth were also uncomfortable returning home. Nonetheless, in a country as small as Rwanda, where a youth's rural home might be within 100 or 200 kilometers of Kigali (or even closer), this was a surprising finding. During field research with youth living in other African capital cities, for example, it was common to learn of their plans to return home for a holiday.[4] Cris Beauchemin and Philippe Bocquier, moreover, note that "in most African countries, migrants still maintain close relations with their birth village even from a distance: they return to visit; they invest in housing, social activities, education and health amenities; they send money and sometimes receive goods or host visiting relatives" (Vidal 1991, cited in Beauchemin and Bocquier 2003: 10). We did not find these trends in Rwanda.

Findings for this research strongly suggest that large numbers of youth in Kigali endure desperate, extreme poverty and social isolation. Hunger appeared to be endemic, employment was sporadic for a great many youth, and connections or networks with those who might assist them were weak or nonexistent. Many poor youth who manage to make money also have difficulty saving it. The government's solution for this and many other urban youth problems was to urge youth to join an association (association members can open bank accounts and invest their savings together). But as for most rural youth, joining an association was a nonstarter, since it cost money, exposed youth to exploitation by association leaders, and was not at all their priority. The difficulties of saving money remained.

Underneath all of this, for a great many urban youth, was a persistent belief that whatever money or success they managed to obtain was entirely tenuous. Most believed that there was little they could do to improve their situation. Fear of bottoming out and becoming an *inzererezi* or a prostitute seemed to haunt many. The moral coloring of male and female youth, so common in big African cities (and beyond), that labels poor male youth as thieves and poor female youth as prostitutes is commonplace in Kigali. Such moral concerns are reflected in the names of two of Kigali's biggest hip-hop groups (circa 2007–8), Bad Boys and Good Guy, as well as one of the most popular foreign hip-hoppers: Tanzania's Mr. Nice.

Similar to government efforts in other African countries to repatriate urban youth to rural areas, some officials, youth, and adults in Kigali mentioned government efforts to corral and shift urban youth to rural areas. But as in countries such as Tanzania (where Nyerere's Nguvu Kazi, which began in 1983, was a famous and expensive flop), youth forced back to rural areas nonetheless return to the capital.[5] In addition, most poor youth in Kigali were found to be living in inadequate or no housing. There is a serious housing crisis in Kigali, too.

Hopeless Youth, Desperation Theft, and the Rise of AIDS

Do male and female youth in Rwanda pose a major risk to renewed fighting and conflict? The short answer is no: the interviews surfaced only one direct comment on this issue. Yet the scenario that one poor male urban youth of twenty-eight detailed is well worth considering, given the sense of entrapment and hopelessness that surrounded so many urban youth:

> This situation is very dangerous. Imagine a city with a hundred thousand hopeless youth. This is a hundred thousand kamikazes. If one comes and tells them [to do] bad things, they would agree. If one gives them weapons, what would they do?
>
> Look, those fellows who were saying that even if they were called in the bush, they would go—do you think they were joking? Others are struggling to get demobilized, but they think the battlefield is better than this life. This is serious for a country that could have enemies, either inside or outside. It can be easier for them to recruit from these hopeless youth around.

The term *urubyiruko rwihebye* (hopeless youth), which is used commonly in Kigali, is also a disquieting one. The evidence suggests that the extreme desperation of such youth in Kigali, including former combatants, make them vulnerable to manipulation and exploitation.

Certainly the fact that so many youth feel trapped in a life of looming failure is hardly a recipe for stable peace. Yet research for this book found no evidence of armed gangs or organized crime outfits operating in either urban or rural Rwanda. Nearly all of the crimes that the research team learned about concerned "desperation theft"—theft by people trying to survive. Remarkably, most youth and adults expressed empathy toward the thieves—even for those who robbed them. Robbers steal roof tiles, crops, and livestock in rural areas. Incomplete and uninhabited houses make easy targets. As noted in chapter 5, reports of theft were regular aspects of rural life descriptions, with one cell-level government official blaming primarily male youth, whose strength would be necessary both to steal the kinds of goods taken and to transport the stolen goods for sale. Despite the regularity of such theft, however, as earlier discussed, few officials, adults, and youth believed that their situation was insecure. As noted, nearly half (45 percent) of seventy-eight rural respondents to the question "Can you tell me about the security situation here?" reported that the security situation in their communities was under control, while another 27 percent of respondents agreed that the situation was essentially fine, with the exception of crimes relating to poverty. Thieves in rural Rwanda, in short, were thought to limit what they did, stealing to survive but not much more.

Much of the crime in Kigali followed a similar pattern. Thieves robbed people of money and food but rarely entered people's homes to rob them. However, definitions of crime were broader in Kigali. Many residents lived by illegally trading goods without a permit, which regularly exposed them to harassment and abuse from the LDF and policemen. A frequently unreported serious violent crime in Kigali, according to those whom we interviewed, was the rape of prostitutes. They are exceptionally vulnerable to being raped because of the apparent impunity of perpetrators. Night patrols were among those whom prostitutes identified as rapists. Despite the stigma attached to prostitution, and the fact that it is against the law, it appeared that raping prostitutes is disturbingly commonplace. Prostitutes risk arrest if they report a rape. And so, evidently, they don't.

The challenges facing prostitutes and other poor female youth in Rwanda are serious and have been, for the most part, overlooked by government and nongovernment officials.[6] Part of the explanation for this may be that both government and nongovernment officials have their hands full with other pressing gender concerns, such as the needs of substantial numbers of Rwandan widows following the civil war and genocide of 1990–94.[7] That said, most poor female youth lack recognition, support, and protection, as young women and as youth. If they are prostitutes, prospects for their present and future appear exceptionally grim.

Among the most serious problems facing female and male youth is the likelihood that they will be exposed to HIV/AIDS. Research for this book indicates that the rate of HIV/AIDS prevalence in the Rwandan population may be substantially higher—particularly in Kigali—than what was reported in the 2005 national survey (3 percent in the nation and 3.4 percent for youth in Kigali; Institut National de la Statistique and ORC Macro 2006: xxix). The likelihood that prevalence rates are higher than those which the 2005 survey states is supported by apparent weaknesses in the survey methodology (noted in chapter 1), which appears to significantly if not severely limit the inclusion of youth from survey participation. In a nation with such a profoundly youthful population, where so many youth endure truly difficult social and economic conditions, and where HIV/AIDS carries with it a punishing stigma, aligning the methods of this sort of survey with the ways in which most youth live is essential. This, however, does not seem to have occurred. In addition, there was limited evidence in all of the areas we visited that current approaches to HIV/AIDS control and awareness were making inroads with poor youth.

Male youth with little hope of becoming men, female youth trapped in prostitution, and the grinding lives that so many youth lead do not inspire cautious sexual behavior. Notwithstanding their knowledge of the dangers of unprotected sex, poor urban youth were disturbingly fatalistic about acquiring the HIV/AIDS virus, and stigma against the infected was so strong that avoidance of testing among Rwanda's poor majority appears to be widespread. Some prostitutes in Kigali reported that they had entered this line of work because they had contracted AIDS and had no other means of survival. In rural areas, some unmarried female youth also fall into the sort of transactional sex where condom use is unlikely. The general desperation of so many rural and urban youth is expressed both through their empathy for youth who steal to survive and by passively exposing themselves to a deadly virus.

Youth Agency in Rwanda

One of the most striking findings arising from this research was how little most youth expected from life. In rural areas, housing and marriage were dominant themes. In urban areas, it was survival. Indeed, many urban youth we interviewed stated that they were hungry during the interview sessions. In both locations, plans for the future mainly emphasized stability over advancement. This reflects the general perspective of poor youth, who see few opportunities for moving ahead and real possibilities of falling further behind. It was an illuminating indication of how few development opportunities are available to most youth in Rwanda.

The low expectations of poor Rwandan youth might be seen as an expression of the risk averse strategies that many poor youth and adults practiced. While many government officials characterized risk-averse practices as signs of backwardness and resistance to development, it was a common approach to garnering a reasonably secure, if limited, profit. Rural youth who became urban migrants were, by comparison to most of their counterparts, forced to become risk-takers. They migrated mainly because they lacked viable options.

The combination of Rwandan youth qualities that surfaced in this research—low expectations and risk aversion as well as muted resistance—generates a complex kind of agency for the poor Rwandan youth majority. To begin with, although "agency is intrinsically connected to power" (Honwana 2005: 48), unforgiving adulthood mandates, and a belief that upward movement in society was unlikely, forced the agency of Rwanda's poor youth majority to operate within narrow parameters. Indeed, their quest for adulthood largely entailed what Begoña Aretxaga considers a "choiceless decision" (1997: 61). To be sure, the situation is not nearly as extreme as it was for many female abductees of Sierra Leonean rebel outfits during the civil war. In that case, female youth had to choose "between becoming a fighter/lover or dying, which is not really much of a choice, more of a matter of bare survival" (Coulter 2009: 150). For poor youth in rural Rwanda, the issue was not survival but avoiding a life of public failure. A poor male youth might remain in his rural home and continue trying to build a house and marry against substantial odds. A poor female youth might remain in rural Rwanda and hope to marry. For some of them, urban migration became a choiceless decision: "escaping" to Kigali sidestepped the prospect of social humiliation in the countryside, even if it was a risky, even terrifying, option.

Despite the dire straits and limited options that so many Rwandan youth face, the expression and enactment of Rwandan youth agency toward government expectations and mandates are a separate concern. Research for this book made it entirely clear that many if not most poor youth quietly resist a great deal of what their government wanted them to do: join associations, attend youth meetings, participate in all *umuganda* activities, avoid working in the informal sector, build houses exclusively on the *imidugudu*, and so on. Jean Comaroff and John Comaroff assert that such actions are part of "the present moment," which has featured "a diminishing of the capacity of governments … to control adolescent bodies, energies, or intentions" (2005: 22). Yet in light of an exacting government whose presence in everyday life was a virtual constant, the Rwandan youth case is, in its way, conspicuous. While some elite Rwandan youth might very well have the ability to express their agency more openly and forcefully, such as finding new ways to gain recognition as adult men and women, Rwanda's poor youth majority have chosen, as much as possible, a fairly imperceptible approach to expressing and enacting their agency. For them, evidently, there's nothing to be gained by being brazen in the face of cultural conservatism and government directives. Stealth worked better.

In the end, members of the poor majority of Rwandan youth exert a combination of what Alcinda Honwana calls tactical and strategic agency. Tactical agency is a kind of coping strategy for people who "have no power base" and "act within the confines of a 'foreign' territory" (Honwana 2005: 49). It is also a concept that Utas sums up as "the art of the weak" (Utas 2005b: 75). In contrast, strategic agency "would imply a basis of power" and "mastery of the larger picture, of the long-term consequences of their actions, in the form of political gain or benefits/profits" (Honwana 2005: 50). Certainly, most Rwandan youth enact a form of tactical agency in the face of adulthood requirements and the option of migrating to Kigali. But their collective response to government directives contains a measure of strategic agency. Regularly and routinely resisting or avoiding the orders and directions of the authorities implies a degree of security, even power, that interprets the role of youth in Rwandan society as active and engaged, albeit mostly on the margins. In a place where government has historically cast a long shadow, Rwandan youth demonstrate agency, in part, through hushed counteraction.

A Question of Masculinity

There was no evidence in the research data of young Rwandans creating alternative paths to adulthood by challenging traditional and government-led definitions. It is likely that such paths are well underway in Rwanda, but mainly among elite youth, whose lives take place in a significantly different context than the poor youth majority. Indeed, the research suggests that elite and poor youth are living lives that are largely parallel and separate from each other. The inability of NYC activities to attract many poor youth is an indication of the degree of suspicion and resistance that the poor youth majority hold for educated, elite youth.

Helping male youth build houses as a means of helping male and female youth become adults both underscores the interdependent nature of male and female identities and represents a departure from mainstream gender work. The lion's share of gender work has long been equated with empowering women through direct assistance. Speaking of Africa, Gary Barker and Christine Ricardo, for example, state that "gender is increasingly used as a framework for analysis and for youth program development in the Africa region. In most cases, gender refers specifically and often exclusively to the disadvantages faced by women and girls; given the extent of gender inequalities in the region, this focus has been necessary. However, a gender perspective and gender mainstreaming have too often ignored the gender of men and boys" (2006: 159). Research on masculinity, such as is contained in this book, provides a basis for revisiting and complementing the pronounced tendency to emphasize the needs of girls and women in the theory and practice of gender development. This is an issue that is subject to considerable debate. On one hand, "the concern that women will disappear from development work once the floodgates are opened to men is prevalent among many providers" (Chant and Gutmann 2002: 279). On the other hand, Sarah White is among those who warn that "if women's empowerment is to be sustained, it must be complemented by a change for men" (White 1997: 20). Andrea Cornwall adds that "working with men as human beings, rather than constructing them as 'the problem'" promises to "have a wider impact on the institutional changes that are needed for greater equity" (1997: 12). However, following through on this complementary objective remains difficult since "the study of men and masculinities in both academic and development settings is in its true infancy" (Chant and Gutmann 2002: 279).

Field research for this book sheds additional light on the sculpting power of masculinity. It is a testament to Gary Barker's assertion that three characteristics reach across cultures to define "what it means to be a man." There is "a cultural mandate to prove yourself, and define which kind of man you are, and to do so in a public way" (2005: 20). In Rwanda, the starting point for normative manhood is a male youth's house. Does he even have one? If so, what kind of roof does it have? Is it finished? Will he ever finish it? If he attempts to build it on his family land and not on an *umudugudu*, will the government order it to be destroyed? Will he *ever* succeed in becoming a real man? If he fails, will he escape to Kigali and never return? A male youth in rural Rwanda must try to build a house because doing so is culturally mandated (yet is seriously complicated by government regulation). The way in which a male youth gains manhood (or not) is easily measured, and it is an entirely public struggle. Watching a male youth succeed or fail to become a man is a shared social experience.

It is in this sense that the theory (or concept) of hegemonic masculinity fits Rwanda's youth situation like a glove. Maria Correia and Ian Bannon state that hegemonic masculinity is "a dominant form of masculinity across societies and cultures" that "is commonly the basis by which men are judged and assess themselves" (2006: 245). For many men, they add, "particularly low-income and poor men, there is a huge gap between this dominant model and the reality of what they can achieve. Due to a range of factors, including chronic poverty, inequality and exclusion, declining economic conditions, and conflict, men are unable to fulfill these external and internalized expectations of what it is 'to be a man'" (245–46). Crucially, avoiding the prospect of failure is not an option: "Even in the face of difficult social and economic circumstances, men cannot afford not to try to live up to the expectations of being a man" (Dolan 2003; cited in Correia and Bannon 2006: 249). Working toward manhood in rural Rwanda is a kind of trap from which it is difficult to escape. Caught by cultural demands and expectations as well as constricting government regulations, too often working on family land that is decreasing in fertility and size over time while economic inequalities are on the rise, all in a postgenocide environment that remains tense, male youth are being squeezed and pressured. What might take place is unclear, and what happens to male youth in similar situations is debated. Correia and Bannon, for example, speculate that male youth lacking options beyond enforced and public failure may lead some of them "to seek other ways of asserting their masculinity, including resorting to illicit and criminal behavior to earn income and status or taking out their frustration and anger through the use of violence, alcohol and substance abuse, and suicide" (249).

On the other hand, Uvin decries "an excessive miserability in much of the masculinity literature." Regarding the issue of violence, he does not deny that men marked by failure will "take it out on others (or themselves)." However, he argues that "the overwhelming majority of men do not turn violent. Faced with stunning constraints, they seek different ways to survive, to innovate, to find respect. . . . In its relentless focus on violent behavior and its almost automatic association between young men and violence, the literature has—mostly unintentionally—created a picture that does injustice to the dignity of men" (2009: 182). Postgenocide Rwanda, with its new opening of an escape hatch from rural Rwanda to Kigali, finds a situation that draws from both sides of this debate. Alcohol abuse is one option available to young men burdened with the prospect of failed manhood. Visiting prostitutes appears to be another important option for male youth who are unable to marry. Domestic violence and substance abuse are certainly available possibilities (the research team, for example, did receive reports of marijuana use among some urban male youth). What is significant, however, is that substantial numbers of male and female youth are heading from rural areas into cities (mainly Kigali) and largely finding exceedingly difficult circumstances upon arrival. And while our researchers did not receive reports of suicide, that does not mean that it does not occur. In addition, the fatalism that so many urban youth related could be construed as a kind of passive suicide. As for crime and violence, suggestions of rape were manifest in interviews with poor female youth in Kigali and constitutes an ignored and potentially terrifying trend. With the significant exception of sexual violence, much urban and rural crime appears to be self-contained: desperation theft and not much more.

Social Distance and the Government Response

Near the end of one interview, a district mayor commented that the research approach for this book was new for Rwanda. The research team members, he said, were "the first to talk to youth who are not in school." The mayor added that the team was "the first to do research on what youth not in school think of those in school." His comments underscore the significance of a primary dividing line in Rwandan society—between those not in school (meaning "uneducated youth," or those who never went beyond primary school in their studies) and those in school (meaning "educated youth," or those who have had at least some secondary education). He also brings to light how out-of-school, "uneducated" youth perceive of the comparatively tiny "educated" youth minority. One wonders whether the mayor mentioned the latter issue out of a concern over what the huge, uneducated majority really thinks of Rwanda's powerful, educated elite.

Although this book examines the situation and perceptions of the vast, poorly educated youth majority, class difference and pronounced inequalities were recurring themes in the narrative. They are present in the story of the educated man who swindled land from a community association and drew protection and favor from government officials, in perceptions of acute social verticality in rural Rwanda and pronounced social isolation among poor youth in urban Rwanda. The separation between those with education and the rest was also highlighted by how most youth view those with education: as the truly fortunate, able to achieve a level of recognition and success that poor youth, in their view, will never attain.

Perceptions of difference in Rwanda are evolving and seem to be sharpening. A report from the National University of Rwanda in the southern town of Butare highlighted how ethnic difference remains potent even as it is illegal to mention it. The "imposed silence" means only that ethnic Hutu and Tutsi students never openly talk about "the one thing always on their minds: each other" (Kron 2010a). The government's hope, as the justice minister, Tharcisse Karugarama, explained, is to "give it ten or twenty years" until you have "a new crop of Rwandans" who don't identify themselves as Hutu or Tutsi (Childress 2010). One challenge is that, at the moment, power in Rwanda mainly lies in the hands of a particular segment of the ethnic minority. Rwandans, as ever, speak in code about things that are too dangerous to state publicly. In this case, students mention their pronounced social separation according to "linguistic lines," which "is code for ethnic groups that dare not speak their names." Accordingly, "'French speakers' means Hutu and 'English speakers' means Tutsi, specifically those who returned from refugee life in English-speaking Uganda after 1994 and now run the country" (Kron 2010a). It is possible that many other ethnic Tutsi belong to the "French speaker" category alongside Hutu, since Tutsi genocide survivors also grew up in Francophone Rwanda, not Anglophone Uganda. Not mentioned here are the ethnic Twa, a small ethnic minority in Central Africa that historically has had a kind of outcast status in the region. "Now they're called potters," a veteran international agency official in Kigali said.

Research for this book indicated that most youth seek assistance from their government. Assisting youth is also a government priority. Indeed, government officials in rural and urban areas demonstrated a firm grasp of a number of critical issues involving the nation's poor youth majority and confirmed the presence and significance of every major finding in this book. The government also had promising structures and policies in place, most notably a national policy for youth, a political structure specially designed to address youth needs and represent their views, a dynamic minister of the Ministry of Youth, and a promising action plan for employing youth. Such developments put the Rwandan government ahead of most governments in the region, the Rwandan government's primary donors (including the World Bank, the U.K. Department for International Development, and the U.S. Agency for International Development) and national and international nongovernmental organizations (NGOs) working in Rwanda, who have yet to raise youth issues to a similar level of prominence. In fact, few poor youth who were interviewed reported that they were receiving support from nongovernmental organizations. When such agencies were present in visited rural and urban areas, they did not focus on youth as much as people with HIV/AIDS, orphans, and other smaller, more targeted groups.

If youth and their government both want the government to "be close" to youth, why is this not happening? Why is Rwandan government assistance to the undereducated, poor majority of youth so underwhelming and ineffective? There are at least three reasons for this state of affairs. First, the NYC, the primary government institution tasked with addressing poor youth concerns, is weak. Most NYC officials are educated but untrained volunteers. They have little or no resources and poor morale. About the only youth who attend their meetings are other educated youth. Most poor youth ignore them. NYC officials, in general, lack the tools to bridge the significant social divide. But much more than that, it is asking far too much of well-meaning but untrained young people to task them with addressing the substantial needs of the massive youth underclass.

A second reason for the current state of affairs between the Rwandan government and poor youth is that there is a communication disconnect. While many Rwandan youth are pressed by their life circumstances to address survival, housing, marriage, and adulthood issues, government decentralization reforms have created pressure on officials to meet existing objectives and goals. One result has been an emphasis on encouraging poor youth and other citizens to follow expansive government regulations. Stressing government-mandated behavior change is hardly a productive environment for cultivating open communication between government officials and members of the poor youth majority. The predominant views of poor youth that government officials reported having—that they were unproductive with their time, unwilling to collaborate or take advice, and that youth leaders represented the views of the poor youth majority—were not supported by our interviews with poor youth. Most youth strived as individuals to improve their lot, were wary of joining associations, and did not trust elite youth. Interviews with government officials further revealed a widespread belief that youth require their advice, guidance, and direction. Listening to the views of the poor youth majority was not part of the skill set of many government officials.

Third, the government established its youth development priorities without discussion with the poor youth majority. What youth seek and what the government is prepared to provide differs.[8] The predominant government solution to nearly every youth problem was to get them to join associations. Yet most poor youth consistently resisted joining or forming associations. Many distrust educated association leaders who might swindle lesser association members.[9] There was also little evidence of active, much less thriving, youth associations in any rural area the research team visited. In urban areas, associations largely took the form of trade associations, which most poor youth either could not afford to join or did not want to join. Cooperatives, a second government solution, were unfamiliar to most government officials and required a level of collateral for membership that most youth did not have. The research data indicated that *ibimina* self-help groups, which do not have government involvement, were far more popular and prevalent among poor youth than associations or cooperatives. In essence, the government wants youth to work in government-associated groups, while most youth want to work either individually or in groups of their own choosing.

Research for this book found that two government regulations were significantly impeding youth efforts to address their most pressing priorities: stabilizing their lives in Kigali and gaining adulthood in rural areas. Informal market trade in Kigali is the economic lifeline for what appears to be a vast proportion of its population. Most of those engaged in this sort of trade (including a great many youth) cannot afford to purchase government permits to sell goods legally. As a result, LDF members and policemen confiscate illegally marketed merchandise and issue fines and arrests. Yet many poor youth and adults in Kigali continue to hawk their wares on city streets illegally because they lack viable options. The virtual absence of street sellers may enhance Kigali's public appearance. But it has severe negative impacts for many if not most of its residents.

The second government regulation mandates that all new houses must be built on government-sanctioned areas known as *imidugudu*. There are three main constraints to the implementation of this policy, and they are all significant: a standard required dimension for an *imidugudu* house, which is far beyond the means of nearly all male youth; a scarcity of available *imidugudu* plots to build on; and, linked to this, difficulties in acquiring *imidugudu* plots. The regulation frustrated most of the Rwandan youth and adults we interviewed. Couples farming and living in a traditional *rugo* on their land, not an *umudugudu*, remains the preferred model of rural life. Yet since creating new households on family land is illegal and building houses on an *umudugudu* is highly unlikely, most male youth are faced with three choices. They can continue to live with their parents and save for a house that may remain beyond their reach, they can resist the *imidugudu* regulation by illegally creating a shelter for themselves and a wife on their parents' land, or they can migrate to an urban area (usually Kigali) or a large commercial farm.

The negative impact of the government's *imidugudu* regulation on rural youth is underscored by research findings in a single rural cell, where government officials took a starkly different approach to the housing needs of youth. A description of this instructive case follows.

A Regulated Life: One Exception

The youth here mind their own business. You see them trading, and you don't see them belonging to associations.
   Cell-level government official

Research for this book indicates that the situation facing most of Rwanda's rural youth is bleak. Yet one case revealed an upbeat example of positive, youth-led action. It arises from counterintuitive circumstances. The enterprising and successful youth described here resided in a remote Rwandan valley, not on a more accessible hilltop. Educational accomplishment did not correlate with success, and none of the successful youth who were interviewed had attended secondary school. Those who were successful included both male and female youth. Their tools of success were not drawn, for the most part, from the direct involvement of government personnel, policies or investments. The elements of success that I examine here, in other words, arise from the sort of location, social background, and connections—youth in a remote location, with low education accomplishment, and with limited or indirect government or nongovernment support—that evoke struggle and failure, not confidence and success.

Some of the youth living in the valley were those who "do their own thing," a government official from their cell commented. As a result, "it's difficult for them to rely on youth leaders" to find a way forward. Instead, they are independent. Many male youth work as "very small scale traders," he explained. This is the sort of work that "can't be done with others," he continued. A twenty-eight-year-old male youth illustrated how a youth just might "do his own thing" and succeed: "Youth without houses don't have plans. What I did was to think about my situation, make my plan, and then save my money. Everything that I save is for building my house. I dig for other people for 300 francs [$0.55] a day, and save 200 francs each day. I sell cigars. I also trade beans. Beans are harvested in December and January. So I buy them then [when the price is low] and then store them until September, when I sell them [when the price is higher]. How do you succeed? You use your head." The verve to trade meant that some male youth saved to get bicycles before saving for roof tiles. This youth also described the benefits of owning a bike: "having a bicycle makes you mobile, so you can go far away and buy things at a cheaper price and then sell them somewhere else for much more." A local government official explained that the youth traders use bikes to buy and sell beer, sodas, and beans. Established traders also hired them to transport goods.

The community in this valley had a longstanding trading tradition. Many older men were traders, and some mentored male youth. As a government official explained, "this cell has a long tradition of trading. [Male] youth and adults are always storing harvests at home, so whenever there's food shortage somewhere, they're ready to sell." Unlike all other areas that the research team visited, most youth in this cell had plans for success. Many male youth believed that they would eventually build their own house and get married. And while success through trading was an established method for advancement, it was not the only one, as a twenty-one-year-old male youth explained: "In our area, you base your plan on digging to generate a surplus. Then you put the surplus in a bank and get a loan. After that, you build a house with that loan, because it's what all youth are aiming for. You also buy a farm animal. Once you've bought a house and an animal, the next step is to look for a wife. Then, after you're married, your loan has taken a bit of a beating. So you have to make an extra effort to buy and store your crops to repay your loan and continue moving up." Repaying one's loan after getting married was part of the youth's plan, he said, because "when there are two of you digging, you have more determination and force."

A female youth who was interviewed displayed a similar level of confidence and vigor. Twenty years old and the eldest of eight children, she had left school in her fourth year of primary school. Then she went to work. She is a member of an *ibimina* savings association (most youth in her cell, she said, were also *ibimina* members), and two farming associations: one for women, the other for members of her Pentecostal church.[10] She had also rented a plot on her own and was farming it herself. She had already bought a cow for her family. Her plan, she stated, "is to get married. I'll give some of the money to my brothers and give a smaller part to my husband. He'll bring his wealth and I'll bring mine [to the marriage], and we'll share it together. We Rwandans struggle. If you aren't lucky to go to school, you dig. That's it." This last statement was expressed without bitterness or resentment. She had apparently accepted her fate and was working hard to achieve her plan.

In addition to hope, spurred mainly by unusually rich soils and local examples of success, there was possibility. This arose from a dramatically different approach to governance. Even with the relatively significant incomes that traders and other youth in the cell achieved, a government official explained that "maybe 10 percent of all youth can afford to build a house." In this way, youth life was just like any other rural Rwandan cell that the research team visited. The same could not be said for how government officials responded. Instead of holding rigidly to the *imidugudu* regulation and ordering houses under construction on family land to be knocked down (and, in one case, commanding the new wife of one young man to return to her parents because the newlyweds had done the culturally unthinkable: they had moved into the home of the young man's parents), the officials of this one remote cell relaxed. Where possible, officials sought to get male youth to build their house near a road—even if the house was not within a government *imidugudu*. Even so, most youth were still unable to build their house near a road: they didn't live near one.

The main thing that government officials in this remote Rwandan cell did about new house construction was to discuss it. They did not order a new house on a family compound to be destroyed if it was not located on an *umudugudu*. Their lone requirement was that the new house, even if it only had banana leaf roofing, had to be able to hold iron sheet roofing—just in case the owner might be able to purchase sheeting at some point. The officials could not bring themselves to knock down new houses. As one explained, "We let them do that [build houses away from roads with banana leaf roofing] even though the [government] regulation doesn't allow it. I'm not supposed to permit it, but what can I do? I can't make the mistake of destroying a house that someone has built. Destroying his house, after all the energy and resources it took to make it, is like destroying him."

Why were success stories so rare among rural youth? The valley described here did not appear to be any wealthier than other areas that we visited, although the richness of the soil may have been better. At the same time, it most certainly did not benefit from high quality education, training programs, youth associations, or infrastructural benefits such as electricity or pumped water. What it did have, however, were examples of success in its midst. Older men had already established trading as a reasonably profitable venture. There were ways to make money, and some youth—though certainly not all—had detailed, viable plans for achieving a stable future. In addition, there was evidence of fairly heavy youth involvement in *ibimina* as a way to access capital for investments.

But in addition, and significantly, youth in this one valley had government officials who took a hand's-off approach to their efforts. It seemed to work: the officials figured as key contributors to relative youth success in the valley by acting against type. Instead of being rigid and authoritative, they were empathic and supportive. The only place in Rwanda where the research team found youth advancing ahead was the only place where officials did not enforce the *imidugudu* housing regulation.

Forward and Backward

We want to be first. We will be very happy to teach all of Africa.

Rwandan provincial governor, speaking about development in Rwanda (quoted in Kinzer 2008)

The potential for future conflict [in Rwanda] rooted in class differences must not be underestimated.

Johan Pottier, "Land Reform for Peace?" 2006

President Kagame is a strong believer in African countries doing things for themselves, managing their own affairs without interference, and his approach to governing Rwanda has been based on this belief.

Colin M. Waugh, Paul Kagame and Rwanda, 2004

The hand of the state is everywhere in Rwanda, and it operates at a finger snap. Kagame has built a powerful ideological machine, complete with all the gears and levers necessary to maintain stability and re-create society.

Josh Kron, "The Country in the Mirror," 2010

There is no consensus about either Rwanda's current situation or its prospects for the future. The debate over Rwanda has only sharpened since the field research period for this book (2006–7). Rwanda's reputation as a "model of development" is, if anything, growing. "The country is increasingly seen as a development model, focused on results and eager to learn from global experience," notes an International Development Association report (2009: 1). The assessment is almost entirely positive about Rwanda's circumstances and projections of the future. The only sign of any concern comes just near the end, when the report blandly recommends that "efforts to restore trust and reconstruct the social fabric need to be expanded to prevent any deterioration in political or social outcomes" (9). That said, the World Bank ranked Rwanda as "the top reformer in Doing Business 2010, having jumped seventy-six places from 143 to 67 in the annual ranking of 183 countries, the biggest improvement ever by any country. As a result of the government's commitment to reform, it is now easier, faster and less expensive to do business in Rwanda" (World Bank n.d.).

Endorsements of the Rwandan government's approach to its challenges come from many quarters. One "abundant asset" that Rwanda has, in fact, is "well-placed friends" (Chu 2009): former heads of state (Tony Blair and Bill Clinton), evangelical pastors (Rick Warren), and corporate kingpins (Google CEO Eric Schmidt), among many, many others. Kagame's strategy, in fact, "relies on wealthy and powerful friends to lure private investment, train a new generation of managers, build a globally competitive economy, and wean the country off foreign aid" (ibid.). If this strategy works, then the government may be able to break its habit of accepting support while chiding aid donors. "Over the past few years Rwanda has acquired a reputation as one of the least corrupt, most serious and most business-friendly governments in Africa," Mauro De Lorenzo writes (2008). Citing President Kagame's intent to shift Rwanda "from an aid-based economy to a trade-based economy," De Lorenzo suggests that "Rwanda seems like a model for how Africa can go beyond aid." Near the end of his upbeat essay about Rwanda's achievements, he notes that its government is "in a sense" a minority government and says that "it is not clear that it has true majority support." De Lorenzo endorses the government's intent to control democratic freedoms and contends that the Kagame government, like China, "can only achieve legitimacy by delivering results."

While the government and its many boosters and benefactors implicitly support this position, criticism of the Rwandan government's attitude toward dissent are harsh and on the increase. As ever, "Rwandan officials are prickly about complaints," Jeffrey Gettleman observes (2010). Yet even as Rwanda "continues to be praised as a darling of the foreign aid world and something of a central African utopia," Gettleman continues, "it is increasingly intolerant of political dissent, or sometimes even dialogue, and bubbling with bottled-up tensions." In just the early months of 2010, President Kagame condemned political opposition leaders as "hooligans" while his government barred most opposition political parties from registering for national elections, attacked opposition supporters in government offices, temporarily shut down the local-language BBC radio service, witnessed the defection of several prominent government officials (who said "they feared for their lives," ibid.), jailed the leader of an opposition party, Victoire Ingabire ("on charges that include collaborating with a terrorist organization and denying the genocide" (African Union 2010: 7)), as well as her U.S. counsel, denied a visa to a Human Rights Watch researcher, shut down several independent newspapers, and assailed one of its closest allies and biggest donors, the U.S. government, "for complaining about restrictions on the media and human rights groups" (Kron and Gettleman 2010). Meanwhile, across the border in eastern DRC, a

UN Panel of Experts report found that "the illegal traffic of Congolese minerals still flows into Rwanda mostly from these violent militias that continue to profit greatly, presumably passing earnings onto their Rwandan backers" (Lasker 2010).[11] A civil society expert in the Great Lakes Region of Africa (which includes Rwanda), moreover, noted that "a large number of civil society members disappeared" in 2007 and that the Rwandan government threatened to shut down the Rwandan civil society organization that tried to trace their whereabouts (it stopped).[12] "Some of our sources say that civil society is largely run by members of the ruling party and the diaspora, and is fairly disassociated from the grassroots," the expert added.

Three shootings in June and July 2010 ratcheted up the tensions within Rwanda still higher. On June 19, Rwanda's former army chief of staff, Faustin Kayumba Nyamwasa, who had fled Rwanda in February 2010 and had become "a top critic" of President Kagame (Baldauf 2010), was shot in the belly in South Africa. South African police "were treating the attempted murder . . . as an assassination attempt" (M. Clark 2010: 2). On June 24, a Rwandan journalist, Jean Leonard Rugambage, who was investigating whether the Rwandan state was involved in Nyamwasa's shooting, was himself shot and killed. The journalist had been the acting editor of a Rwandan newspaper (*Umuvugizi*; the actual editor, Jean Bosco Gasasira, was in exile) and had "complained he was under constant surveillance." He ignored Gasasira's recommendation to flee the country (Smith 2010). *Umuvugizi* published an article online that alleged the government's complicity in Nyamwasa's shooting the day that Rugambage was shot (Peachey 2010). Then, on July 14, Andre Kagwa Rwisereka, the deputy leader of the opposition Green Party, which had been unable to register to participate in the August elections, was found dead, with his head "nearly severed." The murder "followed complaints by senior party officials of death threats, police harassment and intimidation" (ibid.). While the Rwandan government has hotly denied involvement in the two killings and the shooting in South Africa, a message nonetheless radiated from these incidents: challenging the Rwandan government is risky.

Some might attribute the Rwandan government's generally threatening stance toward dissent to preelection jitters in a postgenocide country (August 2010 marked Rwanda's first presidential election in seven years; in both elections, Kagame garnered more than 90 percent of the vote). Concerns over the legacy of a still-recent genocide are real, particularly when some of the former *génocidaires* continue to operate in eastern DRC. At the same time, it is hardly reassuring that such a thumping approach to civil discord was nonetheless met with grenade attacks in Kigali that, together with an army shake-up, "showed

that even one of the cornerstones of the new Rwandan state—personal security—might be in danger" (Gettleman 2010). Taken together, there seem
to be two ways to interpret the Rwandan government's response. Either the
government's projection of confidence and expansive power has shallow roots,
or the government is not nearly as in control of things as is widely assumed.
Neither scenario is encouraging.

Part of the country's real or imagined insecurity draws from the model of
governance it has assumed. Gérard Prunier argues that a linking theme in
Rwandan governance tradition arose from longstanding high densities of
human occupation in Rwanda that, "together with such a high capacity for
producing all the basic necessities of life in plenty, led at a very early stage to
centralised forms of political authority."This combination, in turn, resulted in
"an almost monstrous degree of social control" that successive governments
in Rwanda exercised. Writing in 1995 and arguing that that the governmental
tendency toward social control extends to the present, Prunier also states that
"this obsession with control . . . is due simply to the fact that the land is small,
the population density is (and has always been) high and social interactions are
constant, intense and value-laden" (1995: 3–4). The emphasis on social control
appears to express itself as bureaucratic logic in today's Rwanda. Not only is
it expressed by the national government, it also can be seen in the current
decentralized governance process. Lower-level government officials routinely
deploy their expanded powers by issuing new regulations and fines on citizens
in their locality.

Within this framework, there appear to be two government models that
have been particularly prevalent in Central Africa in recent decades. Both
have inspired a striving for legitimacy. When governments in either Rwanda
or Burundi are largely ruled by members of the Tutsi minority, then mention of ethnicity is outlawed and a shared national identity is emphasized.
During the pregenocide presidency of Juvénal Habyarimana, a member of
the Rwandan Hutu ethnic majority, the opposite was the case: the model of
governance emphasized its identity as an Hutu majority government. When
either model is applied, the reality is that certain ethnic segments dominate
government power. The succession of Tutsi-led governments in Burundi were
actually dominated by the Hima clan, which is found mainly in the southern
province of Bururi, while northern Hutu dominated Habyarimana's government.[13] Similarly, in Rwanda today, as noted in the quotation by Josh Kron,
it is widely believed that former Rwandan Tutsi refugees from Uganda hold
sway over both the government and the economy.[14]

The big picture, for some observers, is that Rwanda really has "democracy with constraints" that are necessary (according to a "senior Western official" in Rwanda) and that Kagame "is the one African leader who gets the basics right" (quoted in Perry 2007). However, the similarities between today's Rwanda and pregenocide Rwanda are worthy of reflection. Analogous to Rwanda's current reputation, under the pregenocide regime of Habyarimana, "Rwanda was poor, Rwanda was clean and Rwanda was serious" (Prunier 1995: 77). In addition, Joseph Sebarenzi recalls that Habyarimana's regime "was hailed as a model of development and stability" (2009)—just as today's Rwandan government is. Similarly, Uvin states that, before the genocide of 1994, "Rwanda was usually seen as a model of development in Africa, with good performance on most of the indicators of development" (1998: 1–2). In his investigation of the ways in which development influenced pregenocide Rwanda, Uvin finds that "the process of development and the international aid given to promote it interacted with the forces of exclusion, inequality, pauperization, racism, and oppression that laid the groundwork for the 1994 genocide" (3).

With Rwanda trumpeted as a venerated development model both before the 1994 genocide and today, is it valid or even appropriate to compare the two? In a country with a government so lauded for success and mindful of the causes of the 1994 genocide, how could today's situation in Rwanda have any similarity to the pregenocide situation? Jefremovas is among those who assert that the connection between the two is entirely clear, and the issue she highlights is not development but governance:

> Overall, little has changed in Rwanda. Every Rwandan government since Rwabugiri took power in the 1860s has followed the same pattern of power: each has centralized power and resources into the hands of a tiny fraction of the elite, each has not tolerated opposition, and each has faced a violent and disputed succession, with a "winner takes all" approach to rule. The end result is a society with increasing inequality, and one in which access to power and resources continues to be based on ethnic and regional politics and personal clientage. . . . These patterns of power created the exclusionary politics of the colonial and the two Hutu-dominated postcolonial regimes. They also led to the genocide. Finally and tragically, these patterns of power also underpin the actions of the current regime. (2002: 125–26)

What appears to be occurring in today's Rwanda is that the government's innovative approaches to prodigious development challenges, together with its generally disciplined and solemn demeanor—Kron asserts, for example, that

"Rwanda has become a case study in autocratic nation-building" (2010b)—are taking place alongside a governance situation that is worthy of considerable concern.

The issue of the conduct of the current Rwandan government again came to the fore in a UN Office of the High Commissioner for Human Rights "mapping exercise" report on human rights violations in the DRC. The report's assertions are damning: that the actions of Rwanda's national army (in concert with its allies, the Alliance des Forces Démocratiques pour la Libération du Congo-Zaire) against ethnic Hutu civilian refugees from Rwanda beginning in mid-1996 might "constitute a crime of genocide" (Office of the High Commissioner for Human Rights 2010: 13). One account of the report put it this way: "the most serious accusations centre on the Rwandan army's pursuit of Hutu militia and refugees following the genocide of Tutsis in 1994. The report says the wholesale killing of tens of thousands of Hutus without regard to their age or gender could amount to genocide" (McGreal 2010). Drawing on this mapping exercise report and many others, Filip Reyntjens has concluded that "there is overwhelming evidence of responsibility for war crimes and crimes against humanity" against President Kagame (2011: 2). The Rwandan government's response was fierce. It asserted, among other things, that the report's authors were guilty of "rewriting history," omitting "the historical context," constituting a "dangerous and irresponsible attempt . . . to undermine the peace and stability attained in the Great Lakes region" and employing a "flawed methodology" that applied "the lowest imaginable evidentiary standard" (Ministry of Foreign Affairs and Cooperation 2010: 3). At the very least, the research methods for the mapping exercise appeared to be extensive and meticulous (Office of the High Commissioner for Human Rights n.d.).

The report's sensational findings have attracted considerable attention and highlighted how Rwanda is regularly judged as a special case. Prior allegations of tens of thousands of people killed at the hands of Rwanda's current military during and following the genocide of eight hundred thousand Rwandans in 1994 (as cited in chapter 1), in addition to allegations of crimes against humanity by the authors of the UN mapping exercise, and an assertive state response to dissent before the August 2010 elections, do not seem to have dimmed Rwanda's glow in the eyes of many. Barely a month after the release of the UN mapping exercise report, for instance, former British Prime Minister Tony Blair "congratulated Rwanda on its latest achievement"—the World Bank announcement that Rwanda was "the second most improved business reformer over the past five years" (Office of Tony Blair 2010). "Rwanda's remarkable story of development has taken another step forward," said Blair. And although donor agencies have mentioned reports of human rights violations and the smothering of dissent in Rwanda over time, rarely have such reports impacted their aid investments.

One might ask whether the Rwandan government can "achieve legitimacy by delivering results" while simultaneously maintaining "democracy with constraints." To address this question, I draw from field notes from two sets of events that took place in the second half of 2008, the first in July 2008, when I returned to Rwanda to share the research findings a final time with international donor and Rwandan government officials, and the second on September 19, when I attended Rwanda Day in Boston, Massachusetts. I end Forward and Backward by considering the development and governance situation in Rwanda, and whether comparisons to the pregenocide era are apt.

JULY 2008, KIGALI

Kigali's landscape in mid-July of 2008 had changed dramatically since my last visit more than a year earlier. However, it was as sprawling and eerily quiet (for a city that size) as ever. Airport officials were still confiscating plastic bags at the airport, and the only streetside hawkers in town were male youth selling newspapers or mobile phone cards. What differed was difficult not to stare at: destroyed homes. Quite unlike in Khartoum, where bulldozing houses is a fairly standard government activity, the destruction mainly takes place far from any main roads and certainly nowhere close to downtown.[15] Not so in Kigali: house demolitions edged right up to main roadways that connected government and international donor offices to the city center. They were impossible to miss. Slowing down to take a look, I could easily see what former residents were doing: where their house once stood, they were picking through the debris for personal belongings. There were no reports of the house demolitions in the press. I learned over the time of my visit that complaints about the demolitions had met with scant criticism from any quarter, including international agencies. The implementation phase of the Kigali Master Plan was well underway and, one might assume, brighter times for a modernizing Kigali lay just ahead.

The government had a plan for the residents whose houses were destroyed, an international official working on urban issues in Kigali told me. It was in line with the 2005 Land Ownership Policy, the official explained. House owners

After one Kigali neighborhood had been bulldozed, former residents
return to search for belongings and to salvage building materials.

This new housing estate features well-built houses for, quite evidently, high-income urbanites.

are entitled to compensation if they supply the proper documents. Even if they can't supply them, "in most cases you get compensated for the house but never for the land." A second challenge is that most Kigali residents are poor youth who do not own their homes but pay rent. Renters receive no compensation.

"The problem is where the renters will go," the official explained. In 2008 there was one low-cost housing project of 250 houses for poor Kigali residents called Batsinda.[16] It is located in Kigali only nominally, however: Batsinda is located in a rural area, very far from downtown, where most of the jobs are. "The Kigali City Council wants to create public transport from the new housing areas to town," the official explained, "But there's no transport." What will happen to the masses of urban poor renters who cannot possibly get into Batsinda? "My impression is that more informal settlements will now be created," the official said. The sense from this account was a rapidly expanding capital city that was moving well beyond the capacity of a city government and its urban planners. For example, new firms seeking land to construct buildings would often be granted land that was illegally occupied. The squatters would then be removed. The Kigali Master Plan, moreover, "is a vision; it's conceptual, and contains no detailed planning, no design of settlements," the official explained. In addition, "there are no building standards [codes] in Rwanda"—an issue that several Rwandan government and international aid officials had related to me about rural Rwanda during the field research period.

My final meeting in July 2008 with ministry-level officials of the Rwandan government about the research findings did not go well. I had been warned that this would be the case. A veteran international agency official, for example, cautioned that the study's findings would be difficult for the Rwandan government to accept because "it's the opposite of what the government says every day. The government doesn't like bad results here." A former Rwandan government official working for an international agency recommended that I think about how I can "situate findings in ways that don't undermine government actions." The problem, of course, is that research findings drawn from a well-constructed design, sample, protocol, and set of questions present themselves as evidence of pertinent realities. The findings are hard to situate because they in effect raise questions about particular government actions and policies.

The meeting was notable for its departure from every prior meeting with government officials about the research findings except one.[17] Now that the research was complete and analysis and publication of the findings would follow, the ministry-level officials weighed in. Gone were discussions with government officials that confirmed the validity of every primary research finding in this book. Gone, too, were the frank discussions about the difficulty of sharing troubling information with government superiors. This was different. The criticism of the research at this meeting had two main strands. The first was to discount the validity of the research because, as one official said, interviews with 335 youth "is almost nothing: you can't take it as a real picture of the image of the country." His reference to the government's sensitivity about Rwanda's image was direct: image really matters. My response to the officials' concerns—that 335 extended interviews with ordinary youth was actually a substantial number for qualitative research, that, in addition, the site selection and sampling procedures strongly pointed to a representative sample, and that many government officials had confirmed the main research findings—fell on deaf ears.

We moved to the officials' second criticism. It was founded in the perspective that, in my experience, is far from uncommon in war and postwar countries with huge youth populations. They rebuked the fact that the research focused on only one "category of youth," although the overwhelming majority of Rwandan youth fell into that group: those who were poor and had no education beyond primary school. Officials claimed that including other youth categories—secondary students, university students, business people, youth cooperative members—would have provided horizontal balance. I responded that gathering the views of youth from different categories was always a good idea, and that the research I had led could most certainly be followed by additional studies. In fact, I argued, more research on Rwandan youth was needed. That said, focusing on the views and perspectives of members of perhaps 90 percent of all youth seemed a useful starting place. The meeting ended with one official providing the following piece of advice to me: "be clear about what purpose you have for poor youth and where you want them to go." If time had permitted me a response, it would have been this: the research aimed to find out what members of the poor Rwandan youth majority thought about their situation and future. The recommendations spring from their priorities and aims. Ministry-level officials had approved this approach at the start, the former Minister of Youth, Culture, and Sports had written a strong letter of introduction for the research team, and government officials from all levels had supported and contributed to the field research work.

Briefings with international agency officials in July 2008 produced a different sort of reaction. They were generally surprised by the findings. Many related that they knew that the situation for youth was serious. But they were unaware of the details. In their way, my findings were a dramatic revelation for them. Donor agencies, for example, had commissioned research work on established development sectors of Rwanda: justice, education, agriculture, health, governance and decentralization, and so on. What had not surfaced often in their work, evidently, was much information on the housing crisis, the inability of most youth to become adults, the plight of poor female youth, and the nature of urbanization. Yet their responses were less about my findings themselves than about the response they anticipated from the government, a further indication of the powerful influence of Rwandan government sensitivities over thought and action in the country. "It may be hard for the government to hear that youth need a house and marriage," an official from one agency predicted. "The government won't buy this, because the government may want to change their mentality, to change youth priorities." Another issue several officials mentioned was what happens when it appears that a policy is not succeeding as planned. "When you leave the ministry level" of the Rwandan government, one international agency official explained, "government officials are afraid to mention any negative realities because they're the ones who will be blamed." The official added that, in general, the government's approach is, "the policies are good; the problem is in the implementation. That's why you must only talk about the positive."

SEPTEMBER 2008, BOSTON

The positive side of Rwanda was the featured theme of an event a couple of months after my July 2008 meetings with Rwandan government and agency officials, in a Boston-area hotel in September. The invitation letter from the Rwandan ambassador to the United States, James Kimonyo, trumpeted "the very first 'Rwanda Day' Conference: Building Bridges between Massachusetts and Rwanda." I eagerly accepted the ambassador's formal invitation, arriving early with a pen and spiral notebook in hand. The conference provided an opportunity to see how the Rwandan government promoted itself and was viewed by some of its many enthusiastic supporters. Bobby Sager, Rwanda's honorary consul to Boston, opened the conference by announcing that "Rwanda is a miracle of reconciliation and progress." "I just think that Rwanda may very well become the Singapore of Africa," he added. The purpose of the one-day conference, ambassador Kimonyo stated in his speech (one of five that formally opened the conference), was to "highlight Rwanda's very attractive business environment." The day was emphatically devoted to promoting Rwanda as a superb location for foreign investment. Prospective business investors were the target audience. Exhibits outside the conference room provided information about successful business ventures in Rwanda. Rwandans in the audience were all impeccably dressed. "I feel safer walking down the streets in Kigali than I do in any other city in the world," declared the veteran U.S. politician, pastor, and diplomat, Andrew Young, in a promotional film called *Rwanda: The Renaissance* that opened the "Rwanda Bilateral Investment Treaty: Leveraging Opportunities" session. David Kanamugire, a member of Rwanda's Office of the President, concluded the first half of the day's proceedings with a short speech. Unrealistically, he announced that "we hope Kigali to be broadband wireless by [the end of] 2008," which was then less than four months away.

President Kagame gave the keynote address. With carefully chosen words and little inflection, the president promoted his country. "We are happy to have you as friends who can give your time and resources to support what is taking place in Rwanda," he announced. Referring to the issue of Rwanda's cleanliness, which Sager and other U.S. speakers had also mentioned, he explained why the emphasis on being clean, literally and metaphorically, was so important in Rwanda: "Let me talk about cleanliness. First, it is very deliberate. We want and intend to be clean in as many things as we can be. What has happened in our history has been very tragic and also very clean. When we hear that visitors say Rwanda is clean, we are very pleased, and we want to be even cleaner. I keep asking myself this question: 'Why are visitors surprised to find cleanliness and tidiness?' So we keep trying to clean up our cities, our villages and our economy and everything else." Then, referring to the genocide, the president said, "The sky will be the limit because we've tasted the worst and know it. So we want to do better and that's what we deserve." Later in his speech, President Kagame told the audience that "the World Bank says that Rwanda is the most conducive environment for business in Africa." He concluded, to thunderous applause, with the words, "we hope to welcome you to Rwanda, to invest in Rwanda, and through Rwanda, to the rest of the region and beyond."

Rwanda's attractiveness for private investment continued to be described in various ways at the conference in speeches by U.S. business investors in Rwanda and by Francis Gatare, the director general of the Rwanda Investment and Export Promotion Agency. Gatare reminded potential investors in the audience that "good governance is the foundation for everything that is done" in Rwanda, that the government there had "a zero tolerance for corruption," and that Rwanda wants "to have an agricultural transformation." Later in his remarks he said, "clearly, Rwanda is still an undervalued stock."

With much talk in morning speeches about Rwanda's knowledge-based economy and its aims to become the information technology hub for the Central African region, what followed after lunch was bracing. The minister of education, Daphrose Gahakwa, laid out in a handful of statistics just how far Rwanda is from achieving the knowledge base that its government seeks. Only 10 percent of primary school graduates go on to secondary school, she said. "We need to build skills between primary and secondary," she added. While the country had 44,000 students in institutions of higher education, she bluntly stated that "the quality [of education] is not very good."[18] She also explained that "we have a critical shortage of professors and faculty." Turning again to the "90 percent of our students who don't continue to secondary school," Minister Gahakwa said that investment was needed in vocational and technical training "so that at least . . . they can be assured of a job." Near the end of her presentation, she plainly stated that "the problem is known: there are not so many schools to go to" in Rwanda.

The education minister's presentation brought home how the situation on the ground in Rwanda confronts the determined ambitions of the Rwandan government. Unquestionably, the Rwandan government has substantial assets. It has risen up from colossal destruction in the aftermath of genocide. The government tackled the problem of genocidal crimes in a comprehensive fashion. A bevy of indicators suggest that the country's economic future is hopeful. Rwanda sports a confident, focused, and disciplined approach to development that mixes state innovation with private-sector investment. It has a reputation for competence, particularly at the national government level, and it has a strong independent streak.[19] While its development plans are ambitious and even audacious, the government's drive to transform the tiny, impoverished, landlocked, heavily populated, natural-resource-poor, rapidly urbanizing nation into a modern, middle-income nation is noteworthy.

Hard to do. It is indeed difficult not to sense that the Rwandan government, amid the welter of accolades surrounding it, is cultivating an air of unreality about itself and its prospects. Concerning Kigali, for example, a veteran international official had shared with the research team his impression that "the Rwandan government thinks that if they make Kigali look like a wealthy city, then it will be a wealthy city." National policies, moreover, are largely treated as sacrosanct scripture: once they are in place, the only question is when implementation will be complete. Questioning a government policy runs the risk of receiving the label of government critic, which is something that must be avoided. With such issues in mind, a former Rwandan government official now working with a nongovernment entity shared his advice on how to shape research findings to address government sensitivities about its policies: "You must interpret your research for a typical elite Rwandan. Look at the policy implications of the research and ask yourself, 'Is it only unearthing sensitive issues for their own ends?' You must draw in policy implications in ways that aren't sensitive. Strike a balance between policy implications and the naked findings." Unfortunately, his advice proved difficult to square with the book's unadorned findings, since they indicate that the government's *imidugudu* and urban housing policies severely hamper youth aspirations, and its policies restricting informal trade severely constrain the economic options of the urban poor—particularly for poor female youth. Our research revealed one rural location where youth were doing reasonably well: in the one place where government officials did not rigidly enforce the regulations on new housing. That location also appeared to be the only place the research team visited where government officials were responding effectively to youth priorities.

A LOOK AHEAD

Perhaps the most disturbing aspect of the Rwandan government's determination to deny many basic realities is that it has so many enablers. Several international agency officials in Kigali privately highlighted their frustration with repeated acts of self-censorship by their institutions. They made it plain that they cannot question Rwandan government policies and actions in meetings or public venues. Their agencies do not allow it. Such actions might enrage government officials and, one imagines, negatively impact agency relations with the Rwandan government. And yet, one can also wonder whether this is a productive approach to a government that appears to be unintentionally self-destructive. Filip Reyntjens has powerfully declared that it is not. He acidly launches wide-ranging criticism at the role of what he derisively calls "The so-called international community," which "has been a willing hostage to Kigali's spin, whether it be on political governance and human rights, on massive violations of international humanitarian law, on the aggression and plunder of the DRC, on its dangerous social and economic engineering exercise, or on the way it has injected structural violence across the country and the region" (2011: 33). Other Rwanda watchers would forcefully disagree with Reyntjens. That said, Rwanda's bright lights cannot blot out the tough questions that persist. Will clamping down hard on public mention of ethnicity and dissent of many kinds, and the press and civil society in general, ultimately make Rwanda more stable? In such an environment, how can national policies that are unproductive or destructive be adjusted or thrown out? Will tensions surrounding ethnic and class difference ease if they cannot be discussed in public and while citizens are urged to report on neighbors who appear to be "harboring divisionism"? Will Rwanda's ongoing involvement in the DRC, and the persistence of *génocidaires* still lodged there, further destabilize the region? Will the growth of a knowledge-based economy also exacerbate growing social and economic inequalities? Are there limits to social engineering in a heavily populated nation where housing and land use are undergoing wholesale changes?

It remains unclear whether the answers to these questions will lead to a Rwanda that is more open, just, equitable, prosperous, stable, and relaxed. Andreas Wimmer's quantitative research suggests that movement toward these ends is needed. Drawing on the statistical model in his 2009 publication (Wimmer, Cederman, and Win 2009), Wimmer measured political exclusion in all governments across the globe and found that Rwanda has the third-highest level of political exclusion (behind Sudan and Syria). His statistical analysis has also found that governments that politically exclude large segments of the population are the most violence prone (Wimmer, Cederman, and Win 2009). Wimmer also calculated the likelihood that today's countries would return to war in the future. His analysis determined that Rwanda has a higher probability of a return to war than any other country in the world.[20]

It also bears mention that James Scott's argument that "many of the most tragic episodes of state development in the nineteenth and twentieth centuries" contain "a particularly pernicious combination of three elements," all of which appear to exist in contemporary Rwanda. The first element is "the administrative ordering of nature and society," which is often expressed in what he calls "high modernism." Its proponents (who include Lenin, the last Shah of Iran, Robert McNamara, and Julius Nyerere) "envisioned a sweeping, rational engineering of all aspects of social life in order to improve the human condition" (1998: 88). The second element "is the unrestrained use of the power of the modern state as an instrument for achieving" the designs of high modernism. The final element "is a weakened or prostrate civil society that lacks the capacity to resist these plans" (88–89). The three elements, in

Scott's conception, work together in the following way: "The ideology of high modernism provides, as it were, the desire; the modern state provides the means of acting on that desire; and the incapacitated civil society provides the leveled terrain on which to build (dis)utopias" (89). In their plans for changing the housing of four of every five Rwandans in rural areas and Kigali (as mentioned in chapter 1) and the array of specific regulations on the Rwandan citizenry (including those pertaining to forestry and land use), the actions of the Rwandan authorities could be categorized as administering nature and society. The Rwandan state's efforts to modernize agricultural production and cities, the *imidugudu* enterprise, and the goals and objectives of Vision 2020 arguably situate Rwanda as "high-modernist." As to the second and third elements, the Rwandan state is using its power to enact Vision 2020, among other things, while civil society's influence is, at best, negligible. What this suggests about Rwanda today is not heartening. It certainly directs concern, and perhaps sheds some light, on the nature of Rwanda's advances and challenges, and how they should be reworked.

The question of whether today's situation in Rwanda harkens back to pre-genocide times will now be addressed. Arguably, there are similarities between the two eras. In both, Rwanda has had a reputation for innovation and has received generally upbeat and strong international support. A rigid style of governance, a weak civil society, a poor human rights record, limited avenues for dissent, and the government's commanding presence in the nation's society and economy are characteristics of the current and prior regimes. Most of Rwanda's citizenry remains poor and under pressure. At the same time, and significantly, the current regime is neither fomenting nor facilitating an environment in which genocide could take place. A second substantial difference between the two eras lies in the ability of Rwandans to move about today. Under Habyarimana's reign in Rwanda, "travelling was tolerated, but not changing address without due cause; one had to apply for permission to move. Unless there was good reason, such as going to school or getting a job, the authorisation to change residence would not be granted—unless, of course, one had friends in high places. Administrative control was probably the tightest in the world among non-communist countries" (Prunier 1995: 77). Kigali's unprecedented and rapid population advance testifies to the fact that Rwandans have a degree of mobility that is entirely new. In addition, the current regime's active support of many vital women's issues is important and noteworthy. Taken together, while differences that separate the two eras are encouraging, crucial similarities between pregenocide and today's Rwanda are manifest.

What follows from this state of affairs is a sense that the Rwandan government will continue to exhibit its current combination of forceful progress and robust social control. In the short term, this will likely continue to yield mixed results. But the longer term prognosis is much less clear. Many youth are tethered to trajectories that currently offer little or no hope. The disquieting prospect that some young people with a looming sense of failure might rebel violently is difficult to dismiss. That said, such a scenario does not entail anything genocidal: pointing out similarities with the past does not equate with predicting genocide. Indeed, no such prediction is being made here. What might become possible one day, however, is that the resistance of cornered youth might be expressed through sweeping violence. Research for this book and the current context make it difficult to rule out such a scenerio. Accordingly, while Rwanda's government may open society and ease state control, the extensive crackdown prior to the 2010 elections, among many other events, points in the opposite direction: toward a government determined to attain its grand goals even if that has meant instituting repressive measures. In this disturbing light, the current status quo seems unlikely to last. Things are just too tight.

The Burundian Youth Contrast

To say that Rwanda and Burundi have much in common is far more than conjecture. The two countries have a shared colonial history, if nothing else: they were part and parcel of the same Rwanda-Urundi colony ruled first by the Germans and then the Belgians. Classic texts (e.g., Lemarchand 1970; Chrétien 2003) and countless articles, reports, studies, and books have covered the two peoples and nations. The Kirundi and Kinyarwanda languages (of Burundi and Rwanda, respectively) are related, as are the landscapes, farming practices, and cultures of Burundi and Rwanda. The two nations share, roughly, the same ethnic composition and demographic proportions of majority Hutu and minority Tutsi and Twa. They also share a significant degree of truly extreme ethnic violence and genocide in their history. The "genocide" label is stridently debated in the region (sometimes depending on which ethnic group you belong to), but at the very least it could be applied to what happened in 1959 in Rwanda, in 1972 in Burundi, and in 1994 in Rwanda. My conversations in Ki swahili with some of the masses of Rwandan and Burundian refugees in Ngara, Tanzania, in 1994 and 1996, for example, revealed identities based not on country but on the violence that had forced them to become refugees. Our discussions about regional issues included mention of refugees from these violent events, whose ordeals are so significant that they enter the language as fixed, proper nouns: *Watu wa Hamsini na Tisa* (the People of '59; ethnic Tutsi refugees who had fled Rwanda), *Watu wa Sabini na Mbili* (the People of '72; ethnic Hutu refugees who had fled Burundi) and *Watu wa Tisini na Nne* (the People of '94; ethnic Hutu refugees who had fled Rwanda).

How striking, despite so many elemental similarities, to realize just how different the views of youth are in these two nations. Rwandan government officials expressed their own realization of the chasm between the two when I shared the contrasting findings with them. As one Rwandan district official confessed, "I'm completely surprised that Rwandan youth are so different" from Burundian youth. What follows is a review of some of the most significant contrasts between the findings in this book and those contained in Peter Uvin's *Life after Violence* (2009), both of which largely employed the same research procedures and protocols. Asking roughly the same sort of youth the same questions in the two countries revealed differences that were, for most, counterintuitive. After all, Rwanda is widely viewed as a beacon of development and progress, whereas Burundi's profile is that of a shaky, still-emerging postwar nation. Linking the two, I was reminded time and again, did not sit well with Rwandan government officials, who no longer considered Rwanda to be a postconflict nation and did not view comparisons with Burundi as relevant, given what they saw as Rwanda's rapid advance versus Burundi's continuing struggles. Yet in many ways, Burundian youth saw their situation in ways that were far more upbeat and promising than did their Rwandan counterparts.

One of the reasons for this is the dramatic contrast in personal freedom. Unlike their counterparts in the rigidly controlled, government-dominated environment that permeates Rwanda, Burundians in the post–civil war era have "a new-found assertiveness." Burundi was "an extremely closed society" until the early 1990s. But no longer. As Uvin notes, an "important change that happened as a result of the war is that the state lost its monopoly on information and organization" (2009: 76). Burundi today has a vibrant civil society that is "a force to be reckoned with." There are also "many quality independent radio stations." Neither is the case in Rwanda; not even close. Remarkably, "reflexive ethnicity is weaker than before" in Burundi—this in a country where it is entirely legal to mention Hutu and Tutsi in public and despite the fact that ethnic violence during the 1993–2003 civil war was widespread and vicious. What is so interesting about this finding is that the Rwandan government has outlawed public mention of ethnicity because it might ignite unrest and violence. That is certainly a possibility. However, across the border in Burundi, public mention of ethnicity demonstrates a new environment of free expression. As Kron notes, "in contrast to orderly Rwanda, the darling of the international aid community, Burundi is violent, dysfunctional, and chaotic. On the plus side, civil society in Burundi is indigenous and true, and unlike in Rwanda, ethnicity is not being ignored. Politics can breathe" (2010b: 2).

A time-honored method for empowering citizens from the national center of government to lower government levels is decentralization.[21] Uvin is harshly critical of these efforts by the development community in Burundi. With Burundi now nearly three decades into the decentralization process, he finds that most of it "is entirely irrelevant to the real potential for citizen-driven democratization in Burundi. It will produce nothing in the way of citizenship or true democracy" (2009: 80). In Rwanda, research for this book found a decentralization effort that may not advance democracy but that was not at all ineffectual. In one respect, the result was similar to findings in northern Ethiopia on the decentralization of a regional education system, which revealed how the logic of bureaucratic action at lower government levels was to act as a command center; to behave, essentially, like a smaller-scale central government (Sommers 1996). The dramatic expansion of regulations and fines that local government levels have instituted in Rwanda to monitor and control the behavior of its citizens aptly illustrates this result in Rwanda. Another aspect of Rwanda's brand of decentralization is illuminated in the appendix, which details the degree to which the central government influenced the process. In principle, the decentralization process is just as the Rwandan government described it: "For services to be effectively decentralized, local governments will need to promote bottom-up planning, so that communities can decide what their development needs and priorities are" (Ministry of Local Government, Community Development, and Social Affairs 2006: ix). But the appendix tells a different story of actual practice: of a national government encouraging *umudugudu* officials to discuss with citizens in their locality what, very specifically, the national government is recommending that they implement. It constitutes, essentially, a method for influencing local decision making, instituting a method for monitoring and marking progress, and defining appropriate citizen behavior for every household in Rwanda. Given the governance climate in Rwanda and the way in which officials responded to the document in the appendix during interviews, it seemed quite unlikely that *umudugudu* officials would refuse to follow precisely the national government's suggestions. Rwanda's government essentially remains an upward-looking one, where central government policies and priorities are paramount. In comparison with Rwanda, Burundi has a much weaker central government but a significantly more open society.

In material terms, the youth situations in Burundi and Rwanda are quite similar. Youth in both countries are generally poor. But right away, in terms of outlook and orientation, a dramatic separation emerges. Uvin states, for example, that "farming is a prison to most Burundians. In the countryside . . . people desperately want to reduce their dependence on the land. The three big ways for young people to escape poverty are education, migration, and hard work" (Uvin 2009: 185). Although youth in Rwanda did not refer to farming as a prison, they did discuss their predicament as devoid of good options. People's dependence on land did not arise often in our interviews, perhaps because few youth owned much. The main focus was on how to get off their parents' land and become adults. In this sense, the ideas of Rwandan youth about escaping poverty are starkly different from Uvin's findings in Burundi. A small proportion of Rwandan youth mentioned education as a viable possibility for them. Rwandan youth in villages and in Kigali primarily viewed rural–urban migration more as an escape from humiliation and failure than as a way out of impoverishment. Urban migration was risky and even perilous. It was a sign of bottoming out, of desperation, much more than a sign of advancement and adventure. In this respect, the views of Burundian youth nearly parallel those of youth in other African nations (Sommers 2009: 17, 21–22). The notion of Rwandan youth as resisting development was an issue that many Rwandan officials mentioned during interviews. Youth might work, but not necessarily in what the officials contended was the right way or toward appropriate ends. The refusal of most youth to join associations (when there were any) was a recurring theme in the comments from government officials about youth challenges. In this way, Rwandan and Burundian youth were indeed similar: they sought solutions to their challenges as individuals rather than as groups.

More than any other issue, Burundian youth viewed education as a kind of fulcrum for self-advancement. Uvin found that "education is the issue that came up most in our conversations about how (young) people try to make it in life. It is at the heart of individual social mobility and family strategies for survival" (Uvin 2009: 86). For Burundians generally, "education means you are not stuck anymore in the prison that rural life represents for many people"

(89). The frame of reference for Rwandan youth, as detailed in this book, is being stuck—but from their inability to become adults, not from the "prison" of farm life. It also must be said that future prospects in rural Rwanda were exceptionally poor for most youth, and they knew it.[22] What captivated their thoughts about the future was trying to become an adult in rural areas and ensuring a measure of stability in urban areas. Rural life for Rwandan youth might also be a prison, but struggling to become an adult was the immediate concern.

The possibility of moving "up" in society was an additional contrast between the research on youth in both countries. What flows from the powerful contrast between young people in Burundi and Rwanda is not their material deprivation but their general orientation. Burundian youth had a "deep sense of potential mobility" (Uvin 2009: 105). While they also believed that "downward social mobility is more likely than upward social mobility," the commanding imprint of risk aversion, so prominent among Rwandan youth, was much less present. In its place was a can-do ethic constructed of "hard work and perseverance, good management, and dynamism." Ironically, Burundian youth seemed to have the sort of attunement to new ideas and innovations that Rwandan government officials tried to inculcate in Rwandan youth: Burundian youth were interested in "trying different things" (117), while Rwandan youth (and adults) largely resisted the new ideas that government officials implored them to adopt. More than that, most Burundian youth had a "capitalist ethos" in a land that had become "a capitalist paradise" (119): "It is through intelligence and studying, through hard work, perseverance and good management, that [Burundian youth] hope to improve their fate. They expect little to nothing from the state or of the aid system. Family members continue to be the main source of support, although there is a significant decline in their ability and willingness to provide mutual aid" (117).

In Rwanda, most youth had little to no expectation that the aid system or families could help them all that much. Their views of the Rwandan government, on the other hand, were a different story. Whether the comments referred to youth being "prisoners" of government regulations or that "the government is our parent," wanting the government to be "close to us" was a recurring refrain. There seemed to be no one else around to help youth, and expecting the government to help remained a possibility. Yet these responses support an outlook on life that seeks help and averts risk. It is not adaptive, experimental, or innovative, as the capitalist ethos of Burundian youth implies. Instead, it is generally careful, resistant, and conservative. Whereas Burundian youth held out hope of improving their lot and perhaps even ascending socially, members of the poor Rwandan youth majority, in words and actions, sought to minimize their chances of collapse.

What accounts for this dramatic difference in outlook for young people in adjacent countries who face many of the same challenges? Certainly one factor is that the lives of Burundian youth did not center on countering failed masculinity, which proved to be a central concern in so many Rwandan youth lives. Uvin's description of this predicament underscores the contrast: "When young men face great difficulty in achieving normative manhood, they do what most of us do when confronted with major challenges in our lives—they try harder than ever, they seek to innovate, they try to move and find opportunities elsewhere, they turn to God for strength, they hang out with friends and complain—but they do not necessarily become murderers" (Uvin 2009: 178–79). Rwandan youth share some similarities: there was no evidence that they became violent, much less murderers, for example. Yet the primary difference boils down to this: they lacked options. In a constrained world of rigid cultural requirements, extensive government regulations, and an orientation that shunned innovation and new ideas as too risky, trying harder than ever and faith in God seemed to be the only options. In rural areas, this mainly meant working for others and trying to save money. In urban areas, it meant trying to get money in some way to stay afloat. While the government offered a prescription for improvement—mainly by joining associations—it was remarkable to realize just how deep the degree of resistance to this option was among both rural and urban youth.

The threat of failing to become an adult, quite simply, did not constrain the lives of Burundian youth nearly as much as it constrained Rwandan youth lives. Uvin does note that traditional expectations of manhood and womanhood "are extremely hard to achieve" in Burundi. But quite unlike Rwandan culture and society, threats of failure for Burundian youth are counteracted, to some degree, by "opposing forces" that do not exist in Rwanda. Uvin found three: "girls and women are encouraged to study as long as they can"; "female dynamism and mutual respect between spouses are increasingly sought"; and "traditional marriage expectations are relaxed" (Uvin 2009: 181). These three forces may well be in play in the lives of the small, elite, educated Rwandan youth minority. But within the impoverished lives that nearly all rural and urban youth inhabit, the conservative, even punishing, combination of restrictive cultural traditions and government behavior did not allow such encouraging forces to surface.[23]

Recommendations

Openings of donor conferences by the heads of developing country states tend toward the predictable. Leaders mix platitudes about their nation's progress with invitations for partnership with powerful international donor agencies. While the themes and tone of such speeches are almost unavoidably genial and a tad bland, the opening to Rwanda's Sixth Annual Government of Rwanda and Development Partners Meeting (held in Kigali on November 22–23, 2006) departed from such expectations. President Kagame used the occasion to address directly some assessments of Rwanda and outline a selection of general parameters for donor and researcher contributions. His remarks were not intended just for the conference attendees: the speech was rebroadcast on national television soon afterward. The local and international media's subsequent focus on Rwanda's imbroglio with the French government at that time, to which President Kagame alluded, overshadowed their coverage of other issues the president raised in his speech.[24] One was his pointed criticism of Transparency International's poor corruption rating for Rwanda and the failure of Transparency International officials to discuss their findings with Rwandan officials before leaving Rwanda.[25] The president recommended that researchers in Rwanda discuss their preliminary findings with government officials.

My research endeavor followed this recommendation. As mentioned earlier, over the course of field research, I regularly met with government officials from the lowest (*umudugudu*) to some of the highest (national offices and ministry) levels.[26] For some officials, particularly those at lower government levels, the main findings were all too familiar. But for many higher-level officials, learning about the breadth and depth of frustration and difficulty in so many Rwandan youth lives was jarring. One shocked district official, for example, requested more discussion immediately after our formal meeting had concluded. We then met into the evening and again during a subsequent field visit to discuss the research findings in more detail.

Two brief sets of recommendations follow: one specific to the Rwandan context and another concerning youth in postconflict and development contexts generally.

1. *Vigorously advocate for crucial priorities.* Rwanda contains a heady mix of dramatic progress and exceptional tension. While the current regime's progressive tendencies have been noted earlier in this book (and elsewhere), the fact that so many Rwandan youth are unable to become adults contributes significantly to the pressurized environment. So does their government. Easing expansive constraints on social, political, and economic life are required to help the current government sidestep its self-destructive tendencies.

Relaxing government regulations on housing and the informal economy immediately is the recommended starting point (subsequent measures are outlined in recommendation 2). An equally important step is to address the following issues that, collectively, run the risk of undermining the capable and visionary dimensions of Rwandan government action if they are not addressed. The government's justified security concerns must be balanced with its ongoing and troubling role in the DRC, which carries with it powerful allegations and damning evidence of war crimes. Similarly, the Rwandan regime's pronounced tendency toward social engineering and control, the nation's acutely constrained civil society, media and political environment, evidence of rising economic inequality and alarming abuses of human rights, and questions about justice require careful reassessment and extensive reform. Reducing and perhaps suspending international donor aid to Rwanda may be a necessary if unfortunate advocacy tool because it may negatively impact members of Rwanda's impoverished masses.

Viewing Rwanda through rose-colored glasses, in short, will not make Rwanda's present and future rosier. But it might help set the stage, quite unintentionally, for an outbreak of severe violence for a nation with a nervous and pressured population, tens if not hundreds of thousands of "hopeless youth," and an innovative but heavy-handed government that is confident to the point of hubris. And that would be tragic.

The absence of viable options for so many youth contains an important cultural dimension, as well. It is probable that those who, consciously or not, carry the torch for traditional definitions of manhood and womanhood do not realize the severe consequences that adulthood expectations place on young Rwandans. With a youth population that is larger than ever before and access to land, housing, and recognized marriages receding for so many, the much more relaxed approach to adulthood that Burundians employ provides Rwanda with an example worthy of emulation. Local and national conversations about how youth gain acceptance as men and women promises to initiate a reconsideration of adulthood mandates. With so many young Rwandans striving hard to meet them, this is the time to implement such an initiative.

2. *Reform government approaches to youth concerns.* The government of Rwanda's youth architecture is substantial. It includes a National Youth Policy, an ambitious plan for expanding access to secondary and vocational schools, a Ministry of Youth, and a National Youth Council that features locally elected representatives at cell, sector, and district levels.

Yet the government's general approach is both directive and directly at odds with the priorities of most Rwandan youth. It emphasizes associations for out-of-school rural and urban youth when the overwhelming majority vigorously resist joining them. Rwanda is a place where youth, as Uvin found in Burundi, "see life improvement as individual[s]" and where "collective development actions are not popular" (Uvin 2009: 118–19). The Rwandan government expects a volunteer institution, the NYC, to deliver results that are far beyond its reach. It has significantly expanded access to secondary education, which is encouraging, while vocational training for poor male and female youth remains woefully inadequate. It seeks to control informal economic activity through regulation and enforcement that negatively, and severely, impact the urban poor. Most of its officials energetically enforce government housing regulations, from *imidugudu* requirements in the countryside to Master Plan implementation and extensive bulldozing in the capital that have inadvertently contributed to the interrelated crises of housing and failed adulthood. The rural cell where the research team found officials who were relaxing *imidugudu* enforcement, and the positive response that this inspired among youth in that cell, underscores the need to reassess the massive housing transformation that government regulations dictate.

A final word on the government's national housing and informal sector ambitions is useful. Researchers have found that wholesale forced housing reforms in the region have failed. Rwanda's government seems to be betting that the results in Rwanda will be the opposite. The need for change seems clear: since there are so many people on so little land, transforming housing patterns is necessary. However, while the urgency of Rwanda's housing and land situation is difficult to question, the government's regulatory approach is not yielding a positive outcome—not even close—for the impoverished youth majority. Evidently, housing is one of the issues that at least some cell and sector officials are afraid to report accurately to their superiors. A similar state of affairs confronts the urban poor concerning regulations on informal economic sector activity. The regulation appears to open the door to low-level corruption among Local Defense Force members and policemen. More seriously, it makes the economic situation for many poor youth far worse, particularly for poor urban female youth, who lack the variety of economic options that male youth have. The consequences of these two regulations are counterproductive and so serious that it is strongly recommended that both should be either significantly reformed or scrapped. Doing so promises to help many more youth become adults and approach economic stability.

Attendant to government reforms is the need for enhanced training for government officials who work with youth. The pronounced class divide between poor youth and most officials, as well as the one-sided nature of their interactions, is also counterproductive. This was starkly detailed by a district-level government official in Rwanda, who noted that

> If you tell the youth what to do, it will fail. They will just run away. They are the ones who have to tell you the solution. As a leader, you have to let youth give their ideas toward a solution. Those youth are very intelligent. They are also strong. They are not ignorant. If you say that they're ignorant, then you have a problem.
>
> It took me one month of going every day, time and again, to get youth to understand that it was [best] to grow beans. Of course there's resistance, but you have to put yourself on the same level of decisions as them, with the same logic. I compare ideas with them. I put on my jeans and go and sit in the grass and talk to them. Then you discuss with them. Again, it's a problem if officials consider them ignorant.

The official highlighted a need for retraining government officials who work with poor youth. "There needs to be an initiative to convince those officials that they have the wrong perspective about uneducated youth," he explained.

The official also highlighted the strong need for wholesale policy reform on youth issues and the dangers of resisting it: "When the youth aren't active and working for themselves, then bad forces can influence them. There are guys opposing the government. They can see that nothing's done for them, and they can get involved in sabotage. So [international] donors should push the government to start a [new youth] policy, and then youth on the ground can contribute their ideas. Our concern is that the government would make a policy without consulting the youth. If you do this, it won't work."

It is probable that issues such as housing and informal market restrictions, as well as jobs, training, and education, would come to the fore if poor youth were able to share their ideas freely. Viable employment for the poor youth majority, moreover, may not necessarily align with current initiatives. For example, creating and developing an information technology (IT) sector, and a knowledge-based economy more broadly, are fields where most poor Rwandan youth—given the educational demands of these fields— will have little or no chance of entering. Instead, it is conceivable if not probable that members of the well-educated youth minority will disproportionately benefit from opportunities in IT and other new economic areas.

It would thus be unfortunate if the growth of exciting new economic sectors in Rwanda significantly expanded social and economic inequalities at the same time. With so much at stake in a country as simultaneously inspiring and unsettling as Rwanda, addressing growing inequality and the priorities of poor youth are crucial.

3. *Significantly expand gender work in Rwanda.* Rwanda's advances on behalf of its women are among the most significant of any developing country in recent years. But gender work there must also address the plight of female as well as male youth. As detailed in this book, a female youth cannot become recognized as a woman in Rwanda until she marries a male youth in a socially accepted fashion (elopement and informal marriage being signs of misfortune and desperation). Not becoming a woman in this way creates severe and negative consequences for female youth. Until male youth can build a house, female youth have no one to marry (the government vigorously restricts polygamy, a former alternative, however unpalatable).

Therefore, first helping a male youth build a house promises to help a great many female youth become women. This recommendation is derived directly from the research findings as an evidence-based, practical means of addressing the adulthood crisis swiftly.

Clearly, such a response is an insufficient means for addressing all the needs of female youth. Among the most important is the situation of poor female youth in Rwanda, particularly those in Kigali, which is thoroughly alarming. This is especially the case for the unmarried and, more than any other subgroup, for prostitutes. Providing immediate assistance and protection for such groups should be viewed as an urgent priority.

4. *Reassess Rwanda's HIV/AIDS prevalence rate and prevention efforts.* Evidence drawn from research for this book, especially in Kigali, indicates that HIV/AIDS infection rates, thought to be 3 percent nationally and 3.4 percent among Kigali youth, may be substantially higher. The focus on households in the 2005 survey (Institut National de la Statistique and ORC Macro 2006) calls for a thorough reexamination, if not an entirely new survey of Rwanda's HIV/AIDS infection rate, because so many youth, urban youth in particular, do not live in ordinary households that were the focus of the 2005 survey. In addition, HIV/AIDS infection is so stigmatized that youth avoid being tested. Finally, the implications of fatalistic behavior among many poor youth (particularly in Kigali) suggest that efforts to inform and persuade poor youth to alter their behavior and avoid infection are unlikely to succeed until the core reasons for their hopelessness—emasculation, female youth desperation and extreme poverty—are concurrently addressed. Appropriately addressing the interrelated adulthood and housing crises, the extreme situation facing poor female youth, and the severe problems caused by heavy informal sector regulation is directly connected to fashioning a more effective strategy for combating HIV/AIDS.

5. *Help youth access capital and save money.* The poorest youth lack entry fees that are necessary to join the popular *ibimina* informal lending associations. Microcredit for these youth is required. In addition, there is a need for youth with cash, particularly urban youth, to find ways to safely save and invest it. While some government officials were certainly aware of this need, the proposed solution was often tied to youth joining associations. As related above, many undereducated youth do not trust educated youth, and many youth resist or are unable to join associations. The government's narrow focus on pushing poor youth to join associations, in short, is a failed policy strategy. Accordingly, other options should be explored. Speaking with poor youth directly about this and other issues promises to yield far more positive results.

6. *Sharply upgrade appropriate attention and support for poor urban youth.* The exceedingly low level of institutional support for Kigali's neglected "hopeless youth" calls for dramatically increased assistance to their disadvantaged and

overlooked lives. Forcibly returning migrant youth to rural areas or tearing down their urban homes without providing a viable alternative is unlikely to work and may prove to be counterproductive—perhaps dangerously so. Both threaten existing arrangements that youth have built and exacerbate their distress.

Reasonable and noncoercive approaches to providing housing for poor youth are vital. Reversing the mainly negative relationships between government authorities and many poor youth is also important. Creating viable possibilities for poor youth, and others, to sell their goods is essential, as the current limitations are creating severe and negative consequences. To this end, the reports of harassment by LDC, police, and night patrol authorities against poor youth, including alleged acts of sexual violence against prostitutes, need to be taken seriously and then addressed swiftly. It is essential that prostitutes be encouraged to report rape and other serious crimes perpetrated against them without risk of negative consequences (such as arrest or harassment).

Kigali's youth are not threats to urban life. They are, instead, two-thirds of the city's residents. Prostitution and crimes of theft are mainly related to desperation. Positive engagement and support, in line with the housing, economic, and rights priorities of urban—and rural—youth, are required urgently.

RECOMMENDATIONS FOR YOUTH WORK IN POSTCONFLICT AND DEVELOPMENT SITUATIONS

I. *Conduct "sectorless" research on the priorities and perspectives of marginalized youth majorities.* The fact that this study's major findings surprised many national-level Rwandan government officials and major donor and other international officials in Rwanda sheds light on the importance of researching the priorities and perspectives of poor youth majorities and then using the findings to inform policy and program work. This is, essentially, the approach that research for this book (and Uvin's *Life after Violence*) provides: an opportunity to find out what youth require and then recommend policy and program reforms based on their expressed requirements. It should be applied elsewhere.

The approach used here also underscores the need to set aside sector priorities for youth until it is clear how they are relevant. In Rwanda, for example, the priority of housing takes precedence over the high value that many youth place on education. In addition, as struggling to come of age figures so prominently in many youth lives, it is important to ask whether and how youth are able to become adults and what happens if they fail to do so. As suggested in this book, male and female youth needs are likely to be intertwined, and poor, unmarried female youth in rural and urban areas may be enduring dangerous living conditions while attracting little or no support.

2. *Countries with youth-dominated populations and policies that are not youth centered need to align their policies with youth priorities.* While the current trend toward creating national youth policies is encouraging, such policies may have inadequate budgets, lack teeth and, even if fully implemented, probably could not adequately address the requirements of youth.

3. *Consider whether mainstream youth leaders adequately represent youth majority views.* Class divisions and animosities among youth can be profound. Relying on eloquent, educated, dedicated, and concerned youth leaders may prove deeply inadequate and even counterproductive if members of the poor youth majority have different, perhaps even conflicting, priorities. They usually do.

Appendix

The original phrase, *imihigo*, refers to the "bets" or "wagers" that each *umudugudu* (village and village leader; the same word is contextual and carries both meanings; in this case the reference is village leader) is expected to address with citizens in his village under the guidance of this document. Another way of thinking of this idea, perhaps, is to think of expectations. The expectation is that this document will help each *umudugudu* leader develop an official Performance Contract. While the original document, titled *Imihigo ku rwego rw'Umudugudu*, lists no source, author, or date, it was distributed by the Ministry of Local Government. It was supplied to me by a Rwanda government official in November 2006, when decentralization activities for *umudugudu* officials were under way. In order to ensure as accurate a translation as possible, several Rwandans translated the original document from Kinyarwanda and I compared their translations. The idiosyncrasies in language remain as close to those in the original text as possible.

Good Governance	Objectives	Strategies
SECURITY	Eradicating (fighting) infiltration	• Knowing people who enter and go out; Identifying individuals who enter and go out of the village. • Eye of the citizen (population); Having a migration notebook, a night patrol (surveillance) rounds notebook
	Fighting sexual violence and rape of children and women	• Public meeting to sanction and shame the trespassers

Good Governance	Objectives	Strategies
SECURITY (continued)	Eradicating wandering around/ways of life	
	Fighting violence (meanness)	
	Fighting drunkenness	
	Fighting drugs	
IDEOLOGY [level of understanding]	Bringing people to love their country (patriotism)	• Participation in all government programs • Protecting the development infrastructures • Participate in *umuganda* (compulsory community labor)
	Eradicating genocidal ideology and its roots	• Sensitizing people to tell the truth • Blaming in public those harboring divisionism • Promoting social harmony (tolerance); unity and reconciliation • Remembering the genocide and its consequences
	Work-driven development ideology	• Promoting a constructive dialogue • Regular evaluation of their work and achievement
	Treating with respect people who come to the authorities	• Welcoming and listening to people who come to the authorities • Avoid delaying the people's claims

Good Governance	Objectives	Strategies
IDEOLOGY (continued)	Promoting hygienic culture	• Having a clean body and clothes • Wearing shoes • Not sharing the same drinks or using the same [drinking] straws • Plastering (embellishing) houses • Planting flowers at home • Check the hygiene of the public latrines • Don't make short calls [i.e., urinate] anywhere • Eradicate the habit of spitting everywhere • Washing hands before eating • Maintaining clean materials (e.g., cups, glasses) in bars and restaurants
DEVELOPMENT	Environment protection; trees near roads and homes	• Keep roads clean • Collecting rainwater at home
	Improve [agricultural] production and poverty eradication	• Terrace cultivation • Modern animal husbandry; farming • Soil protection, antierosion techniques, fertilizers • Vegetable gardens, fruit trees • Saving (crops, money) • Promoting the innovation culture and creative activities
SOCIAL AFFAIRS	Mutual assistance	• Neighbors should visit each other
	Having a nursery school	
	Teaching writing and reading (literacy)	• One library per *umudugudu* [village]

Good Governance	Objectives	Strategies
SOCIAL AFFAIRS (continued)	Providing the population with medical care insurance	• Heath care insurance program [Mutuelles de Santé]
	Promoting culture, sport, and leisure	• Two sports disciplines
	Fighting malaria, HIV/AIDS, etc.	• Mosquito nets for each bed • Planting geraniums • Fighting bush [growth] and water floods around houses • Sensitizing people on HIV/AIDS prevention • Child vaccinations; immunizations • Giving birth in hospitals [not at home]
	Family planning	• Sharing ideas about how to do it in *umudugudu* • Blaming parents whose children suffer from malnutrition (Kwashiorkor) • Educating all youth up to 22 years of age, especially female youth
	Children's education	• Assessing every child's level and quality of education in every household • Knowing the whereabouts of children • Fighting child labor • Fighting child abuse
	Caring about youth welfare	• Sensitization about patriotism • Sensitization about job creation • Sensitization about joining associations • Sensitization about HIV/AIDS prevention

Good Governance	Objectives	Strategies
SOCIAL AFFAIRS (continued)	Fighting prostitution and wandering; debauchery	• Condemning in public those who are "prostituting" and wandering; those who are involved in prostitution and debauchery
	Reduce the number of vulnerable people	• Collecting data on vulnerable groups • Identifying, assisting, and supporting vulnerable survivors of genocide
JUSTICE To oppose the culture of false claims (to say no)	Fighting injustice	• Resolving all kinds of conflicts • To defend any person whose rights are violated • Fighting corruption
	Participation in *gacaca* courts	• Sensitizing people to participate in *gacaca* court proceedings
	Eradicating rumors	• Giving true information
	Avoiding false claims	• To name and shame publicly those who give false claims
	Knowledge of laws	• Inform and exchange ideas about laws in the country
	Gender balance and family promotion	• Sensitizing the families about resource management • Sensitizing men and women about living harmoniously • Ensuring mutual respect between husbands and wives • Legalizing marriages; enforcing legal marriages

Notes

Preface

1. All dollar amounts are in U.S. dollars. The exchange rate used throughout this book is what was valid for the field research period (November 2006 through March 2007): $1 = 540 Rwandan francs.

2. The full list of the Ministry of Local Government's suggestions is in the appendix.

3. Uvin 2009 draws from his research in Burundi.

Chapter One. Youth in Waithood

1. The age range differences are significant: while the UN defines "youth" as all people between the ages of fifteen and twenty-four, many governments have other ideas. In Rwanda, for example, "youth" includes everyone between the ages of fourteen and thirty-five. The definitions are entirely malleable, even arbitrary: I recall a major government donor official declaring, on the spot, that they would narrow the full youth definition range to something like ages twenty to twenty-four as a way to limit access to a youth program that their agency would support.

2. The sentiment is also in a popular, "anthemic" song in Cairo, by Downtown, which includes the lyric, "I want to marry, but I've got no money" (Shadid 2011: 13).

3. Of all youth who were interviewed, 84.5 percent were either poor or destitute while 83 percent of the sample never received any schooling beyond primary (including 8.4 percent of the sample who had never gone to school). More information on the youth research sample is in chapter 2.

4. A Ministry of Youth, Culture, and Sports publication states that there were eighty-eight men for every hundred women in postgenocide Rwanda (n.d.: 9).

5. See also, for example, African Rights 1995, Des Forges 1999, Sommers 1995, 2006a, 2006b, and Uvin 1998.

6. Only five other nations have a younger population; the difference among the countries, excluding Uganda, is infinitesimal. The proportion of Ugandans under the age of thirty is 78.2 percent, followed by Mali (75.9 percent), Zambia (75.6 percent), Niger (75.5 percent), and Burkina Faso (75.3 percent). Two other countries

have the same proportion (75 percent) as Rwanda: Malawi and Yemen (Leahy et al. 2007: 87–91).

7. Rwanda's population density is 302 people per square kilometer. Only two African countries have higher population densities, and they are both small island nations: Mauritius (574 people per sq. km) and Comoros (325 people per sq. km) (United Nations Department of Economic and Social Affairs/Population Division 2001).

Only four nations around the world —Burundi (91.4 percent), Bhutan (88.9 percent), Uganda (87.9 percent), and Trinidad and Tobago (87.8 percent)—have a higher proportion of their populations living in rural areas than does Rwanda, at 86.2 percent (United Nations Department of Economic and Social Affairs/Population Division 2006: 36–45).

Between 1995 and 2000, Rwanda's average annual urban growth rate was 17.92 percent, more than twice the rate of the country with the second-highest rate, Liberia (at 8.83 percent). The average annual rate declined from 2000 to 2005, but it still remained the world's highest, at 9.16 percent (the next highest was Martinique, at 6.88 percent) (United Nations Department of Economic and Social Affairs/Population Division 2006: 77–85). The estimated average annual rate has declined for the years of 2005 through 2010 to 6.5 percent; the world's second-highest rate (Burundi is now the leader, at 6.8 percent) (UNFPA 2007: 90).

8. Rwanda's population estimates continue to drive upward. Philip Gaurevitch, for example, states in 2009 that the population had surpassed ten million (37).

See, for example, Uvin's analysis of "ecological resource scarcity" as a paradigm for explaining the 1994 genocide (2001).

9. While estimates of the number of Rwandans killed during the genocide are as low as half a million (Mamdani 2001: 5), other estimates suggest a much higher figure. Reyntjens, for example, has asserted that perhaps 1.1 million Rwandans died during the genocide (2004: 178). The most commonly used figure, however, is eight hundred thousand.

10. Estimated at nearly 3.5 million people for those between the ages of sixteen and thirty-five (Ministry of Finance and Economic Planning 2007: 70). Charles Twesigye-Bakwatsa put the youth proportion of Rwanda's population as slightly lower: 35.6 percent. His analysis draws from national census population statistics, which state that there were 2,893,468 youth ages fifteen to thirty-four in a total Rwandan population of 8,128,553. The actual proportion is likely higher, since the figure listed here does not include youth ages fourteen and thirty-five (per the Rwandan government's definition of "youth"). Charles Twesigye-Bakwatsa, 2005, "YES Rwanda: Strategy and Operational Plan (SOP) Development Process: A Report of the Situation Analysis of Youth Employment in Rwanda (Revised)," unpublished, provided by a youth leader in Rwanda.

11. Prior Rwandan regimes, in both the colonial and independence periods, severely restricted internal population movements, including to urban areas (Uvin 1998: 116).

12. Both initiatives are described in forthcoming chapters. The rural housing re-

forms are detailed in chapter 5 while the urban housing reforms are explained in chapter 6.

Umudugudu is the singular form of *imidugudu*. The former has three primary uses. It refers to a single community housing area, which is part of the government-led *imidugudu* initiative. But *umudugudu* also means both a village (the smallest administrative level in Rwanda) *and* the leader of the *umudugudu* (i.e., village leader). *Umudugudu* most often refers to the village and village leader (singular and often plural, as well), while a community housing area is often mentioned as an *imidugudu*—even if the reference is only to one community housing area. Thus, *imidugudu* primarily refers to the new community housing areas, while *umudugudu* mainly refers to villages or village leaders.

13. As of this writing I have carried out research work in fifteen countries in the region.

14. One of Gikondo's uses, evidently, is as a jail: several urban youth who had been arrested said they were held in Gikondo.

15. Ironically, Rwanda is about the size of its former colonial ruler, Belgium (http://www.globalissues.org/article/429/rwanda, accessed July 1, 2011).

16. On a scale of 0 to 7, where 0 represents the weakest performance and 7 denotes the strongest performance, Rwanda's ratings for "Accountability and Public Voice" moved from 1.48 to 1.43 from 2005 to 2007; from 2.21 to 1.86 for "Civil Liberties"; from 1.22 to 1.24 in "Rule of Law"; and from 1.97 to 2.48 in "Anticorruption and Transparency" (Burnet 2008: 1).

17. Lemarchand suggests even larger numbers for Rwanda's incursions into the DRC: perhaps two hundred thousand Rwandan Hutu refugees were killed there in 1996 and 1997 (2009: 71).

18. Prunier cites it as just under four million (2009: 338).

19. Significantly, Reyntjens does not account for the deaths and atrocities that other actors in the conflict in DRC have carried out—a sign, evidently, of the author's intentionally partisan purpose. His 2004 article, he notes, "makes no excuse for being mainly concerned with the shortcomings of the present [Rwandan] regime, while leaving its achievements (including institutional reconstruction, relatively good bureaucratic governance, the technical level and cosmopolitan outlook of the new elites) largely undiscussed" (2004: 179). One reason for this is that "these positive aspects have been, and still are, highlighted among the donor community." The second reason is that "the [pregenocide Rwandan] regime also enjoyed considerable favourable prejudice, and this had a blinding effect that caused major warning signs to be ignored. The same mistakes have been and are still being committed since the takeover by the RPF" (179–80).

20. Kinzer also notes that Kagame "angrily condemns and rejects" troubling reports from Western human rights groups (2008: 331).

21. President Kagame, Gourevitch reports, "is commonly described as authoritarian even in the Rwandan press." He adds that Kagame told him that "if he cannot

build the national institutions that allow him to retire and preside over a peaceful transfer of power by 2017, when the Constitution requires that he step aside, then 'It's a failure'" (2009: 38).

22. Strict confidentiality was a core part of the methodological approach for this book.

23. In an interview, a donor agency official described how a supervisor had hotly lectured the official after the official had questioned a Rwandan government policy during a meeting with government officials. The official recalled that the supervisor warned that "we address our concerns with government entities in private."

24. A Rwandan friend of Kinzer's remarked, "People need to understand that if there are controls in terms of security, it's because of what happened in 1994. We need it. We want it. We're happy, so leave us alone. I'm not even remotely political, but Rwanda is free and secure. That's all I require, so who is a human-rights-whatever to tell me I'm not free?" (quoted in 2008: 331).

25. For more on the Millennium Development Goals, see www.un.org/millenniumgoals/bkgd.shtml.

26. *Rwanda Vision 2020* states that "Rwanda is characterized by low but accelerating urbanization" (Ministry of Finance and Economic Planning 2000: 16), while the 2007 follow-up report asserts that "Rwanda has one of the lowest rates of urbanization in the world but it has been rising over the past 10 years" (UNDP 2007: 12).

27. Illustrative of Rwanda's evolution into a nation with a growing urban population is the following statistic: from 1991 to 2002 the proportion of Rwanda's urban population rose from 6 percent to 17 percent of the total population (Durand-Lasserve 2007: 6). The proportion of the population that is urban has continued to expand.

28. Remarkable research from a sample of rural *génocidaires* found that "the perpetrators [of the genocide] were primarily adult men: 89 percent were 20 to 49 years old and the greatest concentrations were men 30 to 39 years old. The median age was 34" (Straus 2006: 104). This research expands but does not necessarily contradict earlier assertions about unemployed youth engaged in the genocide. First, the sample was with rural and not urban perpetrators. Second, since the definition of youth in Rwanda extends to age thirty-five, the sample would confirm that many if not most rural perpetrators were, in fact, male youth—just of an older vintage than others might assume.

29. Gérard Prunier provides a detailed definition of *rugo* (plural *ingo*): "In day-to-day affairs, it simply means the family enclosure or compound around which all life revolves. In a polygamous household each wife has her own *rugo*. But *rugo* is also, at a humbler level than *inzu* (lineage), the basic unit of social life in Rwandese society. *Rugo* is the family. Every hill is dotted with dozens of *ingo*" (1995: 3).

30. Rwanda's phased decentralization reforms included a restructuring of the nation's government levels in 2005. As a subsequent government decentralization document explained, there are "six administrative entities: the Central Govern-

ment, the Province (*Intara*), the District (*Akarere*), the Sector (*Umurenge*), the Cell (*Akagari*), and the Village (*Umudugudu*)" (Ministry of Local Government, Good Governance, Community Development, and Social Affairs 2007: 8). No Rwandan or non-Rwandan official recommended that the research team interview provincial officials. Their authority had been drastically reduced in recent years.

31. About *imidugudu* policy being "voluntarily" implemented, Des Forges observes that "when local officials found people unwilling to leave their homes to move to new sites, they used coercion and outright force, even making people destroy their own homes if they showed hesitation in leaving them" (2006: 362).

32. As of 2002, 42.7 percent of Kigali households were in houses they owned, while 47.2 percent were in rented residences (Durand-Lasserve 2007: 7).

33. Jefremovas supports her assertion by citing Gourevitch (1998) and Wagner (1998).

34. The popular nicknames for ethnic Tutsi who had either returned from different countries or resided inside Rwanda since before the civil war and genocide were mostly derogatory. Many Rwandans nonetheless casually and regularly employed these nicknames in conversation during my seven research visits to Rwanda in 1999–2002. They had become illegal prior to my return to research this book in 2006. The nicknames and their meanings are described in Sommers and McClintock 2003: 40.

35. Ansoms 2009 mentions two Rwandan government sources for the six categories: *National Agricultural Policy* (Government of Rwanda 2004) and *Participatory Poverty Assessment* (Government of Rwanda 2001). Ingelaere 2007 mentions the latter. The titles for the six categories are drawn from Ingalaere's list, which are in the plural, while Ansom's categories are listed in the singular (*umukire* instead of the plural, *abakire*; *umukungu* instead of the plural, *abakungu*, and so on).

36. As is described in chapter 2, this research developed definitions for four economic categories for each of those interviewed: destitute, poor, nonpoor, and wealthy. The research team constructed the categories without reference to the government's set. The aim was to determine difference according to reasonably identifiable distinctions in the field. We also had somewhat different concerns: the kind of housing was a crucial determinant. The conclusions the research team drew were also somewhat different. For example, in our categorization a nonpoor person (similar to an *abakungu*) could hire laborers. We also did not have two categories of destitution.

37. The Rwandan government reported that the Gini Coeffficient, used as a measure of inequality, increased from 0.47 in 2000 to 0.51 in 2006–7 (Republic of Rwanda 2007: 30).

38. The World Bank has added its own concern about implementing decentralization: "Ministerial staff are often not sufficiently aware of the division of labor between sub-national levels and the center and how to effectively supervise activities at the sub-national level" (2008: 11).

39. Primary schools still charge a minimal tuition fee. The government plans to eventually make primary school and the first three years of secondary school tuition free (Ministry of Education n.d.: para. 2).

40. Freedman et al.'s description of the official version of history in Rwanda, and the way that it has been applied, is excellent.

Chapter Two. Doing Research in Rwanda

1. Field research in Tanzania's capital was eventually published as Sommers 2001a and 2001b.

2. A small number of supplementary interviews with government and nongovernment officials were also undertaken in mid-2008.

3. The Institutional Review Board of Tufts University, as well as World Bank officials who were supervising and contributing insights to the field research, approved the research methods.

4. Peter Uvin's research in Burundi resulted in Uvin 2009.

5. The Burundi research eventually included the province of Nyanza Lac, as well.

6. Described in Sommers and McClintock 2003 and Sommers 2006a.

7. While precise population statistics were difficult to obtain, sector officials contributed informed estimates on youth migrant influxes.

8. I chose cells in Kigali instead of sectors in the rural areas because the former's population densities were far higher; the populations of urban cells approximated the populations of rural sectors.

9. The three Rwandan researchers rotated as my translators.

10. Clare Ignatowski supports this determination. "All too often," she writes, "anecdotal focus group perspectives of youth are made to stand in for already existing assessments about youth circulating in the development literature. Attempts at quantifying youth perspectives from small numbers of focus group participants, who are usually the stalwart members of the established NGOs that have organized the focus group itself, are only moderately illuminating. Not only are their perspectives not necessarily representative of all youth in a country or region, but they are usually presented in such generality that not much is learned (such as statements concerning a youth's high valuation of education and jobs). It is much more difficult to access perspectives of youth outside the orbit of the work of NGOs, and to understand youth perspectives in greater depth than focus groups allows" (2007: 227).

11. Our categories aimed to help the research team identify difference in the field. They have no direct connection to the six categories that Rwandan government studies have established (discussed in chapter 1).

Chapter Three. Living in a Vertical World

1. During a subsequent interview, NYC officials debated the possible creation of a soccer field in a distant part of the sector.

2. An NYC official said that youth can't participate in the *ubudehe* program because they "move around" and "don't have a fixed address."

Chapter Four. Low Horizons

1. The primary follow-up question was, "What is the difference between youth who go to secondary or vocational school, and youth who do not?"

2. The definitions of "educated" and "uneducated" youth used in this section draw from the popular definition in Rwanda: that an "educated" person had at least one year of postprimary education (especially secondary education), whereas an "uneducated" person never studied beyond the primary school level.

3. The follow-up questions were: "Can you change categories?" "Can you move up in life?" and "Can you move down in life?" All three were asked as follow-up questions after question 3, which invites respondents to describe the youth situation in their area.

4. The question was, "When someone talks about 'peace,' what does it mean to you?" (question 20 in box 2.3).

5. The question was, "Can you tell me about the social relations here?" (question 19 in box 2.3).

Chapter Five. Striving for Adulthood

1. A fourth option—using grass for roofing—was rarely mentioned by youth or adults during interviews and rarely seen in the countryside.

2. The remaining respondents (12 percent) argued that there was "no difference" between youth life today and youth life a generation ago.

3. In three of the areas visited, the reported daily rate for digging as a day laborer was 200 francs ($0.37). In one sector it was 300 francs ($0.55).

4. Vocational education was largely unavailable in the areas where the field research was carried out. It was rarely mentioned by any youth as a viable option for them.

5. The question was: "What is the difference between youth who go to secondary or vocational school and youth who do not?" Fifty-eight youth answered this follow-up question.

6. A total of seventy-eight youth provided answers that could be trended to the question, "What do/did your parents expect you to be?" (question 10 in box 2.3).

Chapter Six. Desperation on the New Frontier

1. See, for example, United Nations Department of Economic and Social Affairs/ Population Division 2004, 2006.

2. A famous example of state efforts to "repatriate" urban youth to their rural

homes took place in Tanzania beginning in 1983. Called *Nguvu Kazi* (Hard work), and spurred by President Julius K. Nyerere's castigation of the urban jobless as "parasites" and "loiterers," the campaign was both widely publicized and a colossal failure (see, e.g., Kerner 1988, Lugalla 1995, Sawers 1989, Sommers 2001a).

3. There may be no precise code, but there is a government regulation on what constitutes an acceptable housing structure. This regulation, it appears, can be vigorously applied, or not.

4. A cell-level official supported the assessment that NYC officials in his cell were beleaguered. "We don't have many youth activities [in our cell]," the official explained. He added that the youth "know the NYC people but don't come to their meetings."

Chapter Seven. An Inconstant Existence

1. The research team developed this question set for urban youth as follow-ups to question 9 (see box 2.3).

2. The research team developed this additional follow-up question to question 9 to gather specific information on youth motivations for rural–urban migration.

3. Ninety-three respondents comprised the rural sample. Thirty-one respondents highlighted education or an occupation requiring formal education as the primary parental expectation, while 23 percent referred to becoming recognized as an adult man or woman.

4. Regarding religious networks, see, for example, the role of Pentecostal networks in spurring rural-urban migration for refugee youth (Sommers 2001a and 2001b) and across Latin America (Martin 1990).

Chapter Eight. Prostitution, AIDS, and Fatalism

1. The questions were: "Can you tell me about the situation of HIV/AIDS here?" and "How does the HIV/AIDS situation here affect the life of youth?" The research team added these questions after the field research began (see chapter 2 for details), so they do not appear in box 2.3.

Chapter Nine. Stuck Youth

1. There are exceptions to the vigorous repression of polygamy. One executive secretary of a rural sector, for example, related that he was unsure how to address the challenge of an old man of limited means living high up on a hill with ten wives.

2. The same finding surfaced during the course of earlier research in Rwanda (Sommers and McClintock 2003: 53–54). On several occasions during that field research period (1999–2002), I discovered that people did not know the names of

some poor female youth who lived in the rural cells where they resided. This was a singular finding: neighbors routinely pointed out the homes of male youth, men, and women we were looking for in valleys, but not some female youth. It shed light on the degree of invisibility that is a part of life for at least some poor female youth in Rwanda.

3. Curiously, although "the demise of push-pull theory" was widely reported years ago (Boyd 1989: 640), migration specialists continue to highlight its historic influence (e.g., Silvey 2004: 3) and cite factors that "push" or "pull" rural migrants to cities (e.g., Todaro 1997: 28). Evidently, it remains a compelling if imperfect analytical tool.

4. Even urban refugee youth in hiding in Dar es Salaam found ways to return to the refugee settlement homes of their families from time to time (Sommers 2001a).

5. Joe Lugalla provided a compelling analysis of Nguvu Kazi's failures (1995).

6. But not entirely. Among the projects underway are a small World Bank project that targets poor urban female youth in Kigali and a youth employment program run by the Education Development Center and funded by USAID that is also taking place in Kigali.

7. But not widowers. A Rwandan government official in a rural district brought to my attention several years ago the presence and degree of suffering that widowers endure in Rwanda. The official stated that widows often receive assistance from other women, whereas many men make fun of widowers by implying that they are "not men."

8. This is a common characteristic of government and nongovernmental approaches to youth concerns in conflict-affected contexts (Sommers 2007: 112).

9. A government investigation, as reported by a sector leader, would seem to justify youth hesitations to join associations.

10. As in all other areas that were visited, youth associations were weak, and most existed in name only.

11. The title of the UN report is "The 2009 Illegal Exploitation of Natural Resources and other Forms of Wealth of the Democratic Republic of the Congo" (cited in Lasker 2010: 1).

12. Although civil society organizations are often equated with nongovernmental organizations, they may include a broad diversity of organizations, such as trade unions and faith-based organizations, as well.

13. Uvin puts it succinctly: in Burundi, there were "almost three decades of military rule by a small group of Tutsi-Hima from Bururi province: Michel Micombero (1966–76), Jean-Baptiste Bagaza (1976–87), and Pierre Buyoya (1987–93). Their rule constituted the creation of a low-caste Tutsi dictatorship" (2009: 9). Scott Straus notes that Habyarimana "came from Gisenyi Prefecture, and his rule largely benefited northerners, in particular those from the northwest" (2006: 23).

14. The two Central African governance models are elaborated in Sommers and McClintock 2003: 41.

15. A description of bulldozed homes, mowed down like crops on the outskirts of Khartoum, can be found in Sommers 2005: 208–9.

16. The Kigali's official Web site describes Batsinda: "The City of Kigali has embarked on a pilot project to provide 250 low cost houses in Batsinda, Gasabo district, which will employ the model house concept. This project is being funded by the government of Rwanda. Private enterprises that want to participate in providing affordable housing for low income households are also investing in low cost housing models to provide an assortment of choice." "Projects: Developing Batsinda Site," www.kigalicity.gov.rw/spip.php?article139, accessed June 15, 2010.

17. That meeting was with a national government office that, I later learned, was known in nongovernment circles for routinely criticizing their research and activities.

18. Elisabeth King's assessment of education in Rwanda supports the minister's assessment. "Two-thirds of teachers in post-genocide Rwanda," she writes, "have no formal qualifications." She also notes that, as of 2005, "Each student currently shares one textbook with 13 to 22 other students" (2005: 915).

19. Rwanda's assertive (and influential) approach to NGO and donor relations has been noted elsewhere, including Sommers 2004: 64–65, 92–93.

20. Andreas Wimmer, personal communications, January 2011.

21. Decentralization is defined as "the delegation of power from a central authority to regional and local authorities." Merriam-Webster, www.merriam-webster.com/dictionary/decentralization, accessed June 28, 2010.

22. The prison metaphor for farming is strong in Uvin's depiction of Burundian life. For example, he refers to "people escaping the prison of agriculture" as a prime motivator for urban migration (2009: 117).

23. Two UNICEF opinion polls of children's views in Rwanda and Burundi suggest a different story: of over two-thirds of Rwandan children in their sample claiming to be happy and a third of Burundian children responding in similar fashion. The sample in each country was around five hundred children between the ages of nine and seventeen. In Rwanda, the sample was from urban areas in Kigali and rural areas. The researchers stated the issue of security as the reason why "fieldwork was limited" to the capital city's environs (UNICEF 2006b). The methods section in both documents (the question sets and methods appear to be identical) state that "children often tend to be shy and intimidated by older people asking questions" (UNICEF 2006a). Using an opinion poll containing questions on sensitive issues like elections runs the risk of inviting questionable responses. In such a situation, risk aversion may lead Rwandan children toward providing what they consider to be safe answers, not particularly accurate ones.

24. Rwanda ultimately cut diplomatic ties with France soon after President Kagame's donor conference speech in November 2006, restoring them again in November 2009 (BBC News 2006, 2009).

25. Days before President Kagame's speech, the Rwanda News Agency began an article on this issue with the following: "The office of the Ombudsman has strongly contested a report by [T]ransparency International that ranked Rwanda in the 121st position out of 163 countries in the world with regard to corruption perception, RNA has established. The report awarded Rwanda 2.3 marks out of 10 although, as the Ombudsman puts it, [the marks] are unfair [and] contrary to Rwandan government efforts[,] categorically stressing that it is committed to 'fight corruption in all its forms'" (2006: 2).

26. Other members of the research team also interviewed government officials.

References

African Rights. 1995. *Rwanda: Death, Despair and Defiance.* Rev. ed. London: African Rights.

African Union. 2010. "Somalia." *AU Situation Room*, CMD, *Daily News Highlights*, April 22.

Amnesty International. 2004. "Rwanda: 'Marked for Death,' Rape Survivors Living with HIV/AIDS in Rwanda." April 5. Accessed on December 4, 2009, from www.amnesty.org/en/library/info/AFR47/007/2004.

Ansoms, An. 2008. "Striving for Growth, Bypassing the Poor? A Critical Review of Rwanda's Rural Sector Policies." *Journal of Modern African Studies* 46 (1): 1–32.

———. 2009. *Geizichten van armoede in hendendaags Rwanda* (Faces of Rural Poverty in Contemporary Rwanda: Linking Livelihood Profiles and Institutional Processes). Antwerp: University of Antwerp, Faculteit Toegepaste Economische Wetenschappen.

Aretxaga, Begoña. 1997. *Shattering Silence: Women, Nationalism, and Political Subjectivity in Northern Ireland.* Princeton, N.J.: Princeton University Press.

B., Albert. 2006. "Rwanda: Le development à marche forcee." *La Nouvelle Releve* (Kigali) 593 (October 30–November 6): 13.

Baldauf, Scott. 2007. "The African Country Aims to Turn Itself into the 'Singapore of Africa.'" *Christian Science Monitor*, October 17. Accessed November 9, 2009, from www.csmonitor.com/2007/1017/p01s02-woaf.html.

———. 2010. "Former Rwandan Army Chief Shot in South Africa. Was It an Assassination Attempt?" *Christian Science Monitor*, June 20. Accessed on January 18, 2011, from www.csmonitor.com/World/Africa/2010/0620/Former-Rwandan-army-chief-shot-in-South-Africa.-Was-it-an-assassination-attempt.

Bannon, Ian, and Maria C. Correia, eds. 2006. *The Other Half of Gender: Men's Issues in Development.* Washington, D.C.: World Bank.

Barker, Gary. 2005. *Dying to Be Men: Youth, Masculinity, and Social Exclusion.* London: Routledge.

Barker, Gary, and Christine Ricardo. 2006. "Young Men and the Construction of Masculinity in Sub-Saharan Africa: Implications for HIV/AIDS, Conflict, and Violence." In Bannon and Correia, *Other Half of Gender.*

BBC News. 2006. "Rwanda Cuts Relations with France," November 24. Accessed on July 5, 2011, from http://news.bbc.co.uk/2/hi/6179436.stm.

————. 2009. "Rwanda and France Restor Diplomatic Relations," November 30. Accessed on July 5, 2011, from http://news.bbc.co.uk/2/hi/8385887.stm.

Beauchemin, Cris, and Philippe Bocquier. 2003. *Migration and Urbanization in Francophone West Africa: A Review of the Recent Empirical Evidence*. Document de Travail (DT/2003/09). Paris: Développement et Insertion Internationale (DIAL).

Bernard, H. Russell. 2006. *Research Methods in Anthropology: Qualitative and Quantitative Approaches*. 4th ed. Lanham, Md.: AltaMira Press.

Boyd, Monica. 1989. "Family and Personal Networks in International Migration: Recent Developments and New Agendas." *International Migration Review* 23 (3): 638–70.

Buckingham, Stephen. 2008. "Kigali—Miracle City." *Rwanda Dispatch* 1 (1): 24–25.

Buhigiro, Patrick. 2009. "Rwanda: 897 Under-Graduates Complete Ingando." *New Times*, July 19. Accessed December 6, 2009, from http://allafrica.com /stories/200907200358.html.

Burnet, Jennie. 2008. "Country Report: Rwanda." In *Countries at the Crossroads 2007: A Survey of Democratic Governance*, edited by S. Kelly, C. Walker, J. Dizard, 1–27. Lanham, Md.: Rowman & Littlefield Publishers. Accessed on November 9, 2009, from www.freedomhouse.org/uploads/ccr/country-7259-8.pdf.

Chant, Sylvia, and Matthew C. Gutmann. 2002. "'Men-streaming' Gender? Questions for Gender and Development Policy in the 21st Century." *Progress in Development Studies* 2(4): 269–82.

Chauveau, Jean-Pierre, and Paul Richards. 2008. "West African Insurgencies in Agrarian Perspective: Côte d'Ivoire and Sierra Leone Compared." *Journal of Agrarian Change* 8:515–52.

Childress, Sarah. 2010. "Land that Outlawed Hate on Edge as Key Vote Nears." *Wall Street Journal*, March 18, A16.

Chrétien, Jean-Pierre. 2003. *The Great Lakes of Africa: Two Thousand Years of History*. Translated by Scott Straus. New York: Zone Books.

Chu, Jeff. 2009. "Rwanda Rising: A New Model of Economic Development." *Fast Company* 134. Accessed June 16, 2010, from www.fastcompany.com/magazine/134 /special-report-rwanda-rising.html?page=0%2C0.

Clark, Matthew. 2010. "Rwanda Election: Calls Mount for Independent Autopsy of Slain Opposition Leader." *Christian Science Monitor*, July 21. Accessed January 18, 2011, from http://www.csmonitor.com/layout/set/print/content/view /print/315290.

Clark, Phil, and Zachary D. Kaufman. 2009. "Part 1: Introduction and Background, After Genocide." In Clark and Kaufman, *After Genocide*.

Clark, Phil, and Zachary D. Kaufman, eds. 2009. *After Genocide: Transitional Justice, Post-Conflict Reconstruction and Reconciliation in Rwanda and Beyond*, edited by Phil Clark and Zachary D. Kaufman. New York: Columbia University Press.

Coghlan, Benjamin, Pascal Ngoy, Flavien Mulumba, Colleen Hardy, Valerie Nkamgang Bemo, Tony Stewart, Jennifer Lewis, and Richard Brennan. 2008. *Mortality in the Democratic Republic of Congo. An Ongoing Crisis.* International Rescue Committee and Burnet Institute. Accessed January 21, 2010, from www.theirc .org/special-reports/congo-forgotten-crisis.

Comaroff, Jean, and John Comaroff. 2005. "Reflections on Youth: From the Past to the Postcolony." In Honwana and De Boeck, *Makers and Breakers.*

Cornwall, Andrea. 1997. "Men, Masculinity and Gender in Development." *Gender and Development* 5(2): 8–13.

Correia, Maria C., and Ian Bannon. 2006. "Gender and Its Discontents: Moving to Men-Streaming Development." In Bannon and Correia, *Other Half of Gender.*

Coulter, Chris. 2009. *Bush Wives and Girl Soldiers: Women's Lives through War and Peace in Sierra Leone.* Ithaca, N.Y.: Cornell University Press.

De Lorenzo, Mauro. 2008. *The Rwandan Paradox: Is Rwanda a Model for an Africa beyond Aid?* Washington, D.C.: American Enterprise Institute for Public Policy Research. Accessed June 16, 2010, from www.aei.org/article/27476.

Des Forges, Alison. 1999. *Leave None to Tell the Story: Genocide in Rwanda.* New York: Human Rights Watch.

———. 2006. "Land in Rwanda: Winnowing Out the Chaff." *L'Afrique Des Grands Lacs. Annuaire 2005–2006* (July): 353–71.

Desmarais, Jean-Claude. 2004. *Republic of Rwanda: Opinion Survey: The Process of Decentralization and Democratization in Rwanda.* Kigali: National Unity and Reconciliation Commission (March).

DfID (Department for International Development). 2009. "Lessons Go Interactive in Rwanda." National Archives (UK), July 29. Accessed June 24, 2011, from http:// webarchive.nationalarchives.gov.uk/+/http://www.dfid.gov.uk/Media-Room /Case-Studies/2009/Rwanda-volunteer-education/

Dolan, C. 2003. "Collapsing Masculinities and Weak States—A Case Study of Northern Uganda. In *Masculinities Matter! Men, Gender and Development,* edited by F. Cleaver. Durban: Zed Books.

Durand-Lasserve, Alain. 2007. "Market-driven Eviction Processes in Developing Country Cities: The Cases of Kigali in Rwanda and Phnom Penh in Cambodia." *Global Urban Development* 3(1): 1–14.

Economist Intelligence Unit. 2006. *Country Report: Rwanda.* London: Economist Intelligence Unit Limited.

Faulkner, William. 1951. *Requiem for a Nun.* New York: Random House.

Freedman, Sarah Warshauer, Harvey M. Weinstein, Karen Murphy, and Timothy Longman. 2008. "Teaching History after Identity-Based Conflicts: The Rwanda Experience." *Comparative Education Review* 52(4): 663–91.

Gbadamassi, Falila, and Will Chartey-Mould. 2008. "Rwanda to Become English-Speaking." *Afrik.news,* October 18. Accessed April 19, 2011, from www.afrik-news .com/article14716.html.

Gettleman, Jeffrey. 2010. "Rwanda's Mix: Order, Tension, Repressiveness." *New York Times*, May 1, A1.

Gourevitch, Philip. 1998. *We Wish to Inform You that Tomorrow We Will Be Killed with Our Families: Stories from Rwanda*. New York: Farrar.

———. 2009. "The Life After: Fifteen Years after the Genocide in Rwanda, the Reconciliation Defies Expectations." *New Yorker*, May 4: 37–49.

Government of Rwanda. 2001. *Participatory Poverty Assessment*, Kigali: National Poverty Reduction Programme—Ministry of Finance and Economic Planning.

———. 2004. *National Agricultural Policy*. Kigali: Ministry of Agriculture and Animal Resources.

Hilhorst, Dorothea, and Mathijs van Leeuwen. 2000. "Emergency and Development: The Case of Imidugudu, Villagization in Rwanda." *Journal of Refugee Studies* 13(3): 264–80.

Hodgkin, Marian. 2006. "Reconciliation in Rwanda: Education, History and the State." *Journal of International Affairs* 60(1): 199–210.

Honwana, Alcinda. 2005. "Innocent and Guilty: Child-Soldiers as Interstitial and Tactical Agents." In Honwana and De Boeck, *Makers and Breakers*.

Honwana, Alcinda, and Filip De Boeck, eds. *Makers and Breakers: Children and Youth in Postcolonial Africa*. Oxford: James Currey.

Human Rights Watch. 2001. *Uprooting the Rural Poor in Rwanda*. New York: Human Rights Watch.

———. 2006. *Swept Away—Street Children Illegally Detained in Kigali, Rwanda*. 14 May, Accessed April 19, 2011, from www.unhcr.org/refworld/docid/44c764f84 .html.

Ignatowski, Clare A. 2007. "Framing Youth with the Politics of Foreign Assistance." *Research in Comparative and International Education* 2(3): 222–29.

Ingelaere, Bert. 2007. *Living the Transition: A Bottom-up Perspective on Rwanda's Political Transition*. Discussion Paper/2007.06. Antwerp: Institute of Development Policy and Management, University of Antwerp (November).

Institut National de la Statistique du Rwanda (INSR) and ORC Macro. 2006. Rwanda Demographic and Health Survey 2005. Calverton, Md.: INSR and ORC Macro.

International Development Association (World Bank). 2009. *Rwanda: From Post-Conflict Reconstruction to Development*. Accessed June 16, 2010, from http:// siteresources.worldbank.org/IDA/Resources/ida-Rwanda-10-02-09.pdf.

IRIN (UN Office for the Coordination of Humanitarian Affairs). 2003. "Rwanda: U.S. Official Pledges to Mobilise Resources in Fight against HIV/AIDS," December 3. Accessed December 4, 2009, from www.irinnews.org/report .aspx?reportid=47516.

Jefremovas, Villa. 2002. *Brickyards to Graveyards: From Production to Genocide in Rwanda*. Anthropology of Work Series. New York: SUNY Press.

Kagame, Paul. 2009. Preface. In Clark and Kaufman, *After Genocide.*

Kerner, Donna O. 1988. "'Hard Work' and Informal Sector Trade in Tanzania." In *Traders Versus the State: Anthropological Approaches to Unofficial Economies,* edited by Gracia Clark. Boulder, Colo.: Westview Press.

King, Elisabeth. 2005. "Educating for Conflict of Peace: Challenges and Dilemmas in Post-Conflict Rwanda." *International Journal* 60(4): 904–18.

Kinzer, Stephen. 2008. *A Thousand Hills: Rwanda's Rebirth and the Man Who Dreamed It.* Hoboken, N.J.: John Wiley & Sons.

Kirkby, Coel. 2006. "Rwanda's Gacaca Courts: A Preliminary Critique." *Journal of African Law* 50(2): 94–117.

Kron, Josh. 2010a. "For Rwandan Students, Ethnic Tensions Lurk." *New York Times International,* May 17, A9.

———. 2010b. "The Country in the Mirror: As International Darling Rwanda Becomes Increasingly Authoritarian, Neighboring Burundi Experiments with a Unique and Chaotic Brand of Central African Democracy." *Foreign Policy,* June 14. Accessed January 18, 2011, from www.foreignpolicy.com/articles/2010/06/14/the_country_in_the_mirror?print=yes&hidecomments=yes&page=full.

Kron, Josh, and Jeffrey Gettleman. 2010. "American Lawyer for Opposition Figure Is Arrested in Rwanda." *New York Times,* May 28. Accessed June 9, 2010, from www.nytimes.com/2010/05/29/world/africa/29rwanda.html?ref=rwanda.

Kuperman, Alan J. 2001. *The Limits of Humanitarian Intervention: Genocide in Rwanda.* Washington, D.C.: Brookings Institution Press.

Lasker, J. 2010. "Following the Mineral Trail: Congo Resource Wars and Rwanda." Accessed June 16, 2010, from http://towardfreedom.com/home/content/view/1864/1/.

Leahy, Elizabeth, with Robert Engelman, Carolyn Gibb Vogel, Sarah Haddock, and Tod Preston. 2007. *The Shape of Things to Come: Why Age Structure Matters to a Safer, More Equitable World.* Washington, D.C.: Population Action International.

Lemarchand, René. 1970. *Rwanda and Burundi.* New York: Praeger Publishers.

———. 2009. "The Politics of Memory in Post-Genocide Rwanda." In Clark and Kaufman, *After Genocide.*

Lugalla, Joe. 1995. *Crisis, Urbanization, and Urban Poverty in Tanzania.* Lanham, Md.: University Press of America.

Mamdani, Mahmood. 2001. *When Victims Become Killers: Colonialism, Nativism, and the Genocide in Rwanda.* Princeton, N.J.: Princeton University Press.

Martin, David. 1990. *Tongues of Fire: The Explosion of Protestantism in Latin America.* Oxford, U.K.: Blackwell.

McGreal, Chris. 2010. "Delayed UN Report Links Rwanda to Congo Genocide: Rwanda Denounces Report as 'Flawed and Dangerous' and Warns that It Poses a Threat to Regional Stability." *Guardian,* October 2, 20. Accessed January 13, 2011,

from www.guardian.co.uk/world/2010/oct/01/un-report-rwanda-congo
-genocide.

Mgbako, Chi. 2005. "Ingando Solidarity Camps: Reconciliation and Political Indoctrination in Post-Genocide Rwanda." *Harvard Human Rights Journal* 18
(spring): 201–24.

Ministry of Education (Republic of Rwanda). n.d. "Fee-free Education." Accessed
January 21, 2010, from www.mineduc.gov.rw/spip.php?article21.

Ministry of Finance and Economic Planning (Government of Rwanda). 2000.
Rwanda Vision 2020 (July). Kigali: Ministry of Finance and Economic Planning.

———. 2007. *Economic Development and Poverty Reduction Strategy 2008–2012*
(June). Kigali: Ministry of Finance and Economic Planning.

Ministry of Foreign Affairs and Cooperation, Government of Rwanda. 2010.
*Official Government of Rwanda Comments on the Draft UN Mapping Report
on the DRC* (September 30). Geneva: Permanent Mission of Rwanda. Accessed
January 13, 2011, from http://rwandinfo.com/documents/DRC_Report
_Comments_Rwanda.pdf.

Ministry of Local Government, Community Development, and Social Affairs. 2006. *Republic of Rwanda: Making Decentralized Service Delivery Work in
Rwanda: Putting the People at the Center of Service Provision: A Policy Note based
on discussions at the 2005 National Conference on Decentralization, Accountability
and Service Delivery.* Kigali: Ministry of Local Government, Community Development, and Social Affairs.

Ministry of Local Government, Good Governance, Community Development, and
Social Affairs (Republic of Rwanda). 2007. *Rwanda Decentralization Strategic
Framework: Towards a Sector-wide Approach for Decentralization Implementation*,
August. Accessed December 4, 2009, from www.minaloc.gov.rw/spip.php
?article42.

Ministry of Public Service and Labour (Republic of Rwanda). 2005. *Five Year Action Plan for Youth Employment Promotion.* Kigali: Ministry of Public Service and
Labour (provisional final version).

Ministry of Youth, Culture, and Sports (Republic of Rwanda). n.d. *The Republic of
Rwanda Ministry of Youth, Culture and Sports National Youth Policy.* [Kigali: Ministry of Youth, Culture and Sports.].

Momoh, Abubakar. 1999. *The Youth Crisis in Nigeria: Understanding the Phenomena
of the Area Boys and Girls.* Paper presented to the Conference on Children and
Youth as Emerging Categories in Africa, Leuven.

Moore, Jina. 2009. "Ex-Combatants Find Their Way Back to a Changed Rwanda."
Christian Science Monitor, April 8. Accessed December 6, 2009, from www
.csmonitor.com/2009/0408/p06s24-woaf.html.

Musoni, Protais. 2007. *Rebuilding Trust in Post-Conflict Situation through Civic En-*

gagement: The Experience of Rwanda. Paper presented at the 7th Global Forum on Reinventing Government, Vienna, Austria, June 26–29. Accessed on June 24, 2011, from http://unpan1.un.org/intradoc/groups/public/documents/un /unpan026588.pdf.

Nantulya, Paul. 2005. *Evaluation and Impact Assessment of the National Unity and Reconciliation Commission (NURC).* Kigali: Institute for Justice and Reconciliation.

NationMaster. n.d. *Rwandan Education Statistics.* Accessed June 24, 2011, from www.nationmaster.com/red/country/rw-rwanda/edu-education&all=1.

Office of the High Commissioner for Human Rights. n.d. *What Is the "DRC Mapping Exercise?"—Objectives, Methodology and Time Frame: Democratic Republic of the Congo 1993–2003: UN Mapping Report.* Info Note 1. Accessed January 13, 2011, from www.ohchr.org/Documents/Countries/ZR/FS-1_Mapping_exercise _FINAL.pdf.

——. 2010. *Democratic Republic of the Congo 1993–2003: Report of the Mapping Exercise Documenting the Most Serious Violations of Human Rights and International Humanitarian Law Committed within the Territory of the Democratic Republic of the Congo between March 1993 and June 2003: August 2010.* Unofficial translation from the French original. Accessed January 13, 2011, from http://rwandinfo.com /documents/DRC_MAPPING_REPORT_FINAL_EN.pdf.

Office of Tony Blair. 2010. "World Bank Praises Rwanda as One of the World's Leading Business Reformers." November 4. Accessed January 18, 2011, from www.tonyblairoffice.org/news/entry/world-bank-praises-rwanda-as-one-of-the -worlds-leading-business-reform1/.

Obgu, Osita, and Gerrishon Ikiara. 1995. "The Crisis of Urbanisation in Sub-Saharan Africa." *Courier* 149 (Jan.–Feb.): 52–59.

OZ Architecture, EDAW, Tetra Tech, Sypher, ERA, Geomaps, Engineers without Borders-USA, Water for People. 2006. *Kigali Master Plan: Existing Conditions Analysis* (draft). Kigali: Ministry of Infrastructure, Republic of Rwanda.

Peachey, Paul. 2010. "Senior Politician Found Hacked to Death in Rwanda." *Independent,* July 15. Accessed January 18, 2011, from www.independent .co.uk/news/world/africa/senior-politician-found-hacked-to-death-in -rwanda-2026766.html.

Perry, Alex. 2007. "Seeds of Change in Rwanda." *Time Magazine,* September 26. Accessed June 16, 2010, from www.time.com/time/nation/article/0,8599,1665646,00 .html.

Peeters, Pia, Wendy Cunningham, Gayatri Acharya, and Arvil Van Adams. 2009. *Youth Employment in Sierra Leone: Sustainable Livelihood Opportunities in a Post-Conflict Setting.* Washington, D.C.: World Bank.

Peterson, Scott. 2000. *Me against My Brother: At War in Somalia, Sudan, and*

Rwanda: A Journalist Reports from the Battlefields of Africa. New York: Routledge.

Pottier, Johan. 2002. *Re-Imagining Rwanda: Conflict, Survival and Disinformation in the Late Twentieth Century.* Cambridge: Cambridge University Press.

———. 2006."Land Reform for Peace? Rwanda's 2005 Land Law in Context." *Journal of Agrarian Change* 6(4): 509-.37.

Powley, Elizabeth. 2006. *Rwanda: The Impact of Women Legislators on Policy Outcomes Affecting Children and Families.* State of the World's Children 2007: Background Paper (December). New York: UNICEF. Accessed January 30, 2011, from www.peacewomen.org/assets/file/Resources/UN/polpart_impactwomenlegislators_unicef_dec2006.pdf.

Prunier, Gérard. 1995. *The Rwanda Crisis: History of a Genocide.* New York: Columbia University Press.

———. 2009. *Africa's World War: Congo, the Rwandan Genocide, and the Making of a Continental Catastrophe.* New York: Oxford University Press.

Republic of Rwanda. 2007. *Economic Development and Poverty Reduction Strategy, 2008–2012.* Accessed December 4, 2009, from http://web.worldbank.org/WBSITE/EXTERNAL/COUNTRIES/AFRICAEXT/RWANDAEXTN/0,,menuPK:368721~pagePK:141132~piPK:141123~theSitePK:368651,00.html.

Reyntjens, Filip. 2004. "Rwanda, Ten Years On: From Genocide to Dictatorship." *African Affairs* 103(411): 177–210.

———. 2011. "Constructing the Truth, Dealing with Dissent, Domesticating the World: Governance in Post-Genocide Rwanda." *African Affairs* 110(438): 1–34.

Rwanda News Agency. 2006. "Ombudsman Dismisses Transparency International Corruption Report." *Rwanda News Agency*, November 11. Accessed June 21, 2010, from www.rwandagateway.org/article.php3?id_article=3550.

Save the Children UK. 2007. *Rwanda: Development in a Conflict-Affected Country.* Briefing Paper. Accessed June 16, 2010, from www.reliefweb.int/rw/RWFiles2007.nsf/FilesByRWDocUnidFilename/B79EE9CEC3DA2D83C125731700453B28-Full_Report.pdf/$File/Full_Report.pdf.

Sawers, Larry. 1989. "Urban Primacy in Tanzania." *Economic Development and Cultural Change* 37:841–59.

Scott, James C. 1998. *Seeing Like a State: How Certain Schemes to Improve the Human Condition Have Failed.* New Haven, Conn.: Yale University Press.

Sebarenzi, Joseph. 2009. *Rwanda: Heeding History's Lessons Before it's too Late.* Huffington Post, October 1. Accessed June 16, 2010, from www.huffingtonpost.com/joseph-sebarenzi/rwanda-heeding-historys-l_b_306853.html.

Shadid, Anthony. 2011. "Seizing Control of Their Lives and Wondering What's Next." *New York Times*, January 30, 1 and 13.

Silvey, Rachel. 2004. "Power, Difference and Mobility: Feminist Advances in Migration Studies." *Progress in Human Geography* 28(4): 1–17.

Singerman, Diane. 2007. *The Economic Imparatives of Marriage: Emerging Practices and Identities among Youth in the Middle East.* Wolfensohn Center for Development Working paper 6, September.

Smith, David. 2010. "Editor Blames Security Forces after Rwandan Journalist Shot Dead: Shooting of Jean Leonard Rugambage Sparks Fears of a Crackdown in Advance of August Election." *Guardian,* July 26, 21, and guardian.co.uk on July 25. Accessed January 18, 2011, from www.guardian.co.uk/world/2010/jun/25 /rwandan-journalist-shot-dead.

Sommers, Marc. 1995. "A New African World: Rwandan and Other African Youths." *Global Justice* 1(3): 69–74.

———. 1996. *Decentralizing Education: The BESO/Tigray Case Study.* Washington, D.C.: Support for Analysis and Research in Africa (SARA), Academy for Educational Development.

———. 2001a. *Fear in Bongoland: Burundi Refugees in Urban Tanzania.* New York: Berghahn Books.

———. 2001b. "Young, Male and Pentecostal: Urban Refugees in Dar es Salaam, Tanzania." *Journal of Refugee Studies* 14:4, 347–70.

———. 2003. *War, Urbanization, and Africa's Youth at Risk: Understanding and Addressing Future Challenges.* Washington, D.C.: Basic Education and Policy Support (BEPS) Activity and Creative Associates International. Accessed January 7, 2011, from http://www.beps.net/publications/BEPS -UrbanizationWarYouthatRisk-.pdf.

———. 2004. *Co-ordinating Education during Emergencies and Reconstruction: Challenges and Responsibilities.* Paris: International Institute for Educational Planning, UNESCO.

———. 2005. *Islands of Education: Schooling, Civil War and the Southern Sudanese (1983–2004).* Paris: International Institute for Educational Planning, UNESCO.

———. 2006a. "In the Shadow of Genocide: Rwanda's Youth Challenge." In *Troublemakers or Peacemakers? Youth and Post-Accord Peace Building,* edited by Siobhán McEvoy-Levy. Notre Dame, Ind.: Notre Dame University Press.

———. 2006b. "Fearing Africa's Young Men: Male Youth, Conflict, Urbanization, and the Case of Rwanda." In Bannon and Correia, *Other Half of Gender.* An earlier World Bank working paper version of this document, *Fearing Africa's Young Men: The Case of Rwanda,* is available at www.eldis.org/static/DOC21389.htm.

———. 2007. "Embracing the Margins: Working with Youth amid War and Insecurity." In *Too Poor for Peace? Poverty, Conflict and Security in the 21st Century,* edited by Lael Brainard and Derek Chollet. Washington, D.C.: Brookings.

———. 2008. "A Day of Fieldwork in Rwanda." *Praxis: The Fletcher Journal of Human Security* 23:129–34.

———. 2009. *Africa's Young Urbanites: Challenging Realities in a Changing Region.* ADAP Learning Series No. 5. New York: Adolescent Development and Participation Unit, Gender, Rights and Civic Engagement Section, Division of Policy and Practice, UNICEF (December).

———. 2010. "Urban Youth in Africa." *Environment and Urbanization* 22(2): 317–32.

Sommers, Marc, and Elizabeth McClintock. 2003. "On Hidden Ground: One Coexistence Strategy in Central Africa." In *Imagine Coexistence: Restoring Humanity after Violent Ethnic Conflict*, edited by Antonia Chayes and Martha Minow. San Francisco: Jossey-Bass.

Straus, Scott. 2006. *The Order of Genocide: Race, Power, and War in Rwanda*. Ithaca, N.Y.: Cornell University Press.

Todaro, Michael P. 1997. "Urbanization, Unemployment, and Migration in Africa: Theory and Policy." In *Renewing Social and Economic Progress in Africa: Essays in Memory of Philip Ndegwa*, edited by Dharam Ghai. London: Palgrave.

Turner, Victor. 1969. *The Ritual Process: Structure and Anti-Structure*. Chicago: Aldine Transaction (2nd printing, 2009).

UNDP (United Nations Development Programme). 2007. Turning Vision 2020 into Reality: From Recovery to Sustainable Human Development. National Human Development Report Rwanda 2007. Kigali: UNDP Rwanda.

UNICEF (United Nations Children's Fund). 2006. *What Children and Youth Think: Burundi: A Statistical Presentation of Opinions and Perceptions of Children and Youth in Burundi, 2006*. Addis Ababa: African Child Policy Forum. Accessed December 28, 2006, www.africanchildforum.org/Documents/Burundi.pdf.

———. 2006. *What Children and Youth Think: Rwanda: A Statistical Presentation of Opinions and Perceptions of Children and Youth in Rwanda, 2006*. Addis Ababa: African Child Policy Forum. Accessed July 1, 2011, from www.uneca.org/adfv/polls/Rwanda.pdf.

United Nations Department of Economic and Social Affairs/Population Division. 2001. *Population, Environment and Development*. Accessed May 29, 2007, from www.un.org/esa/population/publications/pdewallchart/popenvdev.pdf.

———. 2004. *World Urbanization Prospects: The 2003 Revision*. New York: Department of Economic and Social Affairs, Population Division, United Nations.

———. 2006. *World Urbanization Prospects: The 2005 Revision*. New York: United Nations.

United Nations Human Settlements Programme (UN-Habitat). 2009. *Planning Sustainable Cities: Global Report on Human Settlements 2009*. London and Sterling, Va.: Earthscan. Accessed June 22, 2011, from www.unhabitat.org/downloads/docs/GRHS2009/GRHS.2009.pdf.

UNFPA. 2007. *State of World Population 2007: Unleashing the Potential of Urban Growth*. Accessed November 27, 2009, from www.unfpa.org/swp/swpmain.htm.

Utas, Mats. 2003. *Sweet Battlefields: Youth and the Liberian Civil War*. Uppsala, Sweden: Uppsala University Dissertations in Cultural Anthropology.

————. 2005a. "Building a Future? The Reintegration and Remarginalization of Youth in Liberia." In *No Peace No War: An Anthropology of Contemporary Armed Conflicts*, edited by Paul Richards. Athens: Ohio University Press.

————. 2005b. "Agency of Victims: Young Women in the Liberian Civil War." In Honwana and De Boeck, *Makers and Breakers*.

Uvin, Peter. 1998. *Aiding Violence: The Development Enterprise in Rwanda*. West Hartford, Conn.: Kumarian Press.

————. 2001. "Reading the Rwandan Genocide." *International Studies Review* 3(3): 75–99.

————. 2009. *Life after Violence: A People's Story of Burundi*. London: Zed Books.

van Leeuwen, Mathijs. 2001. "Rwanda's Imidugudu Programme and Earlier Experiences with Villagisation and Resettlement in East Africa." *Journal of Modern African Studies* 39(4): 623–44.

Vidal, Claudine. 1991. *Sociologie des Passions (Côte-d'Ivoire, Rwanda)*. Paris: Karthala.

Voice of America News. 2008. "Sweden Suspends Aid to Rwanda Following UN Report." newsVOA.com, December 17. Accessed November 2, 2009, from www.voanews.com/english/archive/2008-12/2008-12-17-voa68.cfm?CFID=328665778&CFTOKEN=24143743&jsessionid=de3ocfa7afcea0328b72f6b7d66164 01b279.

Voyame, Joseph, Richard Friedli, Jean-Pierre Gern, and Anton Keller. 1996. *La coopération suisse au Rwanda*. Berne: Département Fédéral des Affaires Etrangères.

Wagner, Michele D. 1998. "All the Bourgmestre's Men: Making Sense of Genocide in Rwanda." Special Issue: Crisis in Central Africa. *Africa Today* 45(1): 25–36.

Watkins, Alfred, and Anubha Verma, eds. 2008. *Building Science, Technology and Innovation Capacity in Rwanda: Developing Practical Solutions to Practical Problems*. Washington, D.C.: World Bank.

Waugh, Colin M. 2004. *Paul Kagame and Rwanda: Power, Genocide and the Rwandan Patriotic Front*. Jefferson, N.C.: McFarland & Co.

White, Sarah C. 1997. "Men, Masculinities, and the Politics of Development." *Gender and Development* 5(2): 14–22.

Wimmer, Andreas, Lars-Erik Cederman, and Brian Min. 2009. "Ethnic Politics and Armed Conflict: A Configurational Analysis of a New Global Dataset." *American Sociological Review* 74(2): 316–37.

World Bank. 2006. *World Development Report 2007: Development and the Next Generation*. Washington, D.C.: World Bank.

————. 2007. *Our Commitment: The World Bank's Africa Region HIV/AIDS Agenda for Action 2007–2011*, June 24. Advance copy. Washington, D.C.: World Bank.

————. 2008. *The International Development Association, The International Finance Corporation, and The Multilateral Investment Guarantee Agency Country Assistance Strategy for the Republic of Rwanda for the Period FY09–FY12*. Report 44938-RW,

August 7, 2008. Accessed December 4, 2009, from http://www-wds.worldbank.
org/external/default/WDSContentServer/WDSP/IB/2008/09/04/000334955_200
80904035214/Rendered/INDEX/449380CAS0P1001ONLY10IDA1R200810257.txt.

———. 2009. *Youth and Employment in Africa: The Potential, the Problem, the Promise, African Development Indicators 2008/9.* Washington, D.C.: World Bank.

———. 2011. "Gross National Income per Capita 2009, Atlas Method and PPP." *World Bank Development Indicators database* (14 April). Accessed June 22, 2011, from http://siteresources.worldbank.org/DATASTATISTICS/Resources /GNIPC.pdf.

———. n.d. "Rwanda: Improving the Investment Climate for Private Sector Development." Accessed January 18, 2011, from http://web.worldbank.org /WBSITE/EXTERNAL/COUNTRIES/AFRICAEXT/RWANDAEXTN /0,,contentMDK:22745125~menuPK:368660~pagePK:2865066~piPK:2865079 ~theSitePK:368651,00.html.

Index

Italicized page numbers locate photos, tables, and boxed explanations.

This book is a fine example of the work produced by Senior Fellows in the Jennings Randolph fellowship program of the United States Institute of Peace. As part of the statute establishing the Institute, Congress envisioned a program that would appoint "scholars and leaders of peace from the United States and abroad to pursue scholarly inquiry and other appropriate forms of communication on international peace and conflict resolution." The program was named after Senator Jennings-Randolph of West Virginia, whose efforts over four decades helped to establish the Institute.

Since 1987, the Jennings Randolph Program has played a key role in the Institute's effort to build a national center of research, dialogue, and education on critical problems of conflict and peace. Fellows come from a wide variety of academic and other professional backgrounds. They conduct research at the Institute and participate in the Institute's outreach activities to policy makers, the academic community, and the American public.

Each year approximately twelve senior fellows are in residence at the Institute. Fellowship recipients are selected by the Institute's board of directors in a competitive process. For further information on the program, please contact the program staff at (202) 457-1700, or visit our Web site at www.usip.org.